SOUTHDOWN

Volume One

The History

ISBN 1 898432 07 4

DEDICATION

To the members of the
Southdown Enthusiasts Club

Front Cover Illustration

On a late afternoon run to Arundel in September 1963, No. 720 (KUF 720) an all-Leyland Titan PD2/12 of 1951 crosses the Toll Bridge at Old Shoreham, Sussex, which in those days was a serious bottleneck on the busy A27 south coast road. It was, however, not without charm and highly photogenic, as this picture by John Allpress discloses. Originally built with open platform, No. 720 had been fitted with folding doors some ten years previously at Southdown's Portslade works.

Typeset and produced electronically for the Publishers by
Mopok Graphics, 128, Pikes Lane, Glossop, Derbyshire
Printed and bound in Great Britain

SOUTHDOWN

Volume One

The History

by

Colin Morris

Principal Photographer
Alan Lambert

Venture *publications*

INTRODUCTION

When my first history of Southdown was published in 1985, the process of unravelling the closely-knit structure of the National Bus Company and its subsidiaries was well under way. There were signs at the time, however, that Southdown as an entity of some kind or other was set to survive in the marketplace from which other famous names, particularly in the south, had already disappeared. Few could then have foreseen the eventual outcome of the decentralisation taking place and the restructuring which would follow; nor realised the degree to which the existence the while of a central core at Brighton had been instrumental in the maintenance of Southdown Motor Services Ltd as a holistic operational unit.

Enter Stagecoach Holdings, whose management came, saw, assessed and took the kind of pragmatic steps which no traditionally-attached member of the profession could have had a mind to take. Then, in 1992, the Southdown name went the way of Aldershot & District, Thames Valley and Hants & Dorset – and of the London Brighton & South Coast Railway and the Southern Railway earlier in their turn. Conservative and sentimental by nature as most British folk are, their passing is each time mourned by numerous ex-employees proud of their personal contribution, and by those who became acquainted and developed an affinity with them.

In this context, I am conscious that 1994 is the 40th anniversary of the founding of the Southdown Enthusiasts Club. I am again grateful for their confidence and hope that this celebratory edition proves both timely and appropriate. Some small consolation to them, perhaps – that Southdown outlived all of those firms mentioned and that, from their number, only the LB&SCR enjoyed a longer life.

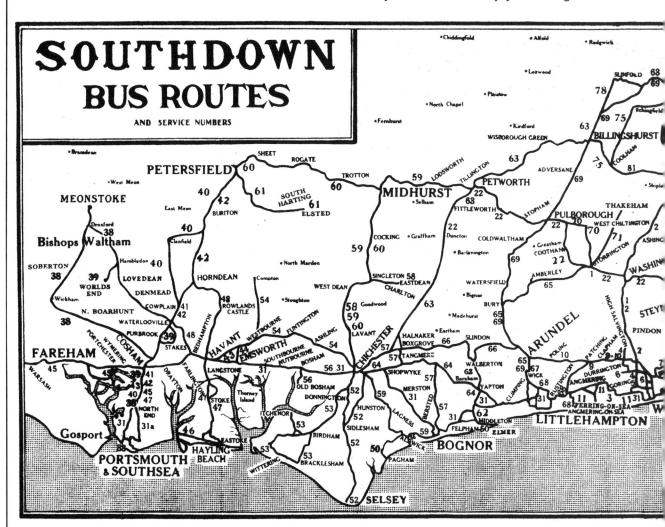

Yet the company which was Southdown Motor Services Ltd still exists. It has simply had its name changed. The original company number, 140534, now refers to 'Sussex Coastline Buses Ltd' – a Stagecoach South subsidiary. Nevertheless, it would not be unreasonable for the current management to wish that in 75 years' time 'enthusiasts' and customers alike will celebrate and say something equally pleasant about the history of Stagecoach and those who founded it.

This book (Volume I) brings the overview of the Southdown history up to its closure in 1992. Once more the generous contribution of Alan Lambert has made the book a feasible project – not least by granting free access to his magnificent photographic collection. Companion to this general history is Volume II, concerned with extensively illustrated detail, to provide pictorially enhanced reference material for the dedicated student of the omnibus industry. It again draws upon the accumulated evidence and knowledge of the company, the Southdown Enthusiasts Club and Alan Lambert. As to whether, side by side, the two volumes represent the 'full-blown definitive tome', which I thought in 1985 should perhaps be written, time will tell; but 'the marker' I had then put down is at least hereby extended.

Colin Morris
Roscote Mews
Heswall, 1994

A map of Southdown's routes as they were in 1939.

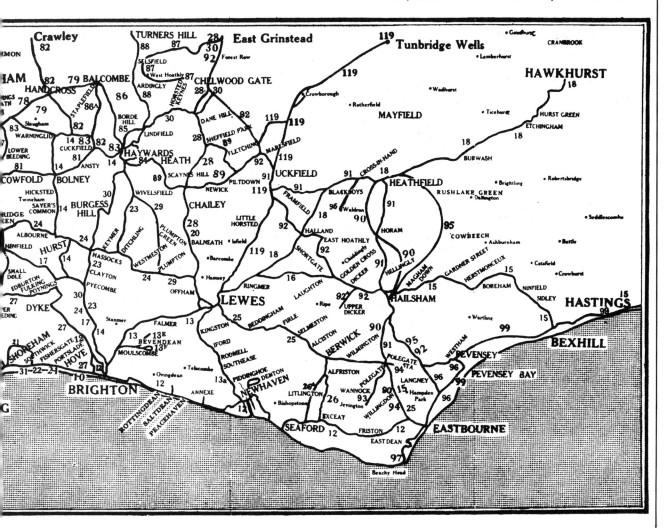

ACKNOWLEDGMENTS

In the preparation of this volume I, was particularly fortunate in being granted interviews by three key officers germane to the history of the company from 1977 onwards. I am grateful to them for their patience, hospitality and follow-up at a time of considerable change in the industry – and in the publishing world too.

First Michael Sedgley, then managing director of the Brighton & Hove Bus & Coach Co Ltd, took a great deal of time and trouble to ensure that the sequence of events relating to the demise of the National Bus Company were properly chronicled. Secondly, Philip Ayers, managing director of 'independent' Southdown kindly put on record at his home in Sussex a candid review of operations in a de-regulated climate.

In a meeting at Chichester Bus Station, Brian Cox, now chairman of Stagecoach (South) Ltd, gave of his precious time to explain the philosophy of his company and the events and reasons which led to the partition and renaming of its Southdown subsidiary.

For reading original drafts, I am also in debt to John Allpress and Paul Gainsbury (and, of course, Alan Lambert) and for their straightening the outline where it had wandered off course. For those wishing to go farther into the recent history of the company, I can do no better than recommend a reading of the Southdown Enthusiasts Club's annual reviews from 1984 onwards. In this context, I found articles by Paul Gainsbury and R. M. J. Maryon particularly helpful, but that is not to detract one bit from the work of other contributors. My thanks to them all, and may their researches continue.

Special mention should be given to the technical assistance and advice granted by my fellow author T. B. Maund.

Lastly, my gratitude to Professor John Hibbs OBE for his good-natured permission to dig him gently in the ribs. This I have done with affection for, as my first editor in this field, he taught me much – "and which you appear to have forgotten" I hear him say. Well, thank-you, anyway.

Colin Morris
1994

PHOTOGRAPHIC CREDITS

All black and white photographs in this volume are the work of Alan Lambert or are from his collection; with the exception of:

Philip Ayers collection   79 (top), 121
A. H. Barkway   32 (top), 36 (bottom), 49 (centre), 73 (top right), 73 (centre left)
A. A. F. Bell   20 (top), 24 (top), 75 (centre), 87 (top right)
J. E. Cull   66 (bottom), 70 (bottom)
R. J. Dallimore   11 (top)
Paul Gainsbury   117 (top), 117 (centre), 119, 120 (centre upper), 120 (centre lower), 120 (bottom)
J. C. Gillham   67 top
W. J. Haynes   66 (top), 66 (centre), 83 (bottom)
Charles F. Klapper   50 (top)
Colin Morris collection   10 (top left), 10 (top right), 12 (bottom), 13 (bottom), 16 (bottom), 17 (top), 42 (bottom left), 69 (top), 70 (top), 82 (top), 83 (centre), 93
E. Nixon   40, 41 (centre)
Portsmouth & Sunderland Newspapers Ltd   42 (top)
G. H. M. Scatliff collection   25 (top)
R. H. G. Simpson   86 (bottom)
Eric Surfleet   26, 28 (bottom), 34 (top), 50 (centre), 51 (centre), 69 (bottom), 76 (top), 76 (centre lower), 85 (top), 87 (centre right)
Sussex Coastline Buses Ltd   8, 31 (top), 33 (bottom), 78 (bottom right), 89 (top), 90 (lower), 101 (both), 102 (centre lower), 106 (top)
Chris Warren   94 (bottom), 98 (top left)

Coloured illustrations:
John Allpress   Front cover
Andrew Gainsbury   64 (top)
Paul Gainsbury   64 (bottom both)
Roy Marshall/Photobus   61 (top both)
Arnold Richardson/Photobus   57 (bottom), 58 (bottom)
John Senior   57 (top), 58 (top left)
Southdown Enthusiasts Club   58 (top right), 59 (all), 60 (all), 61 (bottom), 62 (all), 63 (all)

CONTENTS

'Coach Cruise' – In the early 'fifties, some 7,500 passengers per annum were booking places on the company's tours. Those with sufficient money saved, joined the luxurious Continental Road Services programme operated by Southdown. Guaranteed all the courtesy, care and comfort that had become the watchwords of Southdown, holidaymakers relax elsewhere as their luggage is loaded aboard Leyland Royal Tiger PSU1/15 No. 829 (LUF 829) as another European tour prepares to leave Brighton. The Harrington 'Wayfarer' coachwork provided only 26 seats in order that each passenger could travel in armchair comfort. This air of 'something special' filtered through to all the other aspects of Southdown Motor Services Ltd.

Chapter One: The Founding Fathers

Much has been written in description of the terrain and early modes of communication on the downlands between Portsmouth and Hastings. Roads scarcely worthy of the name after rain followed well-worn tracks through the hills towards London or wound their way east-west throughout the length of Sussex. Carriers, coachmen and smugglers alike struggled to shift their burdens as quickly as they were able whilst latterday highwaymen chanced their luck against them all. In the winter season particularly progress was sometimes bettered by taking to the bed of a shallow stream and, in the middle of the eighteenth century, referring to the depth of the local mud, John Burton was moved to enquire "Why comes it that the oxen, the swine, the women and all other animals are so long-legged in Sussex?"

The need for strong ankles lessened during the next hundred years after local authorities were obliged to attend to the condition of their roads, thus enabling the system of horse-drawn coach routes to be brought to near-perfection; until the coming of the railways creamed off the traffic.

The outstanding personality associated with both forms of transport was William James Chaplin (1787-1859), who horsed and owned coaches and carriages throughout the area, and the best part of England as well. Before becoming chairman of the London & South Western Railway Company, he had taken a look at the possibilities of mechanical traction upon the roads, having travelled as a passenger in Walter Hancock's experimental steam coach "The Infant" which in 1833 set out from London to Brighton. Beaten as much by the state of the road as its own shortcomings, The Infant broke down on Handcross Hill, and his horses survived. Seven years later, in June 1840, Frank Hills' 12-seater steam carriage travelled from Deptford to Brighton, and returned to the Elephant & Castle with a full complement of passengers in 3½ hours. At a fare of only five shillings (25p) per person, the trip, although experimental, showed that passengers could be conveyed by steam vehicles at half the expense and at twice the speed of the horse-drawn stage coach.

From that time onward railways increasingly took custom from the coaches until, in the 1890s, many of the roads saw very little traffic. Long distance coach proprietors retreated into the towns, and horses instead provided the tractive effort for hackney carriages, landaus, wagonettes and bus services operating over urban and local routes. In Portsmouth such services were, in the main, provided by a company with interests at various centres in England and Wales; in Worthing and Eastbourne by individual operators; and across Brighton & Hove by similar proprietors who had joined forces to form a syndicate of considerable significance to the Southdown story.

The best-known of the Worthing proprietors, James Town (1826-1912) has left a nostalgic and highly valuable record of the men, horses and stage-coaches of the nineteenth century in his booklet *Reminiscences of the old*

Coaching Days together with further memories published in the local Worthing press. It would appear that neither coachmen nor 'outside' passengers ever caught cold and, driving some fifty miles per day 'through ten different airs' which produced 'a salutary effect on the system that no medicine can ever do', south coast coach crewmen invariably lived into healthy and great old-age. In addition, these men established a record of getting through on time whatever the weather, of great driving skill and considerable concern for the welfare and safety of their passengers – thus setting a tradition of service and courtesy which remained the hallmark of their successors, Southdown Motor Services Ltd.

The development of the steam carriage upon roadways had been additionally impeded by the constraints upon such traffic imposed by the 'Red Flag' Act which required mechanically powered vehicles to be preceded at a leisurely pace by a man carrying a red flag. By the time the Act had been repealed in 1896 the internal combustion engine had become a much more promising means of propulsion and of the handful of manufacturers who had produced steam-buses thereafter, only Clarkson's of Chelmsford provided anything of significance to the story of Southdown.

Following the Light Locomotive Act 1896, progress with petrol-engined vehicles was rapid, commencing with a celebratory run from London to Brighton. Wade's Garage of Worthing started with a Cannstatt Daimler and Leon Bollee cars and in 1900 provided the first motor coach in the town, a nine-seater Coventry-built Daimler. An earlier start with hot-tube ignition vehicles had been made by Arthur Julian at Portsmouth who, in July 1899, introduced experimental motor wagonette services in the area, which led to the inauguration of his Portsmouth & Gosport Motor Omnibus Co Ltd.

WALTER FLEXMAN FRENCH
(1856-1925)

Although earlier starts with motorbuses had been made at Edinburgh, in Tunbridge Wells, Bournemouth and Folkestone, it is that made between Putney and Piccadilly, London, which is of particular significance here. The proprietor of the MMC wagonettes involved, and who gained his initial experience with motorbuses as a result, was Walter Flexman French, an important contributor to the early history of Southdown Motor Services Ltd – and its first chairman.

Walter Flexman French, the son of a Springfield, Essex, dairy farmer, became an engineering apprentice at the age of twelve. He took honours at the Imperial College of Science & Technology at South Kensington, thereafter spending two years in general engineering and fourteen 'in charge' in locomotive shops. In 1881, he set up on his own account, manufacturing bicycles in a workshop adjacent to his home at Bedford Hill, Balham and in 1889 became

Walter Flexman French: To W. F. French goes the credit for placing upon the streets of London the first petrol-powered stage carriage vehicles. The knowledge gained in that enterprise brought him to Worthing to manage the affairs of the Sussex Motor Road Car Co Ltd, to Brighton in 1912 with his London & South Coast Haulage Co Ltd, and the chairmanship, three years later, of Southdown Motor Services Ltd. He also launched Maidstone & District and Hants & Dorset, and was actively interested in several other companies.

Alfred Douglas Mackenzie: From the moment he set up as consultant to the emergent motor omnibus industry in 1905, until his death in 1944, Douglas Mackenzie was one of the best-known men in the road passenger transport business. Concerned with the day-to-day running of a total of five bus companies, it is with Southdown that his name remains indelibly linked. His methods and sayings became maxims of traffic management; his accumulated knowledge of internal combustion engines was unsurpassed.

totally self-employed as the maker and vendor 'for cash or on easy terms' of his 'Royal Majestic' cycles, with an output of some two thousand per annum. Frustrated by the red flag requirement, his De Dion car, bought on the proceeds, had but few outings until 1896, when he began to search for ways to aid the process by which the internal combustion engine was to oust the horse, devoting much of his time instead to the motor trade.

To French falls the honour of placing upon the streets of London the first fleet of petrol engined wagonettes licensed to operate stage carriage services. Started in the summer of 1899, the service between Putney and Piccadilly gave French's son George (later managing director of Maidstone & District Motor Services Ltd) the opportunity of driving the first motorised stage-carriage vehicle over Westminster Bridge. Too frequent stops and starts however ruined the MMC gear-box brasses within a week and difficulty in keeping the back tyres on longer than a day considerably hampered the enterprise. Instead, on 1st April 1901, his seven-strong MMC fleet, some of them still tiller-steered, was switched to a 'country' route – from Clapham Junction and Balham to Streatham, running under the title 'South Western Motor Car Co Ltd.'

When he eventually gave up the production of bicycles and concentrated upon the motor trade he set up anew at 314, Balham High Road, as French's Garage & Motor Works Ltd, and proceeded to become one of the best-

known figures in the motor transport world – a 'man of remarkable business acumen, of indomitable perseverance and of the strictest integrity', whose letters and every business move were avidly published in the trade press throughout the first quarter of the 20th century.

This then was the man who for two years from 1904 was to move house and home to Worthing to take up the managership of the recently-formed Sussex Motor Road Car Co Ltd – one of the direct progenitors of Southdown, whose first chairman he was later destined to become.

ALFRED DOUGLAS MACKENZIE (1870-1944)

Although French was its first chairman, Southdown Motor Services Ltd was for many years synonymous with what turned out to be the lifelong partnership of 'Mac and Freddie', of Alfred Douglas Mackenzie and Alfred Edward Cannon, respectively traffic manager and general manager of Southdown and joint founders of one of its three constituent companies, Worthing Motor Services Ltd.

Whilst photographs of Alfred Cannon are few and far between, Douglas Mackenzie, in his earlier days both moustached and trim-bearded with naval-style peaked cap planted squarely upon his head, is depicted in numerous photographs of vehicles taken in the first twenty years of the century, in most instances well-placed to listen intently

SOUTHDOWN
MOTOR SERVICES LIMITED

ALL COMMUNICATIONS TO BE ADDRESSED
TO THE COMPANY AND NOT TO INDIVIDUALS

TELEPHONE: BRIGHTON 4033 10 LINES
TELEGRAMS "MOBUS" BRIGHTON

Registered Offices:
STEINE STREET · BRIGHTON · 1

YOUR REF.   OUR REF.

27th October, 1936

PORTSMOUTH SPORTS CLUB

To ALL THOSE who were unable to attend on Friday

evening last, when such handsome presents were given to

us, we wish to convey our heartiest thanks and appreciation

of your generosity and good wishes on this memorable occasion.

The signatures of Alfred Cannon and Douglas Mackenzie adorn this thank-you note to Portsmouth employees unable to attend the 21st anniversary celebration of the founding of Southdown Motor Services Ltd in 1936, when both had been presented with suitably inscribed silver tea sets. Like the man himself, Mackenzie's signature is careful and controlled.

Two Mackenzie innovations embellish this 1906 Leyland X vehicle for the Clacton-on-Sea Motor Omnibus company, one rather longer-lived than the other. Mackenzie always claimed that this was the very first motor charabanc: what is certain is that it was the first (also) of his 'slipper' type bodies which were a feature of his Worthing-based fleet from 1907 until the early 'twenties. The cursive fleetname 'Swiftsure' was a signwriter's tidied-up version of Mackenzie's copperplate handwritten original. He did the same for 'Southdown' – and that could still be found on company vehicles in service as late as 1991.

and knowledgeably to the engines which he nursed and loved throughout his life. In many respects, Douglas Mackenzie was an enthusiast – methodical, cautious and reluctant to throw anything away. Of Ross & Cromarty stock, but born in Kensington, he had travelled to school by train when, according to his own account, he collected locomotive numbers and, long before spotters had it all laid out for them in booklets, devised a system of classification and sequencing to enlighten the task – the first example of that orderliness which was to make Southdown one of the best recorded, ticketed and numbered of bus companies.

The youthful Mackenzie was apprenticed to a firm of marine engineers in Sunderland and undertook several voyages as a trainee ships engineer. Trained upon steam engines, in the autumn of 1898 he was appointed to the secretarial staff of the National Traction Engine Owner's Association, which group required on their staff an engineer to advise its members about the suitability and strength of the country roads and bridges in their area. Mackenzie travelled the country from North Lonsdale in the Lake District to Looe in Cornwall, looking in particular at bridges.

So narrow were most of the country lanes he was obliged to use a bicycle to reach what he quickly realised was some of the most beautiful countryside in England. Apart from rescuing from almost certain destruction a granite clapper bridge in the Looe Valley, his unique two-year tour was to have a lasting effect. First, in his subsequent Worthing days, Mackenzie and his bicycle became something of a legend but, more importantly, his first-hand contact with such terrain, unknown at that time to the majority of Englishmen, caused him to look 'forward to the time when I could get hold of a motor bus chassis sufficiently reliable to send on tours of 500 to 1,000 miles and thus enable others to enjoy the scenery and country I had come to love and value'.

To this experience there may be traced the impetus which led to the provision of an extensive programme of long-distance tours for which Southdown was to become particularly famous.

Meanwhile, in 1901, Douglas Mackenzie joined Allen's of Cowley, Oxford, where he managed a fleet of 80 steam-powered vehicles, including lorries, threshing and ploughing engines and steam-rollers. Never in good odour with the local authorities, because of their weight, his engines made eight-inch-deep ruts in the weak surfaces of the roads as far afield as Salisbury Plain and Southend. Mackenzie realised that the lighter, more easily-managed internal combustion engine had the greater future.

Despite a journey across the Vale of the White Horse, between Wantage and Oxford on one of the earliest of motor cars – and that made astride the bonnet holding his overcoat down on either side to stop an easterly gale blowing out the flame in the car's porcelain ignition tube – the future director and traffic manager of Southdown felt it necessary to up-date his knowledge of petrol engine development by attending trials conducted by the Auto-Cycle Club and the Motor Yacht Club at Southampton. On one such trial on Southampton Water, he encountered a Thornycroft motor cruiser driven by producer gas – a system in which no gas was made unless by the suction of the engine which was actually going to use it. This too was to provide experience which would help him cope with the gas propulsion of buses imposed by wartime restrictions upon petrol.

His introduction to motorbuses was made in 1904, when he was employed by the Motor Traction Co Ltd which had started running double-deck petrol buses in London as early as October 1899. By 1905, he had set up as a consulting engineer, first in the Strand and then at 109 Victoria Street, Westminster, becoming much sought-after in the emergent omnibus industry. The Glasgow & South Western Railway Co, Clacton-on-Sea Motor Omnibus Co and the Isle of Wight Express Motor Syndicate were among the firms which engaged him to advise upon vehicle policy and maintenance. For the Clacton firm he designed what he always claimed was the first motor charabanc. Mounted upon a Leyland X chassis, this was the first of his famous slipper-type vehicles later to become familiar along the south coast. Additionally, its name, "Swiftsure", was applied to the vehicle in a beautiful cursive script which owed much to Mackenzie's own neat handwriting and was the prototype for the elegant 'script' fleetname applied to the Company's coaches.

The consultant now began to move into the actual management of bus companies and, in March 1907, he was appointed to conduct the affairs of the Isle of Wight Express Motor Syndicate Ltd which he undertook from his office at Westminster. At the time this firm was running a fleet of six Milnes-Daimler charabancs – and was already ailing. Fortunately, the company had actually operated three buses in Portsmouth and Southsea the year before Mackenzie arrived and had done some excursion work to Goodwood Races under the watchful eye of a travel agent called Frank Bartlett.

All then was not lost when, in December 1907, Mackenzie was also called upon to act as receiver when

the Isle of Wight Express Motor Syndicate was wound up, for Bartlett was to become the key man in the actual establishment of Southdown at Portsmouth. In addition, Mackenzie kept open an office at Ryde, Isle of Wight, whence he was able to register (and re-register) vehicles for use in his latest, and what turned out to be his permanent venture, in Sussex. For, in April 1907, Alfred Douglas Mackenzie agreed to become full-time general manager of the Sussex Motor Road Car Co Ltd – a position vacated the previous year by Walter Flexman French. To act as engineer, he wooed away from the London Power Omnibus Co Ltd his assistant during his earlier consultancy days, the tall, amiable and 24 year-old Alfred Edward Cannon.

ALFRED EDWARD CANNON
(1883-1952)

A native of Sandford-on-Thames near Oxford. Alfred Cannon (1883-1952) had served his apprenticeship as an engineer in the Great Western Railway works at Wolverhampton – an engineering pedigree as good as any other. Yet it was Cannon's flair for management, coupled with Mackenzie's intimate knowledge of what machines could be expected to do, that was to establish the correct balance of innovation and caution which later established Southdown Motor Services Ltd as one of Britain's foremost bus companies.

Mackenzie, incidentally, did not much like the word **bus. Motorbus** he positively hated, considering it to have "a nasty Yankee flavour that is distinctly unpleasant to British palates". Instead, he called all his buses **cars.** And such was the character of the man, over 40 years after his departure most of the Southdown staff called them that also. The 'Telex' name for Worthing Motor Services Ltd, 'Mobus', later inherited by Southdown, can only be a joke played upon him by Alfred Cannon.

FRANK BARTLETT
(1860-1933)

Frank Bartlett's retirement dinner was held at the City Hall, Portsmouth, in February 1933. It was attended by the Lord Mayor of Portsmouth and all the aldermen of that city. Douglas Mackenzie and Alfred Cannon attended for Southdown Motor Services Ltd and every employee of the company subcribed to his farewell present. Bartlett was neither a director of the company nor a man with engineering experience. He was in fact the first manager of Southdown's Portsmouth depot, in which district he had spent most of his life. Yet his contribution to the presence of Southdown Motor Services Ltd in eastern Hampshire was considerable, having acted as the anchor-man in Portsmouth during Mackenzie and Cannon's attempts to link Brighton with Portsmouth.

Facing page – Alfred Edward Cannon. His early service to the industry interrupted by World War I as a commissioned officer in the Royal Engineers, 'Freddie' Cannon soon regained his footing with Southdown. Becoming managing director at 31, his was the major drive behind the setting up of the express network, and his insistence on the maintenance of standards led to that unmistakable Southdown 'sparkle' – ultra-clean vehicles and staff whose pride in the job they were doing was plain for all to see. His natural flair for man management was the key to that success.

Born at Ryde, on the Isle of Wight, Bartlett became a telegraph messenger in 1872, was a junior clerk until 1877 when he joined the Ryde Pier Company as a booking clerk at the Isle of Wight Joint Railway Companies' offices on the Esplanade and Pier Head stations. He transferred to Portsmouth in 1884, opening the booking offices at Fratton and the one-time Southsea railway station. After a period back at Ryde and six years spent in Canada, he took up local excursion, steamship and emigration work in his own office at 67 Commercial Road from March 1903.

By now a well-established travel agent, Bartlett contacted Clement Rutlin, the secretary of the Isle of Wight Express Motor Syndicate Ltd in 1905 and convinced him that, following the Corporation's decision to concentrate upon its tramways, there was a gap in the market which could be filled by motorbus stage-carriage services and excursions. Although this project ceased and the Isle of Wight company foundered, he thus met Mackenzie and handled the affairs of the Sussex Motor Road Car Co Ltd, and later Southdown, for him until the establishment of a proper depot in the town, when he became the local manager. Comparatively unsung though Bartlett may have been, Southdown's Portsmouth depot owed its origin to his foresight.

Below – Frank Bartlett. Although Bartlett's official position within Southdown was that of manager of the company's Portsmouth depot, his larger importance should not be overlooked. This native of the Isle of Wight trained as a booking clerk for a railway company and moved into his own agency work on the mainland. Having seen the potential for motorbus operation on Portsea, he held the fort first for Sussex Motor Road Car Co Ltd and, when that failed, did the same again until Southdown got established there. He was the Portsmouth pioneer.

Chapter Two : The contributory operators

1: THE 'COUNTRY' SERVICES OF THE BRIGHTON, HOVE & PRESTON UNITED OMNIBUS CO LTD

Upon its formation in 1915, three companies contributed towards what was to become Southdown Motor Services Ltd. Worthing Motor Services Ltd and the London & South Haulage Co Ltd were completely absorbed, whilst the Brighton, Hove & Preston United Omnibus Co Ltd subscribed its country routes, excursion and tours together with the personnel, rolling stock and premises concerned, retaining as an operating entity its stage carriage services in Brighton and Hove which, in turn, were sold to Thomas Tilling Ltd the following year.

Founded in 1884, the BH&PUOC was the oldest of the three companies involved. The London Brighton & South Coast Railway ran its first holiday-makers' excursion into Brighton Terminus in 1844, an event which attracted hotel omnibuses to the station thereafter. Within ten years some 300 horse-drawn conveyances were being licensed by the Hackney Carriage Sub Committee. From among their number there developed recognisable omnibus services upon the London pattern and by 1875, their main assembly point was Castle Square, whose residents complained to the Watch Committee of the obstruction to their businesses and the touting of the conductors. The council promised to take 'steps to remedy the evil'.

In 1877 the several bus proprietors were joined by William Mayner of Westbourne Villas, Aldrington, whose omnibus business in Birmingham had been purchased the previous year by the newly-formed Birmingham Tramways & Omnibus Co Ltd. Mayner ran buses to Cliftonville and between Church Road, Hove and Kemp Town. He and William Taylor Beard, who operated from Church Road to Castle Square and also from North Street to the terminus station, jointly employed a timekeeper to start the buses. Sworn in by a special constable, the unfortunate man's duties extended from 8.30am to 10.30pm each day for 23 shillings (£1.15) per week, the majority of which was paid by Beard.

In addition, there were Walter Tilley's 'Brighton Busses' which operated three services from Castle Square, to Lewes Road, Stamford Avenue and to Tilley's own 'Race Hill Inn', from 1867-1901; the buses owned by A. E. Elliott running between Kemp Town and Cliftonville and Henry Thomas to Tivoli Gardens. Thomas is of particular note for he also ran out of town from the Terminus station and Castle Square along the breezy cliff top eastward to Rottingdean in competition with Welfare's bus.

Still wearing its manufacturer's delivery number and not yet registered CD 103, the first motor bus in Brighton arrived in December 1903, the month that British registration numbers were first issued. It was a 24hp Milnes-Daimler with 'Olympia' style bodywork and entered service with Brighton, Hove & Preston United Omnibus Co Ltd. The vehicle did not survive long enough to be included in either of the transfers of ex BH&D rolling stock to the newly-formed Southdown in 1915 or to Thomas Tilling Ltd when BH&PU sold out the rest of its business the following year.

As early as 1878 road traffic in Brighton and in Hove had reached such proportions that the shopkeepers in Western Road claimed that it was already inconveniently crowded and 159 of them signed a petition to the council protesting against the further issue of licences to omnibus proprietors – a seemingly counter-productive move, for there can be little doubt that tradesmen along the line of route benefited from the growing traffic. The council continued to grant the 5 shilling (25p) licences fairly generously, however, but warned Walter Tilley that after the licensing year 1881-82 they would refuse to license omnibuses of the great size now run by him between New Road and the Cemeteries. Applications by newcomers were nevertheless turned politely aside.

One such attempt – to run small one-horse buses on numerous routes in Brighton – was made by the Brighton General Omnibus Co Ltd in the summer of 1884. Yet it got no farther than the slimmest of toe-holds, before its efforts were pre-empted by a corporate enterprise which was to gather up into a powerful syndicate most of the larger independent operators.

On 11th October 1884, the Watch Committee of Brighton Corporation learned that the Brighton, Hove & Preston United Omnibus Co Ltd had been formed, which proposed to purchase all the omnibuses presently owned by William

Taylor Beard, William Mayner, Henry Thomas and Walter Tilley. The committee quickly informed the new company that it would be pleased to license the omnibuses anew in the name of the company. Indeed, it would have been surprising if it had not, for Aldermen Brigden and John J Clark were members of the board of directors, which also included Major-General W. R. E. Alexander, E. A. Eager, S. Ridley and G. Tatham. Beard became traffic and general manager of the new undertaking, Frank Smith its secretary and, in the early days, Eager was its accountant. William Mayner moved to Seafield Mews, Hove, and set himself up anew as a jobmaster. In the event, Tilley seems to have withdrawn from the scheme and continued to run his own buses along Lewes Road until he was put out of business by the Corporation's tramcars, whereafter he concentrated upon his motion-picture-house.

The grand collection of vehicles and equipment included some 30 omnibuses and 150 horses which were considered to be 'considerably above the average of Omnibus horses' and housed initially in the constituent proprietor's premises – including Upper St. James's Street and Conway Street, Hove. W. T. Beard and Frank Smith (later the first secretary of Southdown Motor Services Ltd) were installed in the offices at 6 Pavilion Buildings, 'the most advantageous spot for collecting the fares from conductors', and set about increasing routes and reducing headways throughout the two neighbouring boroughs. During 1886-87 Brighton alone licensed 42 of its buses, despite fears that the vehicles would 'disturb daily services in many places of worship' and spoil the local cab drivers' livelihood, the high price of corn and hay, a recent epidemic of influenza 'among the visitors and cab-horses' and complaints that buses would bring 'excursionists into the best part of town; an annoyance from which residents have happily not yet suffered'.

In its horse-bus days the company established the practice of painting either the destination or abbreviated route in large letters on the side panelling beneath, or latterly instead of, the company name in full. It was not until 1891 at least that all its omnibuses were fitted with proper staircases, instead of makeshift ladders, thus permitting lady passengers to travel 'on top'. The 'decency panels' which then required placing across the upper rails – lest a shapely ankle distracted other drivers – provided additional revenue in the form of advertisements for national and local businesses.

Urged on by its director E. A. Eager, the BH&PUOC began seriously to consider the possibility of motor traction in 1901. In the event, it was not until December 1903 that it purchased a motorbus, just as registration number-plates were being issued for the first time. CD 103 was a 24hp Milnes Daimler double-decker, the first of 25 bought between then and 1909. In 1906 the BH&PUOC began to build some of its own motorbus bodies at its Conway Street premises – an example later adopted by Worthing Motor Services Ltd. E. A. Eager was now the company superintendent and engineer pressing onward with motorbuses despite the public disquiet felt when, on 12th July

One needed to be pretty observant to discover where these early Milnes-Daimlers were going. 'Brighton & Hove' was the fleetname adopted and gave no certain indication: CD 236 of 1904 has, according to the curved panel over the platform, come from Hove along the length of Western Road. The staircase panel announces that Castle Square will be visited en route and the board above the windows discloses the terminus – Kemp Town, where it is here parked beside the Rock Inn, a Tamplin's pub.

With its strap over the bonnet giving the bus the jaunty air of a Gordon Bennett racer, Milnes-Daimler D 1959 is operating the service between Sackville Road, Hove and Castle Square in Brighton, on 29 May 1913. The vehicle was new to the Tunbridge Wells & Southborough District Omnibus Company in August 1905. Despite being sold by BH&PU before 1915, the vehicle survived, was refurbished in the 'seventies and exported as a museum piece to the United States. In the autumn of 1990, it changed hands at Pebble Beach, California for $253,000 (£137,000 at the then going rate).

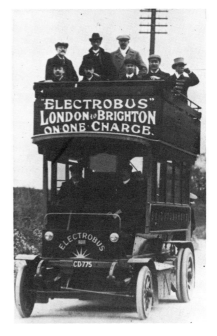

In the effort to placate those in 'the best part of town', BH&PU took their complaints about noise seriously and in 1909 began to invest in some Hallford-Stevens petrol-electric and Electrobus double-deckers whose progress was considerably less disturbing. The first Electrobus battery-electric vehicle was driven down to Brighton from London (complete with grey-toppered 'guard' blowing a post-horn) 'on one charge' – well almost; rumour had it that the lower deck was stacked with batteries for the delivery run. Thirty miles was the usual range for CD 775 and its eleven companions. Since the hill-climbing ability of the Electrobus was not up to the mark, they operated east and west in town.

1906, a London-based Vanguard double-decker en-route for Brighton came to grief with the loss of ten lives on that same Handcross Hill which had stopped Hancock's steam-coach 73 years before. It was Eager who jumped into the driving seat of a BH&PUOC Milnes-Daimler, and collecting doctors, stretchers and appliances, drove to the scene of the accident and took four surviving casualties to hospital in his bus. Eastbourne Corporation, the first municipality in the world to run motor omnibuses under parliamentary powers (from April 1903) had cold feet about them in 1906 and asked Eager to come along and advise the Motor Omnibus Committee of that town on 'matters connected with the management of motor omnibuses'.

Subsequent correspondence makes it perfectly clear that Eastbourne tentatively invited the BH&PUOC to take over the Corporation's bus operations, but the directors came to the conclusion that they should 'keep to the area of Brighton for the present'.

In Brighton itself, if the clip-clop of horses hooves and the jangling of the brasses had disturbed the peace 'in the best part of town', that was nothing compared with the racket set up by a Milnes-Daimler in full stride. The combination of creaking wooden wheels and rack and pinion final-drive produced a continuous chatter not unlike an amplified magpie; it echoed off shop fronts with great effect and did even better off the paling fences which abounded in the more select areas. Taking the renewed and more vigorous bout of complaints extremely seriously in January 1909, the BH&PUOC invested in a Hallford Petrol-Electric bus and three Electrobuses, each capable of travelling some thirty miles without recharging. These placated all but the most hardened complainants and the company purchased all the remaining vehicles of the London Electrobus Company in 1910, placing eight of these in service together with another new Electrobus and three more Hallford-Stevens petrol-electrics, thus providing a fleet of sixteen extremely quiet vehicles.

Eager kept a list of comparative mileages covered by petrol and electric-powered buses from 10th January 1909 to 28th October 1916, until the town services were purchased by Thomas Tilling Ltd. At their zenith in 1911, battery electric buses had covered 277,164 miles against 492,140 by the petrol engined vehicles. In 1915 the figure was 230,406 against 714,807. The petrol engined bus had been seriously challenged but not defeated.

Earlier, the company had made an attempt to lease or otherwise secure powers to run tramcars over the tramways laid down by Brighton Corporation from 1901. The most that BH&PUOC brought away from that discussion was permission to affix some of its 'stop tablets' to the anchor poles. Clauses in the Brighton Corporation Act 1903, however, did safeguard the routes of the company should the Corporation themselves decide to run motorbuses. This of course they did not do in the lifetime of the BH&PUOC or indeed until many years thereafter. Indeed, the Corporation stuck to its tramcars and entered into a series of coordination agreements with the company.

Competition with a different tramway, however, the Brighton & Shoreham Tramways Co Ltd. was another matter. Started in July 1884 with steam-hauled trams, which quickly failed, it relied upon horses stabled in its depot at Halfway House, Southwick, to haul the cars between Shoreham and Westbourne Villas, Hove. The rest of the journey into Brighton had been provided by the

Four Hallford-Stevens petrol-electric buses were operated by BH&PU. These had petrol engines, but final drive to the rear wheels was by separate electric motors, thus eliminating a major source of noise. CD 795 is the first of the quartet, and able to tackle the 108ft hump in the road to Rottingdean. The bodywork came from an earlier Milnes-Daimler and was of the 'Olympia' pattern; passengers inside sat facing inward and those on top faced forward – a combination inherited from horse-bus days. The Hallford-Stevens were outlasted by Electrobuses in BH&PU employ, being in service only some three years.

Although a comparatively noisy 'motor' bus by today's standard, a considerable leap forward in reliability took place in 1914 with the arrival of the Daimler CC type. CD 2156 was one of nine with open-top double-deck bodywork delivered to BH&PU. They were much liked and ran like clockwork, but an event in far-away Sarajevo determined their loss en bloc in September of that same year. On the corporation-owned lamp standard is what was known at the time as a BH&PU 'stop tablet', erected with local authority permission.

horse-buses of William Taylor Beard in the last few months of his independence. Despite their first manager's earlier agreement with the tramway and the fact that it had been purchased by the British Electric Traction Co Ltd with a

The influence of BH&PU is represented twice in this photograph taken in December 1913. Impressed with BH&PU's battery buses, Brighton Corporation decided to go one better and tried out an RET 'Railless' trolley car on a specially wired circuit around the London Road, Beaconsfield Villas and Ditchling Road tramway. However, although Brighton Corporation had received Parliamentary powers to run both trolley and motor buses in 1912, it was not to be until 1939 that it did so. Walter Tilley was originally involved in the discussions which set up BH&PU. In the event, he did not join in, but continued to run his own horse buses on Lewes Road until October 1901 when he was put out of business by Corporation tramcars. Instead he concentrated upon his motion picture house, public house and seedsman's business, delivering fodder for horses; and 'coal blocks' at 5 shillings (25p) per hundred.

BH&PU's decision to invest in Daimlers was one it soon had cause to regret. One of the prescribed war-subsidy types, available at a discount when operators were looking upon the bright side, were of course subject to requisition as soon as war was declared. CD 2167, seen in Hove on 8th August 1913 engaged upon the west-east road to Kemp Town, was duly stripped of its bodywork and handed over to the Army in September 1914.

view to electrification, BH&PUOC now considered it fair game and proceeded to draw off most of the passengers on this route with their far speedier buses, and finally killed it off in 1912.

The Brighton, Hove and Preston United Omnibus Co Ltd began placing single-decked coach bodies on its Milnes-Daimler additions to the fleet and running them along the coast route to Worthing in December 1905 in competition with the Sussex Motor Road Car Co Ltd. Additionally, between then and World War I, it applied for licences to run to Rottingdean, to Hurstpierpoint and to Lewes; curiously, however, there seems to be neither documentary nor testimonial evidence that these were taken up. In 1911, it decided to purchase a pair of Straker Squire coaches and commenced running a series of day excursions from Brighton, building up a fleet of fourteen coaches-cum-single-deck buses and two charabancs. The following January, it entered into an agreement with Worthing Motor Services Ltd – Mackenzie and Cannon's successors to SMRC – whereby the Worthing company retired from the Worthing-Brighton road completely in return for five per cent of BH&PUOC's revenue taken on the route and for concessions to the east of Brighton (see this chapter part 2).

Requisitions made by the War Office at the commencement of World War I reduced this 'country' fleet to eight vehicles. Like operators in other seaside resorts at the time, the company turned again to horses for its excursion work and acquired some taxis as well. In July 1914, it bought as a going concern, staff included, the business of Brighton jobmaster F J Mantell (later to become traffic manager of the Southdown company's Brighton area), together with his licences to ply for hire from the Front, and run to the Devil's Dyke – a service that BH&PUOC had intended to operate with motor buses five months previously.

By the time the Brighton, Hove and Preston Limited Omnibus Co Ltd was ready to make its contribution to the newly-formed pool in 1915, it also owned four horse charabancs, two victorias, sixteen landaus, five six-horse charabancs, each with its own name, one four-horse coach and one light covered-van, together with nineteen horses the army didn't want – and three motor taxi-cabs.

In order to take over the eight coaches, fourteen spare bus bodies and two country routes of the BH&PUOC, the new company had to swallow hard and buy this equine collection lock, stock and barrel – and Douglas Mackenzie 'didn't know one end of a horse from another'.

Tilling-Stevens was a make which did not attract the attention of the military, so TS3 model CD 3036 was among those purchased in 1915 to replace requisitioned Daimlers. They were to remain safely in service at Brighton and Hove with Thomas Tilling Ltd until 1931. The bodywork on this occasion was built by BH&PU in its own workshop and although based upon the 'Olympia' pattern, built by Dodson and other London-based manufacturers, is identifiable by the flat front of its canopy. CD 3036 is at Portslade Station.

2: WORTHING MOTOR SERVICES LTD

If not the oldest of the companies involved in the merger, at least Worthing Motor Services Ltd contributed most in terms of rolling stock, routes, personnel and, above all, its dynamic duo – Mackenzie and Cannon. It is also the best documented and recorded. In many ways it could be said that the founding of WMS' predecessor, the Sussex Motor Road Car Ltd in 1904, marks the real genesis of Southdown Motor Services Ltd.

The last days of the stage coach, the reign of the horse bus, and the emergence of motor traction in the Worthing district has been admirably chronicled by Henfry Smail (1948) in his *Coaching Times and After*, and although much of the story of stage carriage services at the turn of the century seems to have been written without the benefit of documents which have since come to light, it captures nevertheless the spirit and flavour of the period in a manner which only personal reminiscence can express. It therefore has much to lend to the history of Southdown in that area, the cradle of the company. Ironically, it was the reluctance of James Town, one of the major contributors of those reminiscences, to turn from horse to motor traction which provided the opening for the launching of the Sussex Motor Road Car Co Ltd.

As in Brighton and elsewhere, the provision of horse-drawn omnibuses seems to have commenced with the coming of the railway. Numerous small proprietors came and went throughout the next half century, including Jinks, Norris, Scovell, Townley who ran between Worthing and Storringon (later covered by SMRC), and John Stent & Son whose services included much of Worthing to its eastern and western boundaries, together with a joint station-bus in conjunction with James Town.

Although well-established long before, from 1888 Town was running half-hourly headways from Heene, the Pier and the Post Office to Broadwater, and from the Post Office to Heene, latterly at a fare of 4d. (1½p) for the whole journey as a result of motorised opposition. Earlier, his

The best-known of the original horse bus proprietors in Worthing was James Town. Starting with a donkey cart in 1849, he built a business which employed 30 and included stables at Steyne Mews (later a Southdown garage), Marine Mews off South Street and the Royal Mews, behind the Royal Sea House Hotel. His first omnibuses were small and had a near-vertical iron-runged ladder, to the roof, on which the conductor clung between stops. The 'Jubilee', introduced in 1887, was the first with a proper staircase, with 'decency' panels upstairs, so that ladies could travel on top. The basic route was between Heene, Marine Parade and Broadwater.

slogan printed upon his tickets 'James Town's excursion coaches are the Safest and Best' – they ran to Bramber Castle, Arundel and Littlehampton – took something of a knock. In 1890 two horses attached to one of his service buses, fortunately empty and unmanned, bolted from the Town Hall to the Sea House Hotel where they attempted to pass each side of the piers of the hotel portico. The heavy porch was immediately swept to the ground, killing both horses and smashing the bus to matchwood. However, such was the sympathy felt for Town, his fellow townsmen subscribed a considerable sum toward the cost of the damage. Meanwhile, with nothing quite so dramatic befalling them, Jay's buses ran a quarter hourly service between the Thomas a' Becket and East Worthing and Selden Road to the Tarring Fig Gardens for 2d (1p).

In most of the larger municipalities at the turn of the century, electric traction was very much the up and coming motive power. In 1903, both Worthing and its horse bus proprietors survived a British Electric Traction attempt to build an electric tramway in the resort. Brought up with horses and quite unable to bring himself to purchase a motorbus, James Town turned a deaf ear to numerous pleas to try the new form of transport and send some regular motorbus services out into the surrounding countryside. Frustrated, the council commissioned a report upon the feasibility of organising its own municipal motorbus department, but eventually settled for announcing its preparedness to grant licences to the several persons who had been making enquiries on the subject.

This lad would have needed a good head for figures to act as conductor on one of James Town's larger two-horse omnibuses. His half-hunter watch chain suggests he was well-equipped for the task. Eight steps to the top deck were now protected by hand rail and guard of the type which survived in the BH&D fleet on AEC Regent buses until after World War II. On this horse bus, the passengers faced inward downstairs, forward on garden seats on top. Rather than with a bugle or whistle, as on earlier Town buses, the boy conductor would have communicated with the driver by tugging on the bell cord, seen here behind his head.

Sussex Motor Road Car Co Ltd

Accordingly, a completely new syndicate, formed in the summer of 1904, received notification that their plans to link up the railway stations of Worthing and Pulborough would be greeted favourably. Beville Molesworth St Aubyn of Toat Farm, Pulborough, whose idea the project was, had been in Brighton the previous December, when the Brighton, Hove & Preston United Omnibus Company's first motorbus rolled into town. Greatly impressed, he had seen in his mind's eye similar vehicles free-ranging in the Worthing area. St Aubyn thus became managing director of the Sussex Motor Road Car Co Ltd, with his stepson Sir Walter Barttelot of Stopham as chairman, and Newland Tompkins as assistant managing director and joint-secretary. The other directors were Douglas B. Hall and James M. M. Erskine. The managing director's biggest achievement, however, was to convince Walter Flexman French, resident in his summer address at Telville Road, Worthing, that he should become manager and engineer of the fleet.

When French took up his appointment, the syndicate had purchased two Clarkson 'Chelmsford' steam buses to operate the service, which commenced in November 1904. They were parked overnight in Shelvey's Mineral Water Works in Station Road, Worthing, until a garage was rented in the yard behind the Railway Hotel. Facilities comprised two pits, a workbench nine and a half feet by two and half feet, a ticket office the size of a single bedroom and, if the company buses returned before the cars of the hotel guests, a parking lot outside.

After the first few weeks of working, it was found necessary to install large underground tanks to collect rain water for the steam buses at the White Horse Hotel in Storrington, because the hard water of Worthing furred up the boilers which frequently burned out their tubes. The injectors also gave trouble and caused drivers to steer one handed and pump vigorously with the other. French soon realised that chalky Sussex water and steam engines were simply not compatible and convinced the directors that they should be sold whilst still in reasonably good condition. They went to the Vale of Llangollen Engineering Bus and Garage Co Ltd after less than six months service.

In March 1905, a Milnes-Daimler 20hp saloon omnibus arrived to relieve the steamers and further buses of the same make were added for the summer season which was considerably helped by traffic to the Sussex Territorials camp at Washington. By the end of the year, four Milnes-Daimlers had been fitted with open-top double-decked bodywork to French's design. There were seats for two passengers beside the driver and a further cross-seat for four immediately behind him, all of which were preferred, even to those on top, by the travelling public despite a 50 per cent surcharge. The remainder of the seats downstairs faced inward. Rather than engage the owners of numerous overhanging trees in litigation, the seats on the upper deck were arranged to minimise the danger to passengers the first three vehicles with back-to-back knifeboard seating and the other with five garden seats placed down the centre. The others were altered to this configuration by the spring of 1906, by which time the saloon had become a double-decker. Much of the clerical work was undertaken by the Pulborough Estate Office of Newland Tompkins and

The first vehicles of the newly formed Sussex Motor Road Car Co Ltd were a pair of Clarkson 'Chelmsford' steam-powered buses to operate a service between Worthing and Pulborough, where BP319 is connecting with the LB&SCR train service in November 1904. Appointed manager and engineer, Walter Flexman French soon discovered that Sussex water and steam boilers did not suit each other. After less than six months' service, the Clarksons were sold before they had sustained too much damage.

Purchased as a replacement for SMRC's Clarkson steamers was BP345, a Milnes-Daimler 20hp saloon omnibus, the only one in the fleet. It is seen here en-route from Pulborough to Worthing, where it would be shedded overnight at the Railway Hotel Garage. The latter remained the property of the hotel, the covered accommodation being leased to the SMRC company. The registered office of the company was at the other end of this route at the Pulborough Estate office.

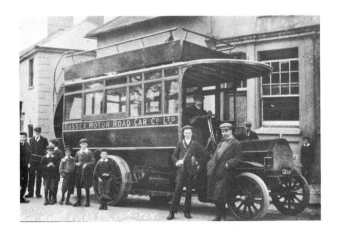

Pausing en route at Storrington is Milnes-Daimler CD 338. Its entry into service had been delayed whilst this double-decked bodywork designed by French was built and fitted. The vehicle was destined to become the oldest bus transferred to Southdown Motor Services Ltd in 1915, though by then carrying a slipper-type charabanc body.

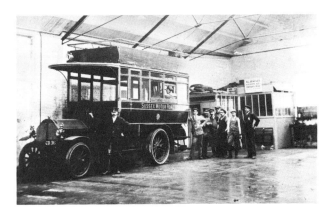

The interior of the Railway Hotel Garage, Worthing in the summer of 1905 with Milnes-Daimler CD 361, which survived to become No. 85 in the Southdown fleet from which it was eventually retired in 1918. The body worn here is one designed by French, and the building in the corner is the original ticket office of the company. It measured 13ft by 12ft, minus a 5ft 3in bite. The small bench beside it was 9ft 6in long and constituted the 'workshop' for the garage's running repairs. The clerical staff lived in French's house nearby.

Actually on the road a day or two before the Sussex Motor Road Car Company got started were the first three buses of the Worthing Motor Omnibus Company. They were Milnes-Daimler 24hp models (slightly larger and more powerful than SMRCs) with 36 seat bodywork and registered BP 311/3/5. This company's vehicles were based at its own Ivy Arch garage on the Broadwater Road which was comparatively well-equipped to deal with heavy repairs.

Two further Milnes-Daimlers with the same capacity completed the fleet and one of these, probably BP317, is at rest beside Worthing Central railway station early in 1905. Several of the founders were interested financially in both companies, so it soon became clear that the creation of one stronger company would be a more effective policy to adopt. The Sussex Motor Road Car Company purchased the WMOC undertaking in August 1905 and both fleets were merged under the SMRC title.

the company's good relations with licensed victuallers along the route was unquestionable. Its parcel offices and waiting rooms were established at *The Railway Hotel*, Worthing, *The Gun*, Findon, *The Maltster's Arms*, Broadwater, *Frankland Arms*, Washington, *The Half Moon*, Storrington, *The Crown*, Cootham, *The White Horse*, Marehill, and the terminus just beyond the railway arch in Pulborough, *The Railway Hotel*. Despite the fact that the drivers were not permitted to imbibe, the journeys were not without incident: on Wiggenholt Common a bus lost all its windows against a telegraph pole whilst avoiding a startled horse and another parted company with one of its wooden wheels whilst descending the Bostal – both without injury to their occupants.

Wooden wheels gave considerable trouble in the early days of motor traction. They were fine on horse-buses, where the tractive effort was provided by some outside force pulling at the bodywork they merely supported, but once the drive was by a live axle through the centre of the wheels, the spokes gradually leaned away from their proper positions, thus loosening the entire structure and adding greatly to the noise of the vehicles' progress. The effect was at its worst in dry spells and the SMRC was not without its pond to soak the wheels on such occasions.

In September 1905, SMRC started a second service between Worthing, Littlehampton and Arundel which did its best to provide connections with the Pulborough buses. The fare for that journey was one shilling and fourpence (6½p) and an extra six pence (2½p) if the passenger wished to sit next to the driver unless, in his subjective judgment, she was young and pretty. SMRC also tried to begin running to Brighton in competition with another company founded in 1904, The Worthing Motor Omnibus Co Ltd. WMOC had been operating local services from Ham Road to Tarring Fig Gardens; Broadwater to West Worthing and West Tarring to the Town Hall, in competition with Town's and Jay's horse buses, with three 24hp Milnes-Daimler open-topped double-deckers which were actually on the road a few days before SMRC's 20hp Milnes-Daimlers. It added two more, all with 36-seat bodywork which was considered at the time to be rather too large for country work, and, in the absence of licences from Brighton, established a service to Palmeira Square, Hove, in June 1905. James Erskine, however, was a director of both companies; by September rivalry was averted and the SMRC vehicles merely provided connections for Hove buses.

Soon after the directors of WMOC realised that a division of interest was counter-productive and, in August 1905, the Worthing Motor Omnibus Company was absorbed by the Sussex Motor Road Car Co Ltd. Worthing Motor Omnibus Company founders David Brazier and 'Major' Harry Gates sold their interest, but secretary Arthur Stubbs continued to act in that role for his new company. B. Molesworth St. Aubyn remained managing director and Walter Flexman French was retained as manager and engineer of a fleet now doubled to ten vehicles. A major asset gained was the WMOC's partially constructed Ivy Arch garage on the Broadwater road, the other side of the railway from SMRC's original depot and potentially twice its size. The working environment of the Ivy Arch premises was already a great improvement on the Railway Hotel garage, from the channels and raised walkways of blue setts which kept the bus washers and crew's feet dry to the

DL208 was the first of two Thornycroft 80 B4 charabancs with Dodson bodywork delivered to Worthing by road from Willesden in July 1907. Their purchase followed the arrival as general manager of Douglas Mackenzie who used his Ryde, Isle of Wight office to register them. The body was the first of his tiered-seating design to enter service at Worthing. DL208 commenced operation on the Worthing-Bognor service: DL209 on the Worthing-Brighton-Seaford.

By the autumn of 1908, the Sussex Motor Road Car Co Ltd was in retreat. It became necessary to run extra journeys along the seafront at Worthing in the evenings to pay the week's wages. The receiver was called in. Mackenzie, however, had purchased six Milnes-Daimlers in London which had not been transferred to SMRC. The receiver declared these to be Mackenzie's property and he and Cannon revived three of them from the bits and pieces lying about the Ivy Arch garage, and kept the Worthing to Storrington service going until the spring of 1909.

provision of a 12ft by 15ft workshop. Its equipment included a 6hp National gas engine, which supplied power and electric light for the building, and enough tools to maintain 25 buses – a clear indication of the expansionist intent of the management. The petrol store was licensed to hold 4,000 gallons which were delivered in 40-gallon steel barrels and mounted on stillages with, optimistically, a New Era fire extinguisher nearby – and to the consternation of the local petroleum inspector, there were 182 more gallons of petrol and 25 of benzolene stored illegally in a greenhouse outside.

Immediately after the merger, the clerical staff was relocated in French's house near the Railway Hotel and it was his policy to train all new drivers himself. The company now planned to move farther afield and, in October 1905, introduced a new service between Pulborough, Steyning and Hove. There was also an over-ambitious plan to operate a Pulborough-Billingshurst-Haslemere-Godalming-Guildford route with six additional buses but clearly the management realised that such a service would

have been too long and the terrain too difficult. Instead, SMRC's renewed efforts to gain access to Brighton were now successful and the necessary licences were issued in January 1906. The Brighton, Hove & Preston United Omnibus Co Ltd actually pipped it to the post, however, gaining running rights over the entire Brighton to Worthing route on 18th December 1905. Brighton Corporation declined to give any reason why they had previously refused to grant licenses to SMRC. Said the journal *Commercial Motor* 'it is ... probable that the extreme jealousy between Brighton and Hove has been allowed to eclipse all considerations of the public welfare'. In fact, if one employs the Namier technique of the historian and looks not at the institution but the people involved, the membership of the board of directors of BH&PUOC tells its own tale.

Perhaps it was SMRC's chosen parking place in Brighton – an undertaker's yard – which presaged disaster. Mechanical troubles with the vehicles were numerous. For instance, the early Milnes-Daimlers were lubricated by an elaborate system of 30 sight-feed bottles of oil on the dash-board with copper tubes leading from each to the part to be lubricated. These the driver, in addition to his main task, had to keep dripping at the correct number of drops per minute and each one at a different rate. French removed the bottles and adopted greasers for most places. With two half-pint bottles for the crank case each driver then had to carry in the bus a quart filler-can and two gallons of oil to keep the crank case bottles topped up. Soon, footboards were covered in oil and the driver got his hands and clothes coated in a mixture of oil and dust. If earlier enthusiasm in the ranks waned somewhat it is hardly surprising. Lubrication problems, gear box trouble and difficulty keeping the tyres on began to accumulate and the crash of the Vanguard Milnes-Daimler on Handcross Hill came at a bad time for public confidence. The route to Brighton was not exactly what SMRC had hoped for either. It had wished to terminate the service at the Aquarium, but conditions imposed by the council insisted that the buses should go on across the unremunerative part of town to Chesham Road, Kemp Town, thus adding unwanted mileage to a route on which it was already obliged to compete with BH&PUOC and the Brighton & Shoreham tramway. Daily breakdowns became more numerous.

In the summer of 1906, Walter Flexman French returned to London and entered the commercial car-hire business. SMRC struggled on with the vehicles under the supervision of engineer A. E. Hartley, until by the early spring of 1907 it was making a heavy loss on the Worthing-Brighton run. Engaged a few months earlier as consulting engineer, Alfred Douglas Mackenzie now accepted the position of general manager of SMRC with his assistant Cannon to act as a very youthful chief-engineer, thus setting in motion what was to prove a thirty-seven-year partnership.

Alfred Cannon immediately set about rationalising the maintenance system and Mackenzie attempted the bold throw – expansion, and far afield at that. Remembering Bartlett, he headed for Portsmouth and on Saturday 12th October 1907, Milnes-Daimler CD 408 rolled to a halt at the Commercial Road office on a trip from Bognor. Three journeys per day were then run via Chichester, Emsworth and Havant. It was planned to close the gap between Bognor and Littlehampton the following spring, thereby establishing a Brighton-Worthing-Littlehampton-Bognor-Portsmouth facility serving all the towns and villages along the line of route. This grand strategy was thwarted, however, by sheer lack of custom at the Portsmouth approaches. On 6th December 1907, Mackenzie obtained permission from Portsmouth Council to transfer two of the four buses used on this route to run within the town itself; from Edinburgh Road to Eastney Barracks via Arundel Street and Fratton Bridge; and from Clarence Pier, where there was an additional booking office, to Eastney via South Parade the following spring. SMRC rented a garage in Rudmore Lane to house the vehicles. That winter an additional bus clawed its way over Portsdown Hill on a route to Hambledon, the birthplace of cricket, and spent three days stranded in a snow-filled ditch. 'Last bus' crews slept overnight at the 'George' inn at Hambledon and the bus was parked in the yard, an arrangement which led to a petrified cockerel taking an unnoticed journey to Portsmouth perched on the back axle, whence he was retrieved by the crew and returned to his hens in a sack.

Mackenzie's plans to save the Sussex Motor Road Car Co Ltd included the purchase of an MOC and two Thornycroft coaches fitted with open charabanc bodies (originally planned for the Milnes-Daimlers) so that body-swaps could provide for seasonal change. SMRC vehicles appeared at Goodwood and Ascot Races, and in addition to the office which Mackenzie retained at Ryde, offices were opened for excursion traffic at Seaford, Newhaven. Eastbourne, Hastings and at the 'George Inn' yard near the Bargate, Southampton. Southampton Corporation was at the time considering restarting a motor bus service – which it first ran in 1900 and 1901 – between the Clock Tower and Northam, and Mackenzie tried to secure it for the SMRC. If he had, it is highly unlikely that Hants & Dorset Motor Services would ever have been founded and Southdown, one may speculate, would eventually have provided stage carriage services all the way from Hastings to Bournemouth. Instead, Harry Lawrence drove a coach, without the benefit of a Southampton licence, from the 'George Inn' yard to Lyndhurst and back for a couple of months in the summer of 1908. If the local police didn't notice, the station master at Totton certainly did, for he was so impressed with the vehicle which paused there upon each trip, he arranged for the London & South Western Railway company to engage Lawrence as the local vehicle mechanic, whence he eventually returned to spend his working life driving for Southdown.

The three new coaches were fitted with what was described as slipper-type bodywork to Mackenzie's own design. Six rows of seats, each five inches higher tier above tier, with two more beside the driver, gave 32 passengers a perfect view of the road. Registered DL 261, DL 208-9 respectively, they were almost certainly ordered by Mackenzie for the Isle of Wight Express Motor Syndicate Ltd, but redirected by him to SMRC. Initially, the MOC worked the Worthing-Brighton service and the Thornycrofts were employed at Bognor and Seaford, their curious shape arousing great interest wherever they went. Meanwhile, the Hampshire adventure of SMRC ended in the autumn of 1908, when the four vehicles based in Portsmouth were hastily withdrawn to Worthing because there was not enough money to pay the garage rent. Things were not much better in Worthing itself either, despite the fact that on one trip Bill West found himself driving Queen Alexandra and the Czarina of Russia from Brighton to Worthing; it became necessary for some additional running along Marine Parade in the evenings to get enough money to pay the wages. In November 1908, the official receiver for Brighton was called in.

Renowned for his reluctance to throw anything away, Douglas Mackenzie had, the previous year, purchased from the London Standard Motor Omnibus Company six of the original Milnes-Daimlers of the defunct Hastings & St Leonards Omnibus Company and stored them about the Ivy Arch garage during the attempted expansion. Since he'd paid only £90 for the lot and 'had difficulty in getting one serviceable vehicle out of the assembled pieces' it is possible they were really intended merely as spare parts. Nevertheless, because the SMRC had not enough funds to purchase them from MacKenzie, the receiver now declared them to be his property. Following the liquidation of SMRC, MacKenzie and Cannon breathed life into three of these buses and, keeping their band of employees together, ran them between Worthing and Storrington throughout the winter of 1908-9.

Formation of Worthing Motor Services

Douglas Mackenzie had been taking out metaphorical insurance in another way also. He had retained his office in Victoria Street. Westminster, and in May 1908 this became the registered office of two allied companies, of which Mackenzie was again the consulting engineer, Western Motor Coaches Ltd of Minehead, Somerset, and Kent Motor Services Ltd of Maidstone. KMS had been started at the request of local residents who assured Mackenzie that there was ample traffic, to run between Maidstone and Sutton Valence, Sittingbourne and Faversham, and from Maidstone to Hastings on Sundays. In fact the Kentish enterprise lasted little longer than two months and its two Milnes-Daimlers and two Thornycrofts were sent along to Worthing.

Formed in March 1909 to acquire the Ivy Arch garage and work the remaining vehicles of both the old SMRC and Douglas Mackenzie, Worthing Motor Services Ltd was registered the following month. In order to keep the registration numbers in sequence, the methodical Mackenzie had used his Ryde office to provide DL series numbers for the ex-Hastings chassis he'd saved from the bits and pieces. The new company retained Mackenzie and Cannon in their respective roles and then afforded them the status of directors. It extended the Worthing-Storrington route back to Pulborough, and plunged into the private hire market in May 1909, providing the transport for the Sussex Royal Garrison Artillery's 'Motor Dash' from Brighton to Newhaven Fort – a journey accomplished in 30 minutes, with Milnes-Daimler double-decker DL 383 well to the fore. Leaving Portsmouth alone for the time being, WMS lost no time in applying for new licences to run into Brighton, and in restarting the local services at Worthing, and to Arundel and Littlehampton – with a total of fifteen buses. Additionally, it acquired rented premises at 23 Marine Parade, Worthing, and into this, from up the stairs at the Ivy Arch, was moved the administrative, clerical and miscellaneous duties section of the company. In this building a clerical assistant spent a laborious week stamping new fares on old Isle of Wight Express Motor Syndicate tickets for use locally and then, when Mackenzie had a better idea, glued paper panels over the Isle of Wight name and destinations upon each ticket and wrote in the Sussex ones instead.

Such economy gives a clear indication of the financial state of Worthing Motor Services Ltd in its first four years and, indeed, it was not until 1912 – when Alfred Cannon himself purchased a Straker Squire chassis and hired it to WMS – that the company managed to add to the fleet. Meanwhile, WMS' entry into Brighton was the subject of new council restrictions. Previously the licences had been granted on a protective-fare basis: now there was to be no plying for hire on the Brighton side of Portslade. Worthing town council retaliated by imposing similar restrictions upon the Brighton Hove & Preston United, leaving each company to bring back only the passengers they had taken

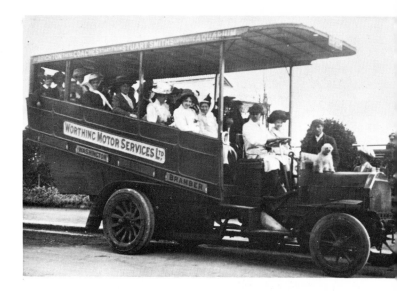

Modifications to Mackenzie's tiered 'slipper' design came thick and fast once Worthing Motor Services Ltd was launched. First, the roofed variety became more commonplace, then the centre of gravity received attention. In this body on Milnes-Daimler CD 354, the weight of a full load is high and behind the rear axle, a recipe for severe roll on a corner – and the road between Washington, Steyning and Bramber was not then noted for its straightness. On CD 390, also a Milnes-Daimler, the combined weight is now marginally in front of the rear axle and the height of the rear passengers above the ground is considerably reduced. A far more stable ride must have resulted.

Opposite page (centre) – Milnes-Daimler CD 408, wearing an SMRC body designed by French, gathering passengers at Worthing for Brighton at a time when protective-fare arrangements in Brighton and Worthing had broken down, to be replaced by a system where WMS could only bring back from Brighton the passengers it had taken there; and vice-versa at Worthing for the rival Brighton, Hove & Preston United company. Both got around this by opening an office in each other's town, and WMS placed warning notices on the vehicles: 'At Brighton passengers must obtain tickets at Booking Office, Steine St, opposite Aquarium'.

Opposite page (foot) – The development of Mackenzie's 'slipper' received continued attention. A little fretwork at the rear end of this smaller capacity body on Milnes-Daimler CD 353 gives a rather more modern appearance at little cost, but fails to give passengers any real protection from on-shore squalls along the seafront. The narrow box-like steps look positively hazardous by today's standards and the body remains decidedly 'seasonal' in character.

Worthing Motor Services not only succeeded in acquiring most of the ex-SMRC Milnes-Daimlers, it also plunged into the private hire business and purchased a small fleet of private cars and taxi-cabs for smaller parties. Vehicles of both types were hired from WMS in May 1909 for the Sussex (Territorial) Royal Garrison Artillery's 'motor-dash' from Brighton to Newhaven. Surgeon-Lieut Harold Scatliff, the taller of the two officers, walks forward to his allotted car as Milnes-Daimler DL383 (re-registered by Mackenzie) brings up the rear in Windsor St, Brighton.

out – which is hardly what a stage-carriage service is supposed to be.

Each company now circumvented the restriction by opening an office in the other's home town and getting the passengers to book in advance. BH&PUOC rented No. 5 South Street, Worthing, and WMS came to an agreement with Stuart Smith to make use of part of his Royal Mews in Steine Street, Brighton. The remainder of those premises was occupied by cabs and their drivers, who viewed motorbuses with undisguised disfavour. One of them lost no time reporting George Cowley to the council authorities when he himself went to the office to buy the distinctive square tickets for the passengers, instead of sending them in to make the purchase. The technique employed by the drivers and which he should have followed was to drive slowly around the Aquarium to attract attention and lead the customers back to the office. In effect, Stuart Smith was WMS manager in Brighton.

Prior to the January 1912 agreement with BH&PUOC which eliminated the need for such antics, it was WMS policy to require all passengers to book at the office, even in Worthing, where it was actually unnecessary, to ensure that they did not travel on the rival buses. Both companies took to wearing flags to identify themselves to the faithful: BH&PUOC a Union Jack, and Worthing Motor Services Ltd a red pennant bearing its initials. It was during this period that driver Wally Turner, who was to retire from

Southdown in 1950, earned his nickname 'Frottle'. "Get down on that frottle" he would say to his conductor when he wanted his colleague to reach under the bonnet to force down the throttle rod and help him outrun the BH&PUOC bus to the next stop.

After 1912, the vehicles released from the competition of the Worthing and Brighton road were able to go in search of new custom elsewhere. The Worthing company's buses now ran from Brighton to Newhaven and Seaford without any attempt at opposition from BH&PUOC, in return – on a reciprocal basis – for five per cent of WMS' takings on that route to be paid to the Brighton firm. Those fares which were subject to this commission were taken in exchange for an unmistakable series of yellow tickets. Fully *au fait* with railway history, and no doubt mindful of the time when the London & Southampton railway found it necessary to change its name to the London & South Western, in case it upset the people of Portsmouth whose town it was about to serve, Mackenzie now decided that the 'Worthing Motor Services' label was a shade too parochial for coaches about to operate in Brighton and as far afield as Seaford, and the name 'Sussex Tourist Coaches' was adopted for excursion work and coaches working east of Brighton.

It was during this period that Mackenzie began to work with the flair which established him as a traffic expert of considerable repute. He had the knack of driving a bus at its lowest oil-consumption, and expected others to follow suit, of knowing by the slightest noise that a vehicle needed attention, of knowing when to change the role in which a vehicle operated. The man whose intention in life was "to get them off their bicycles" would arrive at the Ivy Arch garage as fast as his own bicycle would carry him and call upon everyone in sight to drop whatever he was doing and give a hand with body-shifting – changing coaches to buses and vice-versa – in order to get numbers and usage

in their proper sequence. There was nevertheless a great camaraderie at the Ivy Arch garage and that famous 'Southdown' style came another step along the way. Among those who fielded the pay packets which the young Alfred Cannon handed out was Charlie Harris, the car washer, William Treby who burnished the big ends, driver Len Pearson with his immaculate leggings, Charles Gates, Bill Ellis the leading tipster, R. F. Clement who was to be awarded the MBE in 1953, H. E. Humphrey who became garage superintendent at Littlehampton, W. J. Cooper – a conductor who became area manager at Worthing, Bill Turner – an ex-Brighton horse-bus conductor, and little Jimmy Tee and Scott Fairbanks who were soon to go off to Flanders – and never return. Others were to spend their entire working lives with Southdown. George Cowley who was to transfer to Portsmouth and was always known by Cannon as 'Young Cowley' retired in 1959 with a record of 51 years in PSV driving. The very last to retire was to be conductor William Jay, whose father's horse-bus services in Worthing were taken over by WMS in March 1913.

This was to be the year when Worthing Motor Services began to purchase new vehicles. A pair of Tilling-Stevens double-deckers joined the Worthing fleet which was now operating the following departures each day: Brighton 12, Findon, Washington and Storrington 4, Littlehampton and Arundel 3, Goring Circular 2, Findon and Bramber 1,

An unusual addition to WMS's fleet in 1912 was this Straker Squire U type double-decker with chain drive, whose chassis was the personal property of Alfred Cannon. The bodywork was by Dodson and acquired second-hand from the Metropolitan Steam Omnibus Company. Registered DL621, the vehicle is operating the Worthing 'cross town local' on 19th August 1914 and at this stage, A. D. Mackenzie is named as 'Secretary' of WMS on the address panel. DL621 was destined to become No. 29 in the Southdown fleet.

Amberley and Arundel 1. More importantly, the Brighton, Newhaven and Seaford excursions were greatly enhanced by the purchase of Daimler vehicles for the 'Sussex Tourist Coaches' fleet. Advertising on bill-heads and tickets with the slogan 'Green Cars run Everywhere', Douglas Mackenzie was about to realise his ambition to show 'Beautiful Britain' to a completely new kind of tourist (see Chapter 6).

Much more likely to earn its keep year round was the more sophisticated glazed bodywork fitted to CD 338, suitable for both rainy and cold weather conditions. The pennant, which was red, bearing the letters WMS Ltd, was an identification device worn to aid recognition of the company's vehicles on the Brighton route. BH&PU buses flew a Union Jack for the same purpose. This oddity ceased in January 1912 when the companies reached an operational agreement as custom increased.

Just before World War I, the availability of Daimler chassis enabled the 'slipper' concept to be taken to its elegant conclusion. One of a pair of Daimler CC type purchased by WMS in 1913 was DL702, seen here with Driver Barnes at the wheel, under the watchful eye of Inspector 'Hoppy' Pickford. The occasion was a private hire by the Worthing Brotherhood. By this time, Mackenzie had decided to adopt the name 'Sussex Tourist Coaches' for vehicles operating on private hire, excursions and 'coach cruising'. The chassis is believed to have been among those taken for military service during the war.

3: LONDON & SOUTH COAST HAULAGE CO LTD

No sooner had Worthing Motor Services and the Brighton, Hove & Preston United Omnibus Company reached their 1912 accommodation and subsequent *modus vivendi* than a new company and potential competitor arrived in Brighton. Having left Worthing in 1906, Walter Flexman French had made yet another mark for himself as London manager and agent for the Ryknield Motor Co Ltd, launching French's Ltd (Motor Jobmasters) and hiring out Ryknield lorries on a contract hire basis. This firm became French's Garage & Motor Works Ltd which apart from carrying out the business which its name suggests, became the main agency through which vehicles for Maidstone & District and the future Hants & Dorset Motor Services were acquired and the wages of their employees were paid in

their formative days. French, together with H. E. Hickmott, better known as Major Hickmott with Ribble Motor Services Ltd at Preston, in Lancashire, in the years between the wars, now took an interest in the London & South Coast Haulage Co Ltd, which set up in Brighton with two lorries and a van.

London & South Coast Haulage undertook contract work and cartage for a number of local firms including Hannington's the furniture stores. Within two years, the venture was in danger of imminent collapse as neither the amount of work nor the rates obtainable permitted the company to break even. Turning to a sideline in which he had already enjoyed mixed fortunes, French decided that passenger transport might prove the saving of their faltering enterprise. In Kent, he had already formed omnibus companies at Margate and at Maidstone, his son George now ran the fledgling Maidstone & District company. In

June 1914, French purchased a Daimler CD saloon motorbus and applied for a licence to run from Brighton to Hurstpierpoint. Following an initial rebuff, this was granted after a free excursion followed by tea had convinced the members of the Watch Committee that they could hardly refuse.

To reinforce their entry into the bus field, L&SCH purchased as a going concern the business of William and Anne Ecclestone, whose 'Brighton Queen' charabanc operation was better known as 'Jolly Jumbos' – a reference to Mr Ecclestone's outsize dimensions. The Ecclestones had provided horse-drawn excursion vehicles from their leasehold Middle Street premises and only recently converted to a fleet of five Fiat touring cars and charabancs which they ran from the Kings Head Garage in West Street. At the same time, L&SCH purchased four torpedo-bodied Durham-Churchill charabancs and four further Daimler saloon buses, extending the Hurstpierpoint service to Burgess Hill and opening a second route to Falmer and Lewes. The stage carriage buses bore the somewhat misleading title 'Brighton and South Coast', for its routes went inland.

At the sharp end of the London & South Coast Haulage company's affairs were Driver E. W. Parsons who was to undertake some pioneer work for Southdown, and would be the last of the L&SCH men to retire from its ranks in 1950, Richard Ried conductor and driver, Cecil Pullen, Bill Holland, Frederick Kerman who became garage foreman at Freshfield Road and R. C. Paramor who was Southdown's mechanical inspector at Bognor in the early 'fifties. The best efforts of these men presented a considerable problem to the Brighton, Hove & Preston United Omnibus Co Ltd who had themselves sought licences for the Lewes road. Its difficulty was compounded when the L&SCH added a Straker Squire and Leyland S-type saloons to their fleet and intensified their headways, operating from both of the ex-Ecclestone properties, with additional storage facilities at Ditchling Rise. These were the days when a new saloon omnibus, chassis, tyres and body complete, cost in the region of £800. Two of the L&SCH stage carriage vehicles were second-hand. The Daimlers were particularly modern and attractive to

CD 2649 at Brighton Pier ready for departure on the company's second service introduced – to Lewes. This vehicle has Dodson bodywork of the type which was developed into that company's standard post-WWI Daimler CD19 type. The haulage firm's title was not entirely appropriate to the passenger routes, which went inland, and neither was the fleetname chosen for them, 'Brighton and South Coast'. This lack of nicety seems not to have concerned either principals or passengers. The chassis of the Daimlers were taken for war service: only the bodies were acquired by Southdown.

L&SCH added four Durham Churchill torpedo-bodied charabancs to their fleet in July 1914 and enhanced their entry into the tours business by purchasing a local firm's premises and small fleet of Fiats. In 1915, and just prior to the formation of Southdown Motor Services, French bought three further vehicles for the 'Brighton and South Coast' fleet – a Straker-Squire and two Leyland S type saloons. One of the latter, LH 8977, marked for the Lewes service, poses for its picture at the Aquarium, just prior to entering service with Southdown. The Leyland chassis had been new to London Central, but were purchased third hand from the Wellingborough Motor Omnibus Company and fitted with new bodywork,

Opposite page – CD 2649 at Brighton Pier ready for departure on the company's second service introduced – to Lewes. This Daimler has Dodson bodywork of the type which was developed into that company's standard post-WWI CD19 type. The haulage firm's title was not entirely appropriate to the passenger routes, which went inland, and neither was the fleetname chosen for them, 'Brighton and South Coast'. This lack of nicety seems not to have concerned either principals or passengers. The chassis of the Daimlers were taken for war service: only the bodies were acquired by Southdown.

customers and were some of the first buses to provide drivers with a windscreen to protect them from rain, flies, dust and sprayed tar. It was clear that with the kind of money that French could now rustle up for his operations this, potentially, was a serious time indeed for the incumbents.

Just what kind of battle would have developed between Walter Flexman French and the man who had replaced him at Worthing in 1907 was never to be put to the test. After 24th August 1914, 'French' meant Sir John French or *the* French, as the British Expeditionary Force, tied by political considerations to the strategy of its ally, found itself retreating from Mons – the first battle of The Great War, as it became known until subsequent history renamed it World War I. Commercial battles at home became positively anti-social overnight.

Chapter Three: For 'Coast' read 'down'

If one employs the maxim about silver linings, it could be said that but for World War I, Southdown Motor Services Ltd might never have come into existence. At one and the same time the outbreak of the conflict presented the three companies concerned with both a sudden increase of people on the move and a government policy decision which constrained them from capitalising upon the situation. In the early days, it was not so much the employees who enlisted in the forces, as the British Army's need to bolster its transport columns which created the necessary climate for drastic rationalization.

As early as 1904 it had been recognised by the military authorities that motorised transport would play an important part in future wars. The notion that new officers should be given instruction in engineering was given serious consideration. Several years later Worthing Motor Services participation in the Territorials' 'Motor Dash' to Newhaven marked one of the earliest attempts to move large bodies of men by motor vehicles. In 1911 it was estimated by the War Office that, in the event of a European war, the British Army would require some 900 lorries. Rather than put the Army Service Corps to the trouble and expense of maintaining that many vehicles in peacetime, a subsidy scheme was introduced whereby heavy goods and for that matter passenger-chassis could be acquired at a reduced rate if the operator purchased those built to a specification prescribed as rugged enough to withstand conditions of the field. Prominent features of such vehicles were the relatively high ground clearance and sturdy dumb-irons to which towing hooks could be firmly attached. Among the twelve main manufacturers of these vehicles, Daimler of Coventry was well to the fore – and all three Sussex companies had invested in the make.

Just as, in the Boer War, the best horses had gone from the BH&PUOC stables, army requisition officers now began to visit the depots and arrange for the removal of the better chassis. By the end of 1914, BH&PUOC had fourteen spare bus-bodies, WMS ten and L&SCH five: all of the latter and most of the others marked the passage of army Daimler-collectors. The Army Service Corps entered the war with 950 lorries – and finished in 1918 with 33,500. Clearly what was taken from Brighton and Worthing was but a drop in the national bucket, but the effect locally was immediate. The companies put aside their rivalry, helped each other out with the loan of surviving vehicles and began to talk about ways of resolving their common problem. Amalgamation, it was decided, was the answer.

For all intents and purposes, save the legal niceties, the decision to form one new company had been worked into some detail by the end of 1914 – and it began operating as such with effect from 1st January 1915. Among those involved in the planning, it was Walter Flexman French

Among the oldest vehicles taken into the stock of the newly formed Southdown Motor Services Ltd was CD 338, a Milnes-Daimler which had first been registered on 7 April 1905. Fitted with an early Harrington-built version of Mackenzie's observation car design which seated 25, it survived a further two seasons in the company's employ, becoming No. 84. This unusual view suggests that much of the passengers' safety depended upon the care of the driver rather than on the structural qualities of the coachwork.

who carried the greatest 'clout'. Already chairman of Maidstone & District Motor Services Ltd, he had succeeded in getting the mighty British Electric Traction Co Ltd to take an interest in that firm and Sidney Garcke and William Wreathall had joined the board on BET's behalf in June 1913. To BET, who had already invested in the purchase of the now defunct Shoreham Tramway, and singed their fingers as a result, this was the opportunity to repair their relatively mild embarrassment in some style. William Wreathall would now join the board of the proposed company to represent BET and in return for this vital introduction French was to be made chairman of the directors. Alderman John J. Clark and Sir John Bradford from BH&PUOC and Mackenzie and Cannon from Worthing Motor Services Ltd would complete the board. Between them they raised an initial capital of £51,250. At 31, Alfred Cannon became managing director and Douglas Mackenzie chose to be traffic manager. Frank Smith from BH&PUOC was secretary, his firm giving up its office in Worthing and subscribing to the pool its Steyne garage, Worthing; land at Freshfield Road, Brighton and workshops

140534

"*The Companies Acts, 1908 and 1913.*"

COMPANY LIMITED BY S

𝔐emorandum of 𝔄ssociation

OF

SOUTH ~~COAST~~ *down* MOTOR SERVICES, LIMITED.

1. The Name of the Company is " SOUTH ~~COAST~~ *down.* MOTOR SERVICES, LIMITED."

2. The Registered Office of the Company will be situate in England.

3. The Objects for which the Company is established are—

(*a*) To enter into and carry into effect (with or without modification) an Agreement which has already been prepared and is expressed to be made between THE BRIGHTON, HOVE, AND PRESTON UNITED OMNIBUS COMPANY, LIMITED, of the first part, WORTHING MOTOR SERVICES, LIMITED, of the second part, THE LONDON AND SOUTH COAST HAULAGE COMPANY, LIMITED, of the third part, and SOUTH ~~COAST~~ *down* MOTOR SERVICES, LIMITED, of the fourth part, and is to be signed immediately after the incorporation of the Company, and a copy whereof has for the purpose of identification been subscribed by EMILE MAURICE MARX, a Solicitor of the Supreme Court.

(*b*) To purchase, lease, establish, or otherwise acquire any tramway or light railway, and any trolley vehicle (being any mechanically propelled vehicle adapted for use upon roads and moved by

REGISTERED

63059

2 JUN 1915

count of the vehicles very much in the lap of the War Office, the directors designate now began to think about a name for the company; the new firm was to be 'South Coast Motor Services Ltd' and, as the articles of association were drawn up, this was the name upon the title page and in all correspondence relating to it. The name appeared on the advance publicity, letterheads, timetable booklets and even a sizeable batch of tickets to be issued on the cars. Messrs Emile M. Marx & Colbourne, solicitors of Brighton, sent the memorandum and articles of association to the Registrar of Companies in London and company number 140534 was issued. The date of incorporation was entered as 31st May 1915 – and then someone noticed; the name was not acceptable. It was considered too similar to that of the London & South Coast Motor Services (1915) Ltd, a very old-established firm based on Folkestone which had just been re-registered by its new owner, a well-known pioneer in the business, Percy Allen. With just two days to think about it, Clark and French came up with the name Southdown, hastily amended and initialled the document and returned it to London. Southdown Motor Services Ltd was incorporated on 2nd June 1915.

Among the 27 objects for which the company was established were the following (b) to purchase, lease, establish, or otherwise acquire any tramway or light railway, and any trolley vehicle (being a mechanically propelled vehicle adapted for use upon roads and moved by electrical power transmitted thereto from some external source) motor or other omnibus, ship, boat, aeroplane or airship, or motor and other cab undertakings in the United Kingdom or elsewhere, and to construct any motor omnibus, motor or other cabs, trolley or other vehicles (whether earth, air, or water borne) tramways, or light railways. and to equip, maintain and work, either by wire rope, or by electrical power, or by any mechanical power whatsoever, all tramways, light railways, trolley vehicle, motor or other omnibus, ship, boat, aeroplane, or airship or motor or other cab undertakings belonging to or leased to the company or over which the company may possess a right to run ... and work. (d) To carry on in the United Kingdom of Great Britain and Ireland and elsewhere on the Continent of Europe and in any part of the world the business of Tramways, Light Railways, Trolley Vehicles, Motor or

in Upper St. James Street. As its first, and as it turned out temporary, headquarters the new company was to acquire from the same source an office at 6 Pavilion Buildings. From Worthing Motor Services came a garage on the Amberley Road at Storrington and rented accommodation at Marine Parade, Worthing; the Old Brewery House, Newhaven; the Esplanade, Seaford, and the Royal Mews, Brighton. The London & South Coast Haulage Co Ltd contributed its garage in Middle Street, Brighton.

The Brighton, Hove & Preston United Omnibus Co Ltd was to continue running its town services in the two boroughs under the direction of their superintendent and engineer E. A. Eager (until 1916 when, following the purchase by Tilling he became chief engineer of the Aldershot & District Traction Co Ltd). Finances, who-was-to-do-what and premises sorted out, and with the final other Omnibus, Motor or other Cabs, Carriage and Van Proprietors, and generally of Carriers of Passengers, Mails, and Goods by earth, air or water and of Manufacturers of and Dealers in Tramway and Light Railway Cars, Trucks Omnibuses, Cabs, Trolley Vehicles, Carriages conveyances, Vans, Locomotives, Accumulators, Dynamos, and other chattels and effects required or suitable for the making, maintenance, equipment and working of tramways, light railways, or trolley vehicles, and for the carrying on of the business of carriers of passengers, goods, mails, and parcels by earth, air, or water, and of Omnibus, Carriage and Van Proprietors, Motor Garage and Show and Sale Room Keepers, and of all articles and things used in the manufacture, maintenance, and working thereof; and to carry on the business of Mechanical and Electrical Engineers, Machinists, Metallurgists, Saddlers, Galvanizers, and Packing Case Makers, or to manufacture or employ any person, persons, firm, company, or corporation to manufacture for the Company any motor cars, motor carriages, motor cabs, motor omnibuses, motor carts, cycles, bicycles, tricycles, or vehicles of all kinds whether earth, air, or water borne.

The mark of Walter Flexman French is writ large in all this bet-hedging and is based upon his experience at Balham, Guildford and Maidstone. An almost word-for-word series of objects was used to launch Bournemouth & District Motor Services Ltd (Hants & Dorset), of which he was the prime mover, the following year.

A glance at the map and the name seems obvious; the Southdown Hills provide the beautiful backbone of the territory the company had its eye upon. Yet it is worth noting that Worthing Motor Services' new garage accommodation at Storrington, acquired as late as October 1914, was located in the western-most portion of Adela Powell's 'Southdown Garage' and it is possible that it was this which provided the inspiration. Whatever the answer to that, the substitute did not please all the directors. One at least complained that it reminded him of mutton and, if the nautical counterpart

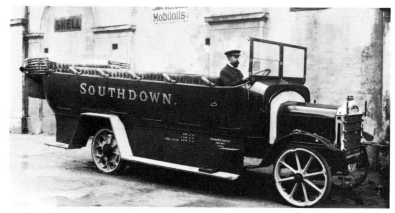

Douglas Mackenzie at the wheel of Daimler CB, IB 703 with Harrington 27-seat charabanc body, which came from the Worthing Motor Services fleet to become No. 3 for Southdown. A new coat of paint does much to raise the image of a very basic design. It was David J. N. Pennels who, in conversation with E. M. Coombes, the founder of the original 'Wilts & Dorset Motor Service' discovered the reason for County of Armagh 'IB' registrations used by Mackenzie. It would appear that the authority was the only one then willing to grant him consecutive numbers for vehicles entering service at widely separated intervals.

Mackenzie had also kept open his Ryde, Isle of Wight, office where, several years before, he had been manager of the Isle of Wight Express Motor Syndicate Ltd, now defunct. This too he utilised to register (DL) the occasional vehicle so that it would fit in with his latest thoughts on numerical sequence – a procedure which simply fascinated him. Leyland X, DL 493, was one such bus purchased in 1915. The weight of traffic outside Mackenzie's Worthing office may be judged by the man who has paused in the middle of the road to light his pipe. Meanwhile, two ladies debate whether they really wish to go to Storrington to play tennis. The vehicle became No. 49, then 149 in the Southdown's fleet.

Believing itself to be South Coast Motor Services Ltd, Company No. 140534 printed tickets in that name and actually began operating as such on – dare one say it – 1st April 1915. In that name too it purchased the motor charabanc business of Arthur Davies in Bognor Regis, principally to lay hands on his licence to operate a stage carriage service to Portsmouth. With that, however, came the trips to places of interest with 'special terms for schools, homes and beanfeast parties'; three Commer WP1 charabancs with Bayley 27-seat bodies – and Arthur Davies to act as local manager. This one had been called 'The Royal Sovereign' in Davies' fleet. The vehicles, BK 2237/45/99, saw out World War I with Southdown as Nos. 97-9.

At Cuckfield on 3rd September 1915, and bound for Hurstpierpoint according to the stickers in the windows, is McCurd CD 3322, which entered service with a 36-seat rear-entrance bus body built locally for Brighton, Hove & Preston United and acquired as one of the spare units on the formation of Southdown. It was longer than normal and consequently of high capacity for the period. The bus became No. 22 in the fleet numbering system which commenced in February 1917. Note the unusually long rear overhang.

With the name of the company altered at short notice to Southdown Motor Services Ltd, the main reason for the founding – the loss of large numbers of motor chassis to the military – now created immediate problems. Orders for new vehicles would have to be placed for makes in which the Army would show no interest. Meanwhile, the horses and carriages which BH&PUOC had acquired from F. J. Mantell, and passed on to Southdown as part of the deal, were actually called back into service for excursions from the Front at Brighton. Mantell's tickets to the Devil's Dyke were dusted off and issued once again. A charabanc drawn by four greys is seen in Dyke Road – the road up to the downs.

The Army's preference for Leyland and Daimler chassis, among others, led to several purchases in World War I which would not otherwise have found their way into the Southdown fleet. Four Caledons were operated for instance, among them IB 614 (below left) with Dodson bodywork and this Scout (right) which came to Worthing from sister company Wilts & Dorset in 1st March.

33

The chassis and engine of this Tilling-Stevens TS3 were purchased from Thomas Tilling Ltd in 1917 as LH 8885. Re-registered IB 616 by Southdown and fitted with Dodson 30-seat bodywork, it became No. 56, as seen here. In 1919, it was again re-registered to the more homely CD 4856 to match the fleet number – and the four others purchased in the same second-hand batch were made to match also. The vehicle's slipboard reads 'Findon & Storrington'.

was anything to go by, a change of name was extremely unlucky. Not so, it turned out, with Southdown. It had from the beginning a well-balanced team of officers who were now to take it from strength to strength.

An impressive-on-paper total of 76 vehicles (and 19 horses and their harness) had been acquired. In fact, only 31 were considered suitable for service as buses, the horses had been valued at £17.10s.0d (£17.50) each and the remainder of the vehicles consisted of small charabancs, lorries, vans, taxis and all those horsedrawn coaches bestowed upon Southdown by BH&PUOC. The latter were pruned and actually kept on the strength, continuing to provide excursions from the Front at Brighton under the supervision of their former owner, F J. Mantell. After the Emergency Provisions of 1916 whose purpose was to protect road surfaces by restricting new licences and the stricter rationing of petrol, the horsedrawn carriages proved an unexpected boon, much to the delight of Mantell, whose tickets to the Devil's Dyke got a new lease of life. So too did many other tickets. Under the waste-not want-not Mackenzie, there was more sticking bits on Isle of Wight ones and those from all three constituent companies, including some of the old Sussex Motor Road Car stock. Some of 'Jumbo' Ecclestone's 'Brighton Queen' charabanc tickets got issued on the excursions from the sea front as well – a case of 'those not skinning, hold a leg'.

The firm which thought it was South Coast Motor Services Ltd actually ran services with effect from 1st April 1915, and the following month had acquired a base in Bognor when it purchased Arthur Davies' charabanc business (see Chapter 4), placed him in charge as local manager and told him that wasn't who he was working for after all. His firm was of interest to Southdown not so much for its charabancs as the licence he had acquired in the spring of 1914 to run a stage carriage service from Bognor to Portsmouth via Chichester. Although not utilised for some while, this enabled Mackenzie to secure for Southdown a route he'd previously served. On its stage carriage routes the new company ran the ageing Milnes-Daimlers and Straker Squire, Daimler, Tilling-Stevens, and Leyland buses and even pressed into service Durham-Churchill charabancs—until Southdown began buying chassis makes of little interest to the War Office. Thus before 1915 was out Ensign, McCurd, Romar and Caledon were represented in the fleet in addition to more of the familiar makes both new and second-hand – a total of 25 additional vehicles, many of which now received the bodywork left spare by military acquisition.

In the summer of 1915, Southdown operated five routes from Brighton to Worthing; Steyning; Lewes; Eastbourne and to Cuckfield, the in-town East and West Worthing route and one from Worthing to Storrington which, to mark its historical importance, remained thereafter Southdown's route number 1. It also offered morning and afternoon charabanc excursions from Brighton, Worthing and Bognor. Meanwhile, keeping strictly within the borough, Tillings arrived in Hove and began the campaign which led to their taking over the remaining operations of the Brighton, Hove & Preston United Omnibus Co Ltd. Clearly, there was growing traffic in the area and, despite the earlier troubles and as long as the right makes were purchased, there seemed to be vehicles available. Within a year, French was able to write '.. at Brighton there are 62 buses on outside service, independent of those strictly confined to the town ... at much less than railway fares'.

Petrol supplies for Southdown were collected from the Silvertown depot of the Anglo-American Oil Company in 50 gallon steel barrels. The railways were still rather anxious about carrying such dangerous cargo and what had been a 20-seat coach was stripped to the floor and, dubbed the 'pigboat' by its crew, carried out most of the fetching and carrying. Eventually, however, petrol rationing became so severe that several Scout and Caledon saloon buses were converted to run on town-gas. George Stocker, who retired as Washington inspector in 1950, always claimed he was the first Worthing driver to take one out on service. The gas was stored in a rubber and canvas envelope fitted to the roof of the cars, whose service was restricted to a reasonable distance from the town supplies of Worthing and Brighton. As the vehicles reached the latter stages of each journey they took on a distinctly dishevelled appearance as the near-empty bag flopped over the side, often threatening the street furniture. Some drivers were issued with poles to poke them back into place. Towards the end of the war – in January 1918 – a Gas Restriction Order came into force making gas for motor vehicles subject to the same restrictions as petrol. A gas permit was now necessary, and this had to be obtained from the Petrol Control Department of the Board of Trade. Southdown went back to petrol.

Alfred Cannon, meanwhile, saw little of the gas-bags. From 1915 to 1919 Douglas Mackenzie was both traffic and general manager whilst Cannon was a lieutenant in the Royal Engineers. Much of his time on war service was spent around Arras, planning layout and operating the rolling stock with the Railway Operating Division – his pupilage with the Great Western Railway having impressed the military rather more than his subsequent road experience. On the home front, Mackenzie kept things moving: a garage was built and brought into use in the autumn of 1916 at Freshfield Road and, following the influx of the previous year, an annual trickle of additional vehicles provided an acceptable level of service. He also convinced Tommy Sturt, the blacksmith, that he should work solely for Southdown. As all good blacksmiths do, he went home each day, summer or winter, in his shirtsleeves, a performance much admired, but not copied. For the first time, women were taken on as conductresses, and Bessie (Hilton) Winters, who signed on at Newhaven, was to remain with the company until 1952, when she retired from the Express and Private Hire department at Eastbourne. The ladies were also employed as clerks and typists from 1915. Their rate of pay was two shillings and sixpence (12½p) per week when they started, rising by sixpence (2½p) per week to six shillings (30p) – rather less than their male counterparts now fighting the war and, although they enjoyed concessionary fares, this was at a time when the single fare between Brighton and Newhaven was one shilling (5p). Yet handwritten letters were now replaced by typewritten ones; the ladies were cheaper and more professional – and they've been there ever since.

In deference to marauding Zeppelins and Gothas, street and vehicle lighting was now restricted and under the wear and tear of wartime traffic, together with monetary priorities deemed to be elsewhere, the condition of the roads, so recently improved as never before, began to deteriorate alarmingly. In Mackenzie's opinion, the worst 'in the whole of Sussex ... was Hove Front, from the Halfway House at Portslade to Hove Street', with potholes over eight inches deep. The springs of the buses on the Brighton-Shoreham service were tested to the limit along this stretch. There was no through service between Brighton and Worthing at the time because an inspection of the chains of the Norfolk (suspension) Bridge over the estuary of the Adur at Shoreham proved them to be nearly rusted through. Brighton and Worthing-based vehicles ran as far as the bridge, where the passengers and conductors with parcels to exchange risked the gap on foot. Farther west, utilising an Act of 1878 aimed at recouping the damage caused by heavy steam-powered vehicles, Westhampnet Rural District Council tried to impose a 3d (1p) per bus mile charge on Southdown in October 1916 for each journey made on its newly-opened service between

CHAR-A-BANC EXCURSIONS. Morning Circular Trips from Brighton

Leave Madeira Road (Aquarium) 10.30 a.m.   Back about 12.45 p.m.   10 mins. Halt on route.

DAY.	TRIP.	ROUTE.	HALT AT	FARE.
Sunday.	PARTRIDGE GREEN	Henfield, Partridge Green, Ashurst, Steyning, Bramber and Shoreham.	STEYNING.	3/-
	WESTMESTON	Patcham, Clayton, Ditchling, Westmeston, Offham, Lewes and Falmer.	LEWES	2/6
Monday	COWFOLD	Pyecombe, Albourne, Bolney, Cowfold and Henfield. Back under Dyke Hills.	HENFIELD	3/-
	BARCOMBE MILLS	Falmer, Offham, Barcombe Cross, Barcombe Mills, Lewes and Stanmer Park.	LEWES	2/6
Tuesday	HAYWARDS HEATH	Clayton, Ditchling, Wivelsfield, Haywards Heath, Burgess Hill, Hurstpierpoint and Pyecombe.	HURST.	3/-
	HENFIELD	Pyecombe, Henfield, Alb'rne, Newtim'r, Patch'm	HENFIELD	2/6
Wednesday	COOKS-BRIDGE	Clayton, Ditchling, Wivelsfield, Cooksbridge, Offham, Lewes and Falmer.	LEWES	3/-
	BURGESS HILL	Pyecombe, Albourne, Hickstead, Burgess Hill, Friar's Oak and Clayton	FRIAR'S OAK	2/6
Thursday	ANSTY	Clayton, Burgess Hill, Ansty, Bolney and Albourne	HICKSTEAD	3/-
	RINGMER	Falmer, Wakelands, Glynde, Foxhound Kennels, Ringmer, Lewes and Stanmer Park	LEWES	2/6
Friday	CHAILEY	Ditchling, Ditchling Common, North Common, Chailey, Cooksbridge, Lewes and Falmer	LEWES	3/-
	TWINEHAM	Pyecombe, High Cross, Twineham, Hickstead, Sayer's Common and Albourne	SAYER'S COMMON	2/6
Saturday	BRAMBER	Under Dyke Hills to Henfield, Small Dole, Beeding, Bramber and Shoreham.	BRAMBER	3/-
	OUSE VALLEY	Rottingdean, Newhaven, Southease, Rodmell, Lewes and Falmer.	LEWES	2/6

Seats may be booked in advance before 10 a.m. on day of trip at Central Garage, Middle Street, Brighton, or Royal Mews, Steine Street, Brighton.   If wet, money returned (on these conditions only) up to within two hours of Coach leaving.   After 10 a.m. book with the Conductor at Madeira Road.

Front Seats 6d. extra.

N.B.—The Company reserve the right to cancel any journey when less than 12 persons have booked seats prior to the advertised starting time of the Coaches.

An extract from a Southdown 'Guide to Motor Char-a-banc Excursions' dated July 1915.

Bognor Pier and Portsmouth. Southdown promptly withdrew the service and appealed to the Local Government Board. Whilst Hampshire made no charge for use of the roads, West Sussex County Council followed Westhampnet's example and tried to charge Southdown and the Aldershot & District Traction Company the same amount when, in November 1916, they tried to open a service between Midhurst and Chichester. This had the effect of curtailing stage-carriage development in that part of West Sussex until after the Armistice.

The gap between Bognor and Worthing was not to be filled until the end of 1919, but the general line of demarcation for the northernmost spread of Southdown was settled as early as 1916, when a territorial agreement was signed with the East Surrey Traction Co Ltd (a forerunner of London Country Bus Services). Southdown's territory – as far as East Surrey was concerned – was south of a line Haslemere-Slinfold-Horsham-Handcross-Crowborough (in other words mostly marginally south of the Surrey county border), with some free-range country between Uckfield and East Grinstead. Apart from some extensions into Surrey, of later date, that is where it remained. Connections with the East Surrey company's services dated from April 1916.

As the war came to a close in 1918, agreement on territorial boundaries had yet to be made with Maidstone & District Motor Services Ltd in the east and with what would become its neighbour in the west, Bournemouth & District Motor Services Ltd (Hants & Dorset Motor Services Ltd from 1920). These would present no problem: Walter Flexman French was chairman of both.

One of Southdown's early efforts to provide a genuine service for rural areas was the provision of 'milk-churn' double-deckers, Presumably, only the fittest of crews were picked for this duty which was a real reversion to the role traditionally undertaken by carriers. The bulkhead behind the driver was rebuilt farther back and the bodywork widened on each side to accommodate the load, creating a very odd-looking vehicle. It was as much the unwieldy nature of the whole exercise as the smell of spilled milk which brought the experiment to an early halt.

An early Tilling-Stevens TS3 double-decker with Dodson bodywork at the Thomas-a-Becket Hotel terminus at Tarring of local Worthing service 3 – as original, but photographed still going strong in 1923 and, like most of its sisters, with many years of life left in it yet. The vehicle has the characteristic 'broken-backed look' caused by the narrowing of the underframe at the front but it was the success of these TS3s which encouraged Southdown to invest in many more Tilling-Stevens in the years ahead.

Chapter Four: The Establishment of 'Areas'

The enforced division of Brighton and Worthing-based operations in WWI caused by the closing and replacement of the Norfolk Bridge at Shoreham, together with the isolation of the new depot at Bognor, doubtless had something to contribute towards the concept of distinct operational areas which now followed. Each of these would have a central garage and administrative facilities capable of coping with most local contingencies. They would be responsible for the day-to-day running of their own series of routes, which would fan out and interconnect with services administered by the neighbouring depot.

In 1919, Alfred Cannon returned from his military service and both he and Mackenzie resumed their original duties within the company. Cannon's policy on local management was simple; wherever possible new posts were to be filled by those who had proved not only their ability but their loyalty to the earlier enterprise at Worthing and at Portsmouth, Douglas Mackenzie now set about his task as traffic manager in earnest, setting many examples which in less expansionist times have proved extremely difficult to follow. To some extent his efforts were aided by an unforeseen development – despite the dismantling of army camps, such as the particularly large one at Seaford, traffic actually increased. Many ex-servicemen, having sampled the bracing and beautiful Sussex coastline for the first time, decided in the peace which followed to bring their families and settle there. Numerous bungalow towns – some of them comprised almost entirely of retired railway carriages – sprang up along the coast and began to reach out towards each other in classic ribbon-development style. Lack of effective planning control resulted in some far from aesthetically pleasing additions to the landscape,

The Sussex coast enjoyed a renewed popularity after World War I, not only as a holiday and excursion locality, but increasingly as an area in which to resettle one's family, and Southdown prospered accordingly. Among the reliable new equipment purchased to cope with the increased traffic was the Leyland N chassis – a development of the M goods vehicle, but with worm drive for smoother running. For the excursionists and private hire work, Harrington's of Hove was the firm mainly called upon to build charabanc bodywork – No. 104 (CD 3534) of 1919 is a 32-seat example – whilst among those equipped to deal with stage-carriage operations that year, and seen below, was No. 103 (CD 3533) from the same order with 31-seat saloon bodywork by Christopher Dodson of Willesden: it was his CD 19 type.

but in the eye of beholders Mackenzie and Cannon this was beauty indeed. Within the first years of the 'twenties over 150 new vehicles had joined the Southdown fleet to help cope with the additional call for transport.

Elsewhere Mackenzie established routes which went inland, increasing the number of departures, even where at first there was insufficient traffic. As he had guessed, this created custom from sheer familiarity and the buses seldom ran empty. When they did, losses were more than recouped by profits made on established routes. Such repetitive bet-hedging built the framework and then infilled the Southdown network of stage carriage services; each route anchored in sizeable centres of population to ensure traffic in both directions. Mackenzie was able to claim "If there's someone walking along one of my bus routes, there's something wrong with the service".

Bognor and Chichester

On 13th May 1915, the new company's purchase of Arthur Davies' licences and three Commer charabancs gave it a base in Bognor before the firm was properly registered. This was located in an office at Beach House on the sea front. Despite the local council's attempt to slap a mileage charge upon the company, from this humble beginning there grew a distinct operational area with garages and outstations as far north as Midhurst and Petworth, where connections were made with the Aldershot & District Traction Co Ltd, and at Chichester, Compton, Eastergate, Selsey, Singleton and Wittering.

Arthur Davies had been in the motor car hire business since 1903. When Southdown made him its first Bognor manager it printed a special series of tickets for his motor trips which met their previous owner's ideas on how such things should be done. No conductors were employed on his Commers and the tickets were collected by the driver before starting on the return journey. Davies had used a similar system since 1908 and the early Southdown tickets actually named him as Bognor manager.

Meanwhile, it was decided that Bognor would act as the anchor-point for the stage carriage service, first to Portsmouth and then eastwards to Worthing, together with another one which was to run to Worthing via Arundel. Chichester, which had enjoyed a double-decker bus service as early as 1906, when the Chichester & Selsey Motor Omnibus Co Ltd began its three-year life, had its service to Selsey restored by Southdown when George Edwards and two colleagues from Bognor started running one bus on a two-hourly headway from 7th July 1920. Twelve years later this service had grown sufficiently strong to run that quaint little train service 'The Hundred of Manhood & Selsey Railway' off its rails and into history. An office was opened at Chichester in June 1921. The route to West Wittering – originally motorised by George Theobold with a Siddeley-Deasy 14-seater on 5th November 1919 to the accompaniment of fireworks thrown beneath its wheels by supporters of the village horse bus – was added following the acquisition of Alfred Trickey's business. Trickey, whose garage was at Birdham, owned a red Vulcan VSD saloon which entered the Southdown fleet in June 1923 and was quickly turned into a charabanc. Based thereafter at Portsmouth, Tricky was to serve with Southdown for over 40 years.

In November 1923, C. G. Shore of Bognor contributed his 'Royal Blue Services' Aldwick to Middleton stage carriage service, an excursion licence, three Guy B saloons and three Ford T 18-seaters to the Southdown operation, and two months later, at a time when the company had only two buses based at Chichester, the purchase of W. G. Dowle's 'Summersdale Motor Services' between Chichester and East Dean added a Ford 1 ton model, two further Vulcan VSD saloons and a small office at the Dolphin Hotel in the city. A curiosity of that service had been the issue of ticket sets of a different colour for each of the three conductors. Dowle was to retire from Southdown in 1948 as the company's manager at Chichester. It took the stringent regulations imposed by the Road Traffic Act 1930 to bring George Tate's 'Red Rover Motor Services' licence for the stage carriage service from Bognor to Pagham under the control of the company in October 1932. Throughout this period – and until 1950 – E. A. Cooksey was manager at Bognor, his thirty-odd years in that post constituting something of a record among local managers. Shore and Dowle's vehicles helped recoup the losses suffered when, in the early hours of 9th July 1923, the Bognor garage burned, destroying fourteen buses in the process. Vehicles brought in from other depots arrived in time to start the local services and not a journey was lost, Southdown had passed the first test of its abilities to cope in an emergency of such magnitude.

Early in September of 1934 Bognor Regis bus and coach station was opened on what had been the site of the old municipal offices and, for its time, had well-appointed offices and public accommodation and a garage with no supports in the modern manner. Chichester, however, was to wait another 22 years before it got similar facilities. Although Southdown had a garage in Northgate, and, from March 1926, an office in West Street by 1938, as many as six or eight buses at a time hovered beside the cathedral to the consternation of local councillors. During the early years of the war the depleted ranks of cars because of fuel rationing nearly led to the establishment of a small bus station on the roadside West Street car parking area, but this was not to be.

Opposite page lower left:
The Tilling-Stevens Express B10A2 was Southdown's standard saloon bus of the 1928-31 period. Bodywork to a Southdown specification was by Short Brothers or Harrington, batch by batch. Number 640 (UF 4240) is a 32-seater by the latter, delivered in 1929, and is working on the anti-clockwise version of service 51, the well-patronised and long-lasting Bognor Town circular route. The vehicle has paused beside Bognor Regis bus station on 24 August 1939 in the last days of peace before World War II. It was requisitioned by the War Department the following year. Southdown's ideas on destination display were far superior to those of most fleets at this time.

Opposite page lower right:
Number 623 (UF 3823), a Tilling-Stevens with 30-seat bodywork by Harrington on service from Arundel, where it was photographed in the 'thirties, to Littlehampton. This was a short distance local journey, but guaranteed good custom in the 'thirties with a tourist attraction at one end and the seaside at the other. Of particular note is the extremely low position of the headlamps common to these vehicles – the extra need for cleaning compensated for by the increased night vision on country routes during fog, mist and, what they call in Sussex, 'sea-fret'.

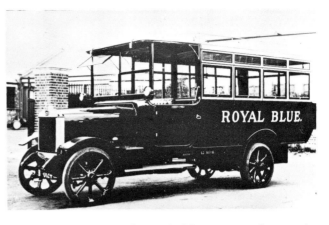

Alfred Trickey of Birdham, on the Chichester Channel, sold his business and a Vulcan CSD saloon to Southdown in June 1923 and put in 40 years' service with the company at Portsmouth. What looks like a village honeymoon departure has attracted onlookers who include a boy with a cricket bat. The vehicle is a Guy 14-seater (bearing Trickey's 'Sapphire' fleetname) which was sold off separately.

C. G. Shore's 'Royal Blue Services' of Bognor were taken over by Southdown in November 1923, together with an excursion licence, a stage carriage service and six vehicles – three Ford and three Guy saloons. All were numbered and operated locally by Southdown; the largest of the Guys – a 1921 model – going as far afield as Petersfield, Hants, on service 39 from Bognor and Chichester. This vehicle is seen on delivery as BP 0124. It became BP 5963 – No. 323 with Southdown.

Trickey's Vulcan (BP 7485) had been in the Southdown fleet only a matter of weeks, when it was badly damaged in a disastrous fire at Bognor's Station Road garage, built of corrugated iron in 1919. The spillage of fuel in July 1923 wrote off four Tilling-Stevens TS3 charabancs with Harrington bodywork and caused irreparable damage to the bodies of ten other vehicles. A victorious and smutty-faced Bognor Regis fire brigade poses proudly among the ruins. The building was rebuilt in brick. The Vulcan is on the right.

Among the Tilling-Stevens TS3 charabancs sent to Bognor Regis was No. 63 (IB 863), delivered in April 1919. It was fitted with an earlier in-stock Harrington body, originally the property of Brighton, Hove & Preston United, and featured this uncompromising way of taking the running board over the rear wheel, employed by Harrington at the time. Yet this was the direct ancestor of the beautiful Harrington Cavalier of the 'sixties. The TS3 is at the junction of Bognor's High Street with Sudley Road.

Portsmouth

Waiting open-armed at Portsmouth for Mackenzie and Cannon's triumphant return was, of course, Frank Bartlett. Southdown's conductors paid in at his office near the Theatre Royal whence publicity, timetables and tickets were issued. Its vehicles were parked at various sites nearby until, in 1923, the company opened its own premises in Hyde Park Road (now Winston Churchill Avenue). Before this depot opened, any vehicles arriving spare at Bognor from Worthing were sent on to Portsmouth on Sundays and Bank Holidays, where Bartlett loaded them with day returns to Bognor at five shillings (25p) per head. Five or six vehicles in addition to the normal hourly service would be despatched and one eye-witness claims to have counted 90 passengers off an open-topper at the other end of the journey. Waiting for the return journeys passengers stood good-naturedly in queues for up to three hours, and the last got home after midnight.

In the Portsmouth area particularly women enjoyed their newly-won emancipation and hauled their menfolk off into the surrounding countryside by Southdown bus. In the evenings the flow reversed, as increasing numbers of picture palaces brought people into Portsmouth from all the neighbouring towns and villages, the cinemas quickly upstaging the old established theatres. Despite economic troubles on the horizon, these were simple pleasures which thousands of local folk could afford and Southdown's resultant growth on Portsea Island and the surrounding area was rapid. Portsmouth Corporation Tramways Department was not quite sure what to do about this increased traffic into the town and at first asked for, got and enforced a 6d (2½p) minimum-fare ruling.

During May 1921 Southdown's neighbour to the west, Hants & Dorset Motor Services Ltd, had established itself on a route to Fareham, where it later opened an office at 12 West Street, and SMS Tilling-Stevens saloons and the occasional double-decker were dispatched there to make connections with Hants & Dorset's Leyland saloons from Southampton. June 1922 saw this become a joint Portsmouth-Fareham-Botley-Southampton service (No. 35), terminating at the aptly-named Sussex Place in that growing commercial port – and subject to a 6d minimum fare there also to protect Southampton's trams. An occasional Saturday traveller on this service was a Southsea prep-schoolboy and his equally anonymous classmate who, according to his own much later account, (see his first autobiography, *The Moon's a Balloon*) visited Southampton to do some shopping in that town without the benefit of money. He was to become the actor David Niven.

A similar joint-service (No. 36) with Hants & Dorset started running to Winchester in December 1922 with driver A. M. Mountifield at the wheel of one of the first Southdown buses on the route. Portsmouth Corporation relaxed its minimum fare policy in 1925 and both companies were able to charge penny fares on five stages between Victoria Hall, Portsmouth, and First Avenue, Wymering. But then came the last of the boundary agreements which – with one later exception – sealed Southdown's western frontier for the best part of 60 years. In February 1926, both companies retreated to their original terminus at Fareham and passengers wishing to travel beyond that point changed to the other company's buses. A new series of through-tickets was issued in celebration of this retrograde step, which handed back considerable traffic to the Southern Railway

Believing that Southdown could be suitably sweetened by the removal of the 6d minimum-fare ruling, in the summer of 1925 Portsmouth Corporation began running its own buses beyond Cosham to Drayton and charged 1d (0.42p) for the journey – against 2d (0.83p) by Southdown. The management of the latter, not noted for its insouciance, retaliated with a penny fare over the same section and proceeded to saturate the route between the Theatre Royal and Cosham with vehicles in excess of available custom. Over some stages, the company's buses actually charged less than the trams. Portsmouth Corporation then sought to impose conditions upon the continuing use of licences to what it called the private companies, and when Southdown appealed against this, the Ministry of Transport decided that the tramways would be suitably protected if Southdown charged one penny in excess of the tram fare. Whilst this ruling was awaited, April-December 1926, Southdown buses actually ran unlicensed within the Borough of Portsmouth.

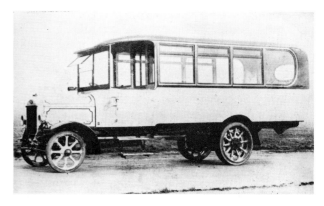

In order to take over Frank Plater's 'Southsea Tourist Co Ltd' in March 1925, it was necessary for Southdown to dip into the red at the bank. Plater had achieved a remarkable degree of standardisation; all 30 vehicles acquired were of Dennis manufacture. One of the earlier saloons, BK 4051, delivered in 1920, was fitted with 25-seat bodywork by Bartle who dubbed it their 'Portsmouth' type and claimed it to be 'the most elegant bus on the road'. It was certainly more curvaceous at the rear than the rest.

Most of Plater's work was concerned with tours and excursions from Southsea and North End, Portsmouth. Eight vehicles were specifically built for stage carriage work and this consisted of taking on the electric trams of Provincial's 'Portsdown & Horndean Light Railway'. Some of the journeys, however, went beyond Horndean to Petersfield, a considerable extension northward through the Hampshire Downs at Butser. One of a pair of 1920 30-seat saloons prepares for this journey at Southsea.

A smaller Dennis saloon, new in 1920 to Southsea Tourist, is Southdown's No. 374 (BK 4348), although the 3 ton chassis is somewhat older. The 'vee' windscreen suggests bodywork by London Lorries, but with its 24-seat capacity it looks an ungainly beast. Nevertheless, it has been afforded the full Southdown paint job and is parked beside the company's enquiry office and garage at Littlehampton, earlier the home town of Plater's other mainland company – 'South Coast Tourist'.

Picking up some of the route variations along the way to Horndean from 1924 were two Dennis 4-tonners fitted with open-top, double-decked 57-seat bodywork by Hickman and registered TP 29 and 30. One of the pair, enjoying its single brief season in Plater's grey livery, poses on South Parade, the traditional terminus at Southsea beside the promenade and shingle beach. The pair became Nos. 375-6 in the Southdown fleet.

Fortunately not a common occurrence with such a normally reliable type, a Leyland G7, attempting to reach Portsmouth in 1926 probably suffered a tyre failure with disastrous consequences to the front assembly. Under the anxious gaze of an AA patrolman – Southdown were, of course, members – company staff with jacks and baulks of timber shore up the patient where it stands. The vehicle, bound for Southsea, via the Town Hall (Portsmouth was not created a city until that same year, when it became the Guildhall) is No. 159 (CD 7719) with 51-seat Tilling bodywork and was delivered in 1923. Not forgiven, the bus was sold in 1929.

Meanwhile, in 1925, Southdown had gained the Fratton Road route to Southsea and consolidated its position in Portsmouth with the purchase of another company administered by Frank Plater, the Southsea Tourist Co Ltd (for the first, see 'Worthing' section of this chapter). This was the largest firm that Southdown had taken over by that date and it was necessary for the company to incur a bank overdraft to complete the deal. Transferred to Southdown on 1st March 1925 were 70 employees: a garage in Clarendon Road, Southsea; the tours office at North End; stands on the sea front; 30 Dennis vehicles; and the goodwill and licences for tours, express and stage-carriage work. For some while after the takeover, the ex-Tourist crews continued to wear their

The Leyland Titan double-decker was to sharpen Southdown's competitive edge considerably. As well as being the instrument by which the enterprising C. R. Fuger of Warsash was defeated, its lively performance enabled more traffic to be taken from the Portsdown & Horndean Light Railway operated by the Hampshire Light Railway (Electric) Co Ltd – a Provincial subsidiary. In a specially posed 1935 picture, two 1931 Short Brothers-bodied TD1 models, Nos. 930 and 927 (UF 7430 and UF 7427) compare their carrying capacity with P&HLR car No. 2, marked 'Through Car: Portsmouth & Horndean'. The picture represents, better than any other, the fatal squeeze put nationwide on the tramcar by the Leyland Titan bus.

Fewer vehicles were taken into stock from businesses acquired in the 'thirties, but eleven Thornycroft buses came into the Southdown fleet from F. G. Tanner's Denmead Queen concern of Hambledon in March 1935. This one, an A6 with 20 seat Wadham Brothers bodywork dated from 1928: it became No. 40 (TP 6601) in the Southdown list. The photographer was H. Marshall of Waterlooville, whose connections with transport began with pictures of local horse buses, then the products of Wadham Brothers through to the late 'forties.

Tanner's red-liveried 'Denmead Queen Motor Services' represented the largest single purchase by Southdown of another operator's stage-carriage vehicles in the Portsmouth area – some of the vehicles themselves were also large for the time, this 32-seater with Brush bodywork being one of four with such a capacity. It had originally been built at Basingstoke by Thornycroft as a demonstrator of that firm's products and had been purchased at a discount in 1934 – the last addition to Tanner's fleet. The interior of the Brush-bodied Thornycroft gives a fair indication of how advanced passenger comfort had become by the early 'thirties – sprung, upholstered seats, luggage racks, good wide windows, ample electric light and a general feel of spaciousness to go with the smooth running of a six cylinder engine. Little wonder that the vehicle saw three years' service in the Southdown ranks as No. 46, then 546 (CG 7119): it was a CDF 'Cygnet' model. Tanner's main route had extended from the densely packed Guildhall area of Portsmouth to the then aptly-named village of Worlds End. The body was to BET Federation specification, something Southdown avoided until the early 'sixties.

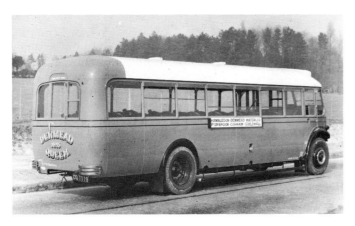

grey uniforms, and its personnel seemed well-pleased to be part of Southdown. 25 years later 27 of them would still be in the employ of the company. Plater had run eight stage-carriage vehicles, including two double-deckers, on a route – with variations – to Waterlooville, Horndean and Petersfield. Over much of the route this service of pale grey buses had been in competition with the sea-green and cream tramcars of the Portsdown & Horndean Light Railway. Southdown's arrival doomed the trams by much stronger opposition.

Taking much of the weight from Frank Bartlett's shoulders throughout these days of expansion was Benjamin H. Ogburn who signed on at Hyde Park Road in July 1923 as cashier and assistant to the local manager. He had undertaken a rudimentary training in transport with Provincial Tramways' other Hampshire undertaking, Gosport & Fareham Tramways. He was also to take much of the detailed work off the shoulders of subsequent Portsmouth managers (Walter Budd, later general manager of Southern Vectis, J. B. Chevallier. A. F. R. 'Michael' Carling – a future general manager of Southdown – and G. R. Wakeling) for the best part of 30 years and was able to boast that he had 'trained area managers very satisfactorily'. During the latter part of the 'twenties Bartlett was thus able to concentrate upon being, in effect, traffic superintendent for the Portsmouth area of the company. As such, he was able to organise further expansion and the provision of Dennis chasers against Millard's Safety Coaches who ran some GMC saloons from Fareham, West Street, to Portchester Castle and, from the Portsmouth end, against 'Portsmouth & District' who ran services as far afield as Denmead, Fareham, Hambledon and Westbourne. In both cases the operators simply withdrew from the route without need for Southdown to effect a purchase.

It seems to be part of the British character that requires an exceptional event to get people talking one to another. In September 1929, it was the international speed contest for seaplanes at Spithead, the Schneider Trophy, which provided the spur for a week. Both Corporation and Southdown buses beavered away harmoniously to shift the crowds of spectators who saw the Supermarine RAF team win the trophy for the second time running. Again both operators strove for a working arrangement in the city and, on 8th October, a renegotiated agreement was announced. Buses from both undertakings were to be run in accordance with timetables agreed by the respective managers. Tickets for issue on Southdown buses within the city were to be printed by the Corporation and all such fares were to be paid to the Corporation transport department. The Corporation were to pay to the company a sum per bus mile run by Southdown buses within the city, equal to the sum per bus mile shown to have been the all-in working expenses of the company each year. Transfer and season tickets were to be continued and the fares charged on Southdown buses fixed by the tramways general manager.

The joint omnibus service came into being on 1st January 1930. People living within the city thus gained a much more frequent and efficient service, but on outward journeys they tended to crowd out Southdown's long-distance passengers. The 'cordial spirit of co-operation' lasted exactly two years: on 13th November 1931, Southdown appealed to the Traffic Commissioners against eight licence applications by the Corporation and had nine

of theirs objected to by the municipality. A compromise solution pulled all the Corporation buses back south of Cosham railway gates – beyond which they had previously strayed to Drayton – and removed objections to Southdown working within the city on condition that protective fares should be reintroduced. These were to be on a sliding scale of 1d-2d (0.42p-0.83p) in excess of the Corporation fares, thus affording the municipality a degree of protection and as it turned out – reducing the problem previously encountered by long-distance travellers. Despite a protracted argument in 1934, this arrangement remained in force throughout the 'thirties and until after World War II, by which time the trams which the Corporation had originally sought to protect had long since been replaced by the rapid and popular trolley bus.

Other private operators within the borough still had to charge 6d (2½p) excess. Not included in their number was one which in the spring of 1929 had set out to challenge the growing weight of Southdown and lost the battle in the space of twelve months. The story is of particular interest, because it took the co-operation of a sister company to achieve victory, and the final outcome was not quite what its ally had expected, since in 1924 Southdown had already given up the territory in its favour after just one year's service.

C. R. Fuger of Warsash, on the River Hamble and well within what was to become the area of Hants & Dorset Motor Services Ltd, started running buses to Fareham from his home village in 1919. Ten years later he'd come to the conclusion that the majority of his passengers went on to Portsmouth in Southdown buses and, to the company's disbelief, applied for and was granted licences to run a total of 28 journeys per day at half-hourly intervals (against 44 by Southdown) beyond Fareham to the Victoria Hall, Portsmouth – which he now set out to do. Fuger's 'Warsash & Fareham District Bus Service' as it was called was ill-equipped to deal with the counter-punch which now followed. Hants & Dorset withdrew from the route, whilst Southdown based two brand-new Leyland Titan double-deckers in an old strawberry-packing station which it acquired at Fleet End, near Warsash and proceeded to saturate the entire route from Warsash to Portsmouth with 32 return journeys per day and with the fare on the section to Fareham down to 6d (2½p) return. Fuger capitulated on 1st May 1930, selling his fleet to Hants & Dorset for considerably less than that company had originally offered. He transferred the title of his Warsash to London express coach service to his wife, Mrs M. V. Fuger, but this, too, was to be sold in 1935 – to Southdown (see Chapter 7). Southdown, however, remained on the Warsash route well within Hants & Dorset territory, with whom it now ran the service jointly west of Fareham. It was to continue operating on the Warsash road for over fifty years.

Another acquisition in 1929 was made far less traumatically and involved the transfer to the company of the licences and four Dennis vehicles of W. E. Pinhorn's 'Meon Valley Services' of Catherington, which operated a stage-carriage service into Portsmouth from East Meon and Clanfield. Southdown settled for the Clanfield to Portsmouth section. Three years earlier it had consolidated a place upon Hayling Island by purchasing Holt's Motors' Rowlands Castle to Hayling service: together with a stage carriage service from Hayling to Waterlooville and a small Morris saloon bus from W. Stride. On Monday 1st November

1926, Frank Bartlett had launched its Hayling presence in some style. He took the councillors of Waterlooville on the inaugural run and entertained them to tea at the Ship and Bell Hotel, Horndean. Hayling had enjoyed a railway service since 1867, but despite vigorous efforts to develop the island, including the establishment of a race course, it remained something of a retreat, the weight of traffic considerably curtailed by a road bridge which later imposed curious operating conditions upon Southdown. Despite the building of a grand Victorian parade on the southern shore, all that followed was an extremely modest series of seaside amusements. Two other small operators – P. C Belier and G. W. Meekings – had, however, found enough seasonal traffic to offer stage-carriage services along the sea front, and the licences for these were acquired by Southdown in July 1933. Well used to their own sea front, a sufficient number of Portsmouth and Southsea's citizens now proved interested enough in what Hayling had to offer to make an island-to-island service a viable proposition.

Most fascinating of the contests for custom, however, was that going on between Southdown and the tramcars of the Hampshire Light Railway (Electric) Co Ltd. The trams, which left Cosham on an embankment and a series of bridges over both railway and roads, climbed Portsdown Hill at a speed which had the edge over the rival buses, ran along roadside track in the countryside and up the middle of the road through the townships to Horndean. They had their loyal supporters, but it was the ability of the buses to make route variations and go beyond the tramway terminus which eventually won the day for Southdown. The tramway was purchased by the company and Southdown buses took over the route on 10th January 1935, leaving the parent 'Provincial' company with only its Gosport & Fareham operation to represent what had once been the major provider of road transport on both sides of Portsmouth Harbour.

Walter Budd having gone over to the Isle of Wight to take up the general managership of the Southern Vectis Omnibus Co Ltd, supervision of activities in Portsmouth was now the responsibility of J. B. Chevallier. To him fell the task of securing for Southdown a complete monopoly of stage-carriage traffic from Portsmouth to the surrounding countryside. In March 1935, F. G. Tanner of Hambledon at last agreed to part with his licence for the World's End-Hambledon-Cosham-Portsmouth route of his red liveried 'Denmead Queen Motor Services'. The eleven Thornycroft saloons which entered the Southdown fleet represented the largest single purchase of another operator's stage-carriage vehicles in the Portsmouth area and firmly established the company in another village with historical connections for Mackenzie and Cannon. A clean sweep of the area followed in September with the acquisition of the licence for the Meonstoke-Droxford-Wickham-Southwick (Hants, pronounced 'Suthick')-Portsmouth & Southsea Service of Blue Motor Services (Southwick) Ltd of Boarhunt, to the northwest of Portsdown Hill. This all helped to change Portsmouth Corporation's views on co-operation with Southdown and it now began to think seriously about a proper co-ordination agreement, particularly since the company's operations had grown so large that, in 1934, an impressive new garage-cum-coach station had been opened at Hilsea on the northern edge of Portsea Island. But, as Southdown's businesslike fleet of Leyland Titan double-deckers got steadily larger, the Corporation

concentrated upon the replacement of its trams with trolley and diesel-engined buses. The territorial ambitions of Nazi Germany were to postpone such an arrangement until an even later date.

When war was once again declared in September 1939 there was little doubt that Britain's major naval base would attract the attention of the Luftwaffe. There was immediate work to be done in the evacuation of children from the city to the surrounding countryside – although during the 'phoney war' many of them drifted back again. After Dunkirk, Portsmouth was to share with Southampton in excess of 1,500 air-raid alerts with extensive bomb and landmine damage both in and outside the Dockyard. Vehicle-dispersal at night removed buses from the menace of incendiary bombs, but during the particularly severe raid of 11th January 1941 two of the company's coaches which had been converted into ambulances were destroyed. The following year saw the re-engagement of conductresses, and one, Madge Joslin, was to be appointed inspector some 33 years later.

Eastbourne

Eastbourne is, of course, somewhat famous in the transport world as the municipality which was the first to gain parliamentary powers to run a motorbus service. This it commenced to do on 12th April 1903, after representatives of the town's Motor Omnibus Sub-Committee had gone

The majority of acquired business in the Eastbourne area was concerned with excursions and tours. One of the exceptions was the stage-carriage work of H. J. Twine's Hailsham-based small fleet of Dennis and Thornycroft saloon buses which he had operated from Eastbourne to Polegate and around Willingdon Hill to Jevington. This small Thornycroft model A2 20-seater was one of the vehicles acquired, becoming No. 383 (HC 9159) of Southdown.

Running west from Eastbourne on what was then service 26A is No. 472 (UF 3072) a Tilling Stevens Express with Short Brothers bodywork seating 32 and built to Southdown specification. Its journey took it over the steep and spectacular eastern end of the Southdown Hills, to Seaford via the appropriately known High & Over. The B10A2 model Tilling Stevens was the large-capacity saloon workhorse on Southdown country routes during the 'thirties and, historically, must be considered one of the more important types operated by the company.

Although restricted to the use of single-deckers on the Beachy Head run, there was no restriction as to how many vehicles Southdown could provide to operate it as long as there were passengers to shift. The use of a coach-standard specification for the vehicles was a good move; it gave that extra 'holiday' feel to the service rather than that of a more prosaic stage-carriage duty. Tiger TS8 No. 1183 (EUF 83) with Harrington bodywork weighs in at Eastbourne Pier to support the 3-axle Tigers (see Chapter 5). Its folding canvas roof made it ideal for such work.

over to Hastings to see a Milnes-Daimler at work and had been much impressed by it. Recent research suggests this vehicle was among those which Douglas Mackenzie later purchased for use at Worthing. Eastbourne's buses ousted the horse-buses of F. Bradford and William Chapman & Sons, the latter turning to excursions and tours with wagonettes and brakes. Chapman had thus captured the lucrative Beachy Head traffic, despite the efforts of Mackenzie, on behalf of the Sussex Motor Road Car Co Ltd, who in March 1908 had unsuccessfully approached the Corporation for licences to run motor coaches to the headland, some 575 feet above sea level. Chapmans had also secured for themselves what would prove to be a quarter of a century's reign as the town's leading proprietor of excursions and, latterly continental tours (see Chapter 6).

As early as July 1915, Southdown had run motor coach excursions and a short-lived twice-a-day bus service to Eastbourne. It arrived in the town as fully committed stage-carriage operator in 1920, when pockets of post-World War I settlement along the coast developed into the positive housing boom which was to make the company's march eastward from Brighton a major feature of its rapid expansion. A completely new community with a name now evocative of those heady post-war years sprang forth, and sought transport.

It was called Peacehaven – and its brave new-world citizens wanted to go into Eastbourne, as well as Brighton. Southdown now provided the means by extending its Brighton to Seaford route. Once in Eastbourne, it started a service which went north west to Hailsham and Uckfield and another which strode on eastward to Bexhill and Hastings, run jointly with Maidstone & District Motor Services Ltd. Additionally, for some two years, Southdown buses turned off at Ninfield and went to Battle – an evocation of somewhat earlier vintage. These services passed along the Polegate to Hailsham road, considered at the time to be the worst in the country. The county councils faced a serious dilemma. WWI traffic, steam traction engines and a lack of money to spend had ruined many roads, which were now heavily potholed. To run the rain off those that they repaired, the roadways departments gave them a heavy camber. This meant that double-decker buses in particular leaned heavily to the side, where they knocked street lamps out of their holders and swept away awnings from shop-fronts. To counteract this, drivers kept to the middle and got accused by irate fellow motorists of hogging the road. Solid tyres wore tracks in the flimsy road surface and in places it was necessary for the bus to be put into a lower gear in order to make headway *downhill*, or to turn to left or right. Only the combination of a good tarmacadam crust and the introduction of pneumatic tyres for the buses from the middle 'twenties onwards solved a problem which posed difficulties for everyone concerned. East Sussex lagged somewhat behind West Sussex in its efforts to repair its roads, despite the latter's unsuccessful attempt to impose a mileage charge upon Southdown. At one stage, in 1921, it actually suggested closing the coastal road between Seaford and Eastbourne to anything heavier than a private motor car. Southdown, however, continued manfully to strain its springs along these routes until East Sussex council caught up with the rest.

As befitted its foundation upon the estate of the Dukes of Devonshire, Eastbourne was found to be attracting a rather more staid holidaymaker, eager to go farther afield with a purpose, usually to see something historical and to see it in comfort. Accordingly, Southdown's excursion traffic from the resort grew apace, with the majority of the numerous acquisitions of rival businesses being in the excursion and tour sector. The exceptions were T. A. Piper's 'Red Saloon Motor Services' stage-carriage service into Eastbourne from Hellingly, and H. J. Twine's Hailsham-based fleet of four saloon motor buses together with services from Eastbourne to Jevington and to Polegate. Both operators gave up their licences in favour of Southdown in 1929, the year that it purchased the old Lion Brewery site to build the Pevensey Road bus station. Post-Traffic Act difficulties caused J. Haffenden of Vines Cross to follow suit with his Heathfield to Eastbourne service in March 1932.

Despite a mildly unhappy start at Eastbourne, when the municipality sought unsuccessfully to set and regulate the times of departure for the company's buses running out of the borough, Southdown was to establish an extremely cordial relationship with the town. However, whilst some routes were clearly of no interest to Eastbourne Corporation's Motor Omnibus Department, such as those which the company was to establish to Heathfield and the extremely long run to East Grinstead, others like the Stone Cross circular, the Wannock and Jevington, and the Pevensey Bay routes had their termini tantalisingly close to the municipal boundary. The most contentious route proved to be that to the top of Beachy Head, so long the territory of Chapmans. In August 1931, the Traffic Commissioners for the South Eastern area sat at Eastbourne and heard applications for stage-carriage licences for this route from six operators including the incumbent Chapman & Sons, Eastbourne Corporation and Southdown. The latter proved to be the successful company, on the condition that they used only single-decker buses (later relaxed to include open-topped double-deckers) and did not take up and set down the same passengers between the Redoubt and the foot of Beachy Head. In 1934 Southdown realised that the single-deck restriction could be lessened by purchasing vehicles of greater carrying-capacity for this service, and invested in the first of four petrol-engined Leyland Tiger six-wheelers built to a suitably coach-like specification. By their presence in Eastbourne, embellished with their Mackenzie-style fleet name, they added to the Southdown image of something special and did good business accordingly.

World War II was to hit Eastbourne particularly badly. Declared a restricted area in 1940, the resort was an easy target for Luftwaffe aircraft coming in low from the Channel, and numerous bombs were lobbed into the town, often without warning. With its holidaymakers temporarily lost and large numbers of its inhabitants evacuated, the municipality was to loan to Southdown ten petrol-engined Leyland Titan double-deckers of various marks and vintage. For some three years, these, together with others borrowed from East Kent, were to provide a welcome relief at Worthing and elsewhere to the difficulties encountered by Southdown following the requisition or converting into war-time guise of many of its vehicles. Despite the danger on the coast, it was inland at Heathfield that a bomb dropped directly beside a Southdown bus and blew it over a hedge into a field, killing five passengers and the conductor – the company's worst incident of the war.

Worthing

It was to be from the premises at 23 Marine Parade, Worthing that Mackenzie and Cannon were to plan the rapid expansion of stage-carriage services into the Sussex and east Hampshire countryside. It was from here too, incidentally, that for many years, and together with their longtime friend Percy Lephard, they were to run the affairs of Wilts & Dorset Motor Services which they had taken over and registered as a limited liability company on 4th January 1915 – four months before the official launch of Southdown. The specifications for Wilts & Dorset vehicles, the arrangement of their colour schemes (albeit basically red) and the Mackenzie-style fleet name on its coaches were to remain 'Southdown-style' almost until World War II and in some cases into the post-war years. During that period, Wilts & Dorset vehicles were sent to Worthing for overhaul and new ones were marked down to that address by manufacturers. The association was also to lead to the establishment of the South Coast Express coach services – an excuse to use the name previously denied them.

Number 23 was a rambling premises: one was greeted at the entrance by notice boards listing the services and the times of departure. In the basement was Douglas Mackenzie's pride and joy – his ticket store. Arranged on its shelves in sequence and by route and price, each bundle was tied with string. Each piece of string was saved as it came off and was measured against a rule on the front of his desk drawer marked to represent the size of bundle it would hold – and was put into a compartment for further use. He wasted nothing. In the front room upstairs the conductors paid in their money and at the back the ladies typed and kept the waybill book. Mackenzie's office ran across the front of the building on the next floor above. In the attic, Philip, the regulator, and his wife lived on the premises, devoting their entire time to the company. Acting as Worthing manager initially was chief cashier Parker. Upon his death in 1922, Inspector E. James was to begin his twenty year duty as local manager. Also working in the building was the man who would succeed him in World War II, Inspector W. J. Cooper, and Mackenzie's secretary, Miss Hilda Botting. The original garage, now used as the coach station, was located behind the Clarendon Hotel. Two further garages were constructed nearby as the business expanded.

Until Douglas Mackenzie married Eva comparatively late in life, he always gave the Marine Parade office as his private address. Miss Winnie Bravant, who worked for Southdown from 1920 to 1964, is of the opinion that he lived nearby in small hotels and spent more time in the office than he did anywhere else. He was always there first thing in the morning and the staff invariably left him there at night; he seemed never to leave the office for meals and appeared to live on bars of chocolate. He would take such a bar from his pocket and present it to a driver asked unexpectedly to do some overtime, in order to keep him going. His emergence from the office was now restricted to crossing the road to listen to the engine of a bus the driver was doubtful about – an engineer to the last. Marriage changed his lifestyle somewhat. He found a new interest in his Scottish origins, joined Caledonian societies and went so far as to call his first proper home in Mill Road, Worthing, 'Scatwell' – a seat on the River Conon in Clan Mackenzie country.

James Town had died at the ripe old age of 86 on 1st January 1912. His son George kept the services running and did what his father could never bring himself to do - he turned to motorbuses. In June 1916, he placed his first on the Heene to Broadwater route, with his daughter acting as conductress. Fittingly, perhaps, he was the first local operator to run his buses on town-gas during the WWI petrol-shortage, and whereas most other operators carried the gasbag on the roof, at least one of his was towed behind on a trailer. George Town finally brought to an end his family's long association with transport in Worthing by selling his three remaining double-decked open-toppers to Southdown on 18th November 1918. They had been operating on the Broadwater to Elm Grove route.

Having gained what at that time constituted a virtual monopoly in Worthing, the company now set out to establish, with variations, a basic eleven routes in, across or starting from the resort with, of course, the famous route 31 going through all the way from Brighton to Portsmouth On the morning of its inauguration Mackenzie had emerged from the office to wait, watch in hand, for the first arrival from each direction. He was not disappointed, remembered William Jay, conductor of the first Brighton-bound vehicle. Starting with Horsham in 1919, at the end of the route via Ashington, Southdown's Worthing office was to assume responsibility for garages in eight other locations, ranging from the dormy-shed at Dial Post to what would eventually become a 55-car depot at Horsham.

Littlehampton depot had its origins in the office opened at the Dolphin Hotel in Surrey Street and supervised by Inspector R. Howe. From its initial two buses, Littlehampton

Douglas Mackenzie always preferred to run his side of the business from his office at Marine Parade, Worthing. One of the few things which could coax him away from his meticulous back-room organisation was an excuse to cross the road to listen to an engine giving cause for anxiety – an engineer to the last. On a summer's afternoon in 1915 Mackenzie, the driver and his conductor listen to the faltering engine of Milnes-Daimler CD 397 (ex BH&PUOC), on its last legs before withdrawal.

Originally X30 in the London General Omnibus Co's fleet, George Town's LGOC X-type double-decker is here reduced to single-deck only during World War I as the upstairs is taken-up by a gas-bag. Fittingly, he was the first local operator to run his buses on town-gas during the petrol-shortage, but regained his lost seats by transferring the bag to a trailer. LN 4588 had been returned to petrol by November 1918 when Town's local Worthing services were acquired by Southdown. The 'Picturedrome' advertisement was to lend itself to a Tilling-Stevens restoration programme completed in 1993 at Amberley.

was to gain a garage capable of housing 30 vehicles, in East Street, with H. E. Humphrey as garage superintendent. In 1924, Southdown took over the Littlehampton-Arundel-Angmering service of the South Coast Tourist Company Ltd the first of the 'Tourist' companies controlled, in this instance with Norris Brothers, by Frank Plater together with its excursion licences and eight vehicles. In its running battle with Southdown, Tourist had brought the fare from Littlehampton to Arundel down from 10d (4p) to 4d (1½p), at which figure Southdown retained it until 1951.

Back in Worthing that year of 1924, however, a new and what proved to be a minor trendsetting operator gained a stage-carriage licence to operate along the Front. Walter Gates, a Londoner, had returned from a lengthy visit to New Zealand and noticed that the elderly at Worthing had difficulty in mounting the steps on Southdown's high-framed buses. Accordingly he asked Shelvoke & Drewry, the manufacturers of the 'Freighter' refuse-wagon, to provide a chassis for bus work and from a garage in Wordsworth Road put the first of his curious little vehicles, which initially he drove himself, on service along Worthing Front. Some fifteen of these 'Tramocars', red with white roofs and gold lettering, were placed in service between then and 1935. Eleven of them were to survive long enough to be purchased by Southdown in August 1938. The latter continued to run them in decreasing numbers until 1942, when they were replaced by more modern conventional buses which by now had relatively lower steps and floor level. Older residents continued to call the replacement Southdown vehicles 'Tramocars', much to the puzzlement of visitors.

Meanwhile, Southdown's operations in the Horsham area increased following a spectacular but disastrous fire at the Barns Green garage of W. H. Rayner & Sons. Because of a curious allotment of their responsibilities, the Horsham brigade did not respond to the call and the Steyning brigade had to go fifteen miles to find aluminium and burning oil flowing down the road and a bucket-chain doing its best to save Rayner's house and furniture. Only one bus was saved from the seven-strong fleet and this, plus the goodwill of services from Horsham to Coneyhurst, Horsham to Brooks Green and the Horsham town service, Rayner sold to the company in January 1935. That same month T. W. Carter of Horsham relinquished his service to Steyning. The newly acquired routes were added to those gained in January 1933, when S. S. T. Overington, trading as the Blue Bus service, sold his licences for

Representing the influence of Thomas Tilling Ltd on the Southdown board at the time, No. 202 (CD 6835) of 1923 is a Tilling-Stevens TS3A with Tilling 51-seat bodywork – one of 48 delivered between 1922-6. They were thought worthy of conversion to pneumatic tyres in 1927, but had been sold out of service by 1931 as the all-conquering Leyland Titan TD1 became established in the ranks. Number 202 is operating the local Broadwater, Worthing Town Hall, Marine Parade and Elm Grove service acquired with George Town's business.

South Coast Tourist Co Ltd of Littlehampton was the first of the two companies acquired by Southdown in which Frank Plater had an interest – in this instance with Norris Brothers. With it, in 1924, came a stage-carriage service to Arundel and Angmering, excursion licences and eight vehicles. One of these was this Dennis 3ton 37-seat charabanc (BK 2879 or 80) which became No. 341 or 342 in the Southdown fleet. It is pictured, before acquisition, at Arundel.

Extensive refurbishment of the shop-fronts at The Arcade, Worthing, is under way as one of Walter Gates' Shelvoke & Drewry 'Freighters' rolls past with a full load. Gates' 'Tramocar' services, as he called them, were introduced in 1924 primarily so that the elderly could climb aboard easily – and the vehicles would be stopped on request at any point along the routes. The vehicles operated in a red and white livery, and most of them had tram-type controls and epicyclic gearbox. This is one of the earlier Hickman-bodied examples (probably PX 1593) with solid tyred wheels.

In contrast, the final two, already on order when Tramocar was purchased by Southdown, broke new ground in being of a new and very rare rear-engined type. Harrington had provided bodywork for Tramocar from the early 'thirties and for this pair came up with a 26-seat design whose front-end owed much to their earlier body for the much larger AEC 'Q' coach (for Elliott Brothers, Bournemouth and others). Southdown took delivery of T16 (FCD 16) in 1938, keeping the 'Tramocar' trading name but applying its own traditional livery. T7 (PO 1748) of 1930 brings up the rear.

49

Southdown supplemented its newly-acquired 'Tramocar' fleet in 1939 with a pair of specially-built low-loading Dennis Falcon saloons with 30-seated, centre-entrance bodywork, again by Harrington, the experts in this, as in many other fields. Once again, the vehicles were in Southdown colours, but carried the 'Tramocar' legend also, although their design was far removed from anything remotely resembling a tram. No. 81 (FUF 181) and sister vehicle 80 were later employed on Hayling Island.

W. H. Rayner & Sons 'Horsham Bus Services' was put out of business overnight by an intense fire at Barns Green garage. This Vulcan VSD is thought to be one of those that perished, for only a Dennis 30 cwt saloon bus (PX 5776) survived to be purchased by Southdown in January 1935, together with the goodwill of Rayner's three local services. The Vulcan, a 1924 model, stands at The Carfax, Horsham in the early 'thirties.

In 1937, a diminutive 30 cwt Dennis 18-seater with Short Brothers bodywork clambers over the railway crossing at Ferring and sets off in vain pursuit of a Southdown double-decker. The bus is from the fleet of R. J. Smart and his Ferring Omnibus Services, based at Ferringham Garage, Worthing – it had previously been the property, new in 1928, of Mackenzie and Cannon's 'other business', Wilts & Dorset Motor Services Ltd. Southdown acquired the goodwill only of Smart's service to Goring.

the Balcombe and Maplehurst routes to Southdown. One further acquisition in the years before World War II was that of R. J. Smart's 'Ferring Omnibus Services' to Goring.

Brighton

Even if Cannon and, particularly, Mackenzie were reluctant to move eastward along the coast from Worthing, the official registered offices of the company were, from the first, in Brighton. To start with they were at the 73 Middle Street premises once owned by 'Jolly Jumbo'. Some administrative work seems to have been undertaken also at 6 Pavilion Buildings, before part of Stuart Smith's house at 5 Steine Street was acquired for the role of head office. Whilst Frank Smith from BH&PUOC assumed the role of company secretary, Stuart Smith, previously manager at Brighton for WMS, took on the role of supervisor of the

Arrived at Worthing Pier from Brighton is No. 114 (CD 5114) of 1919 with bodywork built by Hora to Mackenzie's semi-observation specification. The chassis is the rugged Leyland N type which served Southdown well, putting in at least ten years apiece with the company. In 1934, No. 114 was still at work in London as a lorry, a common second use for the type, when its worm-drive gave a particularly gentle ride to its load.

At work on Brighton-Hurstpierpoint-Ditchling-Lewes-Brighton circular service, one of Southdown's longer-lived, is No. 12 (CD 6012) a Daimler W whose chassis was purchased in May 1919. The 30-seat bodywork, new in January 1921, is another interpretation of Mackenzie's designs, this time by Brush of Loughborough, then a BET-connected company. The crew wear the original rectangular Southdown cap-badge and the conductor's Bell-Punch ticket machine and leather bag are at the ready.

Well able to cope with the long run from Brighton to Portsmouth is No. 228 (CD 9228), a Tilling-Stevens TS6 with 51-seat bodywork built by Tilling at their Wren Road, Camberwell factory. It is photographed at Brighton in June 1925. The board in the front window shows that it will travel westward via Bungalow Town – a reminder of the ribbon development which took place along the Sussex coast after World War I. Delivered that year, it was one of Southdown's first forward-control, half-cab buses.

In April and June 1927, a batch of twelve ex-Birmingham Corporation Daimler Y-type open-toppers was acquired by Southdown via the Associated Daimler Co Ltd. The vehicles had been quite extensively rebuilt, though the chassis dated from 1916. They had Brush bodywork built in 1922 and had later received windscreens and cab half-doors. They had also been fitted with AEC engines in 1925-27, and some had also gained AEC radiators, as shown by No. 319 (OB 2102), seen at The Carfax, Horsham in its leafier days. All those metal railings disappeared in the 1940 armaments drive.

Southdown's first covered-top double-deckers began to arrive in October 1929 with the first of the Leyland Titan TD1 model incorporating Leyland 48-seat bodywork – the type which ushered in the era of the weatherproof modern bus. As we are reminded from time to time, living in paradise carries its penalties. Number 842 (UF 5642) wades through Sussex floodwater en route to Brighton from Petworth, via the aptly-named Washington, in the 'thirties.

In concert with other large bus companies, Southdown organised a parcel delivery service from the outset. A complete parcel-ticket system was devised by Mackenzie and agents' offices were established throughout the Southdown area at newsagents, village post offices and other retail premises. The company was able to offer same-day deliveries to named agents premises for collection by the forewarned recipient. A Southdown conductor in summer rig obliges en route.

company's clerical and private-hire work.

Initially traffic operations and the engagement of staff were undertaken by French's colleague, H.E. Hickmott, but when he went first to war and then north to Ribble, at Preston, as Major Hickmott, his duties were taken up by Frederick Mantel – until his retirement in December 1932 In 1918, Stuart Smith moved across to the opposite side of Steine Street and made the whole of his house available to Southdown. The first workshops in Brighton were located in Upper St. James's Street, but the new (in 1916) Freshfield Road garage incorporated improved facilities. Any chance of competition which could have arisen as a result of the purchase of BH&PUOC's town services by Thomas Tilling Ltd was averted in February 1917, when Thomas Wolsey, representing the Tilling organisation, was elected to the Southdown board, He was the younger brother of Walter Wolsey, Thomas Tilling's son-in-law. At the same time Southdown was converted from a private to a public company.

In 1921 a joint service with Maidstone & District was started between Brighton and Hawkhurst, whilst other services had already been established from Brighton to Worthing, Eastbourne, Lewes, Lingfield, Horsham, Uckfield, Petworth and, of course, the long journey all the way to Portsmouth. A depot was opened in Haywards Heath in 1925, although operation had already been established from a dormy-shed at nearby Scaynes Hill. By the summer of 1921 it was possible to travel all the way from Brighton to London by stage-carriage bus: Southdown to Handcross– 2/6 (12½p): East Surrey to Reigate– 2/5 (12p): London General– 2/- (10p): a total fare of 6/8 (34½p). Although this took some 5½ hours it was considerably cheaper than the contemporary charabanc fare of £1.

The following summer, there began a controversy over Brighton Council's decision to grant tentative permission for Southdown to build a garage for 200 coaches in the eastern end of the Aquarium on a 60-year lease. The town divided into two hostile camps: 'attend a meeting at the Dome and protest' ran the posters. Said one councillor prophetically "Messrs Tillings are a very large shareholder in the Southdown and some day they may be a very large combine: not only the Southdown and Tillings, but the London General Omnibus (also). What would happen if we were to have thousands . . . of people put down on the Brighton Front all day?" The Council decided by one vote not to proceed with the lease. So ended Southdown's first attempt to build a bus station – and in the long run the company was never to embrace the notion of the need for bus stations as avidly as most of its sister companies.

The frustrated architect of the Aquarium garage plan was C. E. Clayton, who had designed Southdown's Freshfield Road garage and Tilling's one in Conway Street. He was one of those rounded men who was also an educationist, JP, reformer and chairman of Brighton College of Art. Another in similar mould was John Henson Infield, whose deep knowledge of the area was to lend renewed local strength to Southdown when he joined its board of directors in May 1924. Latterly, and until his death in June 1942, he was to become vice-chairman of the company which enjoyed his talents, legal, social and practical: sagacious and kindly, he was a barrister at law, JP, director of Brighton's 'Grand Hotel' and of the 'Theatre Royal', Brighton and chairman and managing director of

the Southern Publishing Company. Interestingly, that firm had from the beginning printed and published Southdown's timetables and publicity. Meanwhile, in 1925, Southdown had moved into a further new garage built in Edward Street.

The General Strike of May 1926 had comparatively little effect upon Southdown. Whilst the Brighton trams and Tilling's buses were at a standstill, Southdown had buses out along the coast roads and on country routes, but on the first day none ran out of Brighton until 2pm when they were driven by the large proportion of non-union men. They were haranged to some extent by pickets at the Aquarium pick-up point, and were actually guarded by police, but this was largely unnecessary for none of the strikers attempted to interfere with passengers.

But Southdown took a strong line with the strikers: "All employees who have not remained at work during the present crisis are regarded as no longer in the service of the company. The insurance cards of these employees will be returned at once and they will be called upon to return their uniform and other property of the company". It announced that an agreement entered into with the crews' trade union on 27th April, now violated, was forthwith terminated and that in future it would not recognise any trade union or engage union labour. By 14th May, almost all the strikers had taken the opportunity to rejoin the company as new employees and the service had returned to normal. This had been standard BET policy; if the TUC had been ill-prepared for the strike, it met scarcely more effective opposition to trade unionism than that put up by BET's subsidiaries – and trade unionism didn't get a foothold in Southdown worth the name until after World War II.

Sidney Garcke, son of BET's founder Emile Garcke, had joined the Southdown board in March 1924 and had been elected chairman of the company in January 1926 following the death the previous month of Walter Flexman French. In view of events taking place in the bus world at national level this would stand Southdown in good stead. In 1922, Thomas Tilling Ltd had taken a large holding in BET's subsidiary, the British Automobile Traction Co Ltd. This somewhat untidy marriage was smartened up in 1928, when Tilling & British Automobile Traction Ltd was formed – under the chairmanship of Sidney Garcke. This practically ensured that in any parting of the ways Southdown and its chairman would end up in the same camp.

In November 1928 the four main-line railway companies started talking with Tilling & BAT about investing in its subsidiary bus companies rather than in their own road passenger services for which recent powers had been granted them by Acts of Parliament. Both parties approved the railway acquisition of shares equal to those held by Tilling & BAT in the appropriate bus companies. Thus the Southern Railway Company paid £3.5s.0d (£3.25) per £1 share for one third of Southdown's stock which stood at £200,000. It was considerably more than Southern paid for a similar share in East Kent and Maidstone & District. As a result of the agreement, the assistant general manager of the Southern, Col G. S. Szlumper joined the board in February 1930 followed by Ralph Davidson in September – the advance guard of numerous railway representatives until the establishment of the National Bus Company in 1972 rendered the system obsolete.

Incorporated in the Road Traffic Act 1930, was a group of clauses which brought thoroughgoing changes to the omnibus industry. These required the crews to be licensed centrally, the vehicles to be submitted to strict mechanical tests, each bus or coach service, tour or excursion to be separately licensed, with opportunity for objections to be aired in special traffic courts by other operators or the railways, should they feel that their own trading prospects were at stake. The country was divided into traffic areas administered by 'Traffic Commissioners', transgression of whose rulings would carry severe penalties. Independent operators saw such close control of their affairs as the beginning of the end, and a considerable number chose or were obliged, to sell up soon after the Act came into being, Southdown, well represented in the courts by extremely sound legal advocacy came out well on balance and, in the nine years between the enactment and the outbreak of World War II, absorbed the goodwill of no fewer than 44 rival operators throughout its area, against 26 in the fifteen previous years. Apart from H. J. Sargent's East Grinstead-Ashdown Forest stage-carriage service, acquired in September 1937, such takeovers in the Brighton depot's area consisted of excursion, tours and express services.

If truth be told, the new legislation probably put an end to the vestiges of the more unusual activities engaged in by Southdown in its first fifteen years. In the early days, no reasonable offer was refused. Charabancs had been changed into lorries, by removal of their seats, and carried such diverse cargoes as shop-fronts, flour from mill to bakery, groceries to wholesalers, and even a totally unmanageable load of loose sprats for Billingsgate fish market. Two ex-RAF type Leyland lorries, which were later transformed into saloon buses, worked on the removal of chalk from the foundations of Brighton's 'Regent-Cinema'. Stage-carriage vehicles on service had carried churns of milk into town from outlying farms, mail for the Post Office, pigs, goats or calves in pig-nets and sides of bacon and carcasses of pig or sheep up the ladder and on to the roof-rack. Conducting such a bus was not just a question of collecting the money and issuing tickets.

Until the establishment of the London Passenger Transport Board in 1933, Uckfield was the meeting point of services operated by Southdown, the East Surrey Traction Co Ltd and Autocar Services Ltd. Southdown now gained some extra territory: services previously provided by East Surrey and Autocar south of Crawley and East Grinstead, not being part of the area prescribed for LPTB, were allocated to Southdown, and the co-axial point moved eastward to Heathfield, which was now shared with Maidstone & District.

Back in Brighton, the Steine Street coach station had been enlarged and Pool Valley was in use as the Brighton stage-carriage terminal. It had soon become clear that attempting to cope with the maintenance of the fleet at the comparatively new Freshfield garage was an overwhelming problem. Further land had thus been purchased at Portslade and a new central overhaul workshop had been opened there in 1928. From the beginning its main functions were dealt with in the chassis shop, the body shop and the paint shop – each with its own sub-sections and stores located around it. The integral office block became headquarters for the chief engineer – R. G. Porte, initially – the assistant engineer and the stores superintendent, who rivalled Mackenzie in his meticulous system for numbering the parts in their separate bins. The tailor's shop was also located at Portslade - the summer staff handing over their uniforms to a full-time tailor who cleaned, renovated and placed them in store for re-issue the next summer.

The seasonal nature of Southdown's traffic also dictated the way the central workshops would operate. For instance, at the beginning of April 1938, 467 vehicles were licensed: in August 699, covering two-thirds as much again as the winter mileage of 1,500,000. During the summer every vehicle in the fleet save those for sale, had to be on the road. In winter, the canvas-roofed coaches, which only covered some 10,000 miles each season, were either laid up or formed a spare-time docking job. They, and the company's 23 open-topped Titans were de-licensed during the winter months, the comparatively light use of the latter enabling them to put in over 20 years service with Southdown. Fifty dual-purpose employees were one of the most important factors of the seasonal organisation. During the winter they worked on overhauls at Portslade; at the beginning of summer they transferred to the depots, to act as drivers, conductors or tradesmen. Other seasonal crews were given, on a rotational basis, the chance of permanent employment as vacancies occurred – and, being Southdown, where long-service was the norm – this was not quite so often as some would have liked.

At overhaul time, the bodies were also refurbished, from upholstered seats outwards, but the days of Mackenzie's body-swaps had gone. Now they were never separated from their original chassis at any stage of their Southdown lives. Service buses exclusively were attended to in the summer, and work on excursion and tours vehicles took place in the winter. The works and facilities were, of course, added to over the years as further vehicles and new technologies demanded. Both the facilities and the level of craftsmanship of the work-force were second to none in the industry and, quite simply, that was the way it remained. A standard-image was never likely to go down well at Southdown; everyone concerned wanted to provide that extra sparkle.

From the earliest days, employees had been provided with facilities for refreshment and recreation, and these improved and enlarged with the opening of each new building. Sporting activities at the depots started humbly with a dart board and went from strength to strength with table tennis, billiards and snooker, football, cricket, road-walking and full-blown athletics meetings being added to the social calendar. A large array of cups, shields and other trophies suitably named after their donors, both company and outside, handed-out at well-organised presentation nights, turned each programme pamphlet into a roll-call of Southdown officials. Company dances, dinners, and presentations of long-service awards, had their origins in this period.

For many years, such events, and much other business concerning the company, was recorded in a house journal called at first 'Tweenus' and, later, the 'Southdown Chronicle'. This extremely well-designed newspaper had its origins in the example set by Midland Red. R. J. Dallimore, area manager later of Brighton and then Portsmouth depots and a man who had much to do with the running of Southdown's sports and social clubs, bought a Midland Red house-magazine from the conductor of a bus in Birmingham in 1935 and carried the notion of something similar for Southdown back in Portsmouth. The first number

Departing from bay No. 7 at Brighton's Pool Valley is No. 878 (UF 7078) the first of the Short-bodied Titan TD1s. The over-elaborate 'vee'-front upstairs reminds one that bodybuilders had not yet learned that an upright profile could mean four extra seats. Number 878 was one of 41 Titan TD1s transferred to sister company Wilts & Dorset in June 1939, together with 17 other buses, from Southdown, as part of a massive input to that company from twelve different operators. The extra vehicles were required to cope with the military build-up on Salisbury Plain and the construction of Blandford Camp.

of 'Tweenus' were compiled, in 1937, at that depot, before production was transferred to Brighton. There, over the years, it recorded for posterity the names of hundreds who have contributed to the progress of the company – among them Cherriman of Hurstpierpoint and Bannister & Evans of Burgess Hill, each of whom transferred to Southdown their stage-carriage services to Hassocks in 1938 and 1940 respectively.

In the final months of peace, when Britain prepared – as A. J. P. Taylor nicely put it – to go 'reluctantly to war', Southdown's old ally Wilts & Dorset found itself desperately short of vehicles. The Army was making large extensions to its facilities on Salisbury Plain and the local company couldn't cope. Nearly all the vehicles it normally could have expected to replace, Southdown transferred to Wilts & Dorset – and then found itself short when War Department requisitioning and military production at the vehicle manufacturers became the order of the day. Yet when World War II started Southdown, with its nominal fleet of over 700 cars, was the sixth largest omnibus company in the United Kingdom and its annual revenue had exceeded £1 million.

At the commencement of the war, Douglas Mackenzie devised a scheme to beat the delays caused on the country roads by the black-out. He simply added an extra minute in ten to all the schedules; so that there was a much greater chance of making connections even though a completely over-cast sky might greatly reduce the possible speeds. Saloon buses were converted with perimeter seating to take 30 seated and 30 standing passengers. Twelve were allowed to stand downstairs in double-deckers. The company's war effort included a tax-free loan to the government of £50,000, followed by a War Weapons Week donation of £26,000 subscribed by management and employees. Far more effective than the charming 'Walmington-on-Sea' example, however, was the company's contribution to home defence.

The Local Defence Volunteer organisation, started in the early summer of 1940, provided the inspiration for Southdown's traffic manager to approach the Home Guard Commander and suggest the setting up within the company of a separate unit composed of employees and Southdown vehicles. Accordingly, the traffic manager became Lt Col Alexander H. Burman, officer commanding the 12th Sussex (Southdown Motor Transport) Battalion, Home Guard. Over 1,000 employees joined and trained as members of the Royal Army Service Corps – the first battalion to be formed for Motor Transport Service, with its own cooks and clerks included. Until stand-down in December 1944, they put as many as 35 coaches at a time at the disposal of numerous military manoeuvres and field-days at regular intervals throughout the darkest days of the war.

Until 1939 a proud member of the National Scheme for Disabled Servicemen, the company increased the number of conductresses that year to help replace what would be an eventual 987 employees who joined the armed forces. Initially, drivers aged 25 and over were declared to be in a 'reserved occupation', but this group also became depleted. The transfer of all those buses to Wilts & Dorset, together with military requisition, now left Southdown with a vehicle shortage. In 1941, 23 Brush-bodied Titan TD1 open-toppers were denied their usual winter storage, given waterproofed stretched-canvas top-covers (in dark green) for the duration of the war and pressed into continuous service. The covers had four glass windows at the front, the rest celluloid. Number 815 (UF 4815) is in service at Emsworth with hooded headlights and white wingtips.

As soon as the LDV came into being, Southdown asked for volunteers and got an enormous response. A Southdown battalion of Home Guard was formed in June 1940 and based at Brighton. The panoramic rear-window design of No. 1426 (DCD326) Leyland Tiger TS7, with Harrington 32-seat bodywork, gives one of the newly appointed conductresses a good view of her colleagues on manoeuvres in Grand Junction Road, Brighton, beside the beach. They are taking on, some with bayonets fixed, a regular army unit equipped with a Bren gun carrier – by standing in front of it. The censor has blanked out the destination screen of the bus, so that the enemy might not discover where such dedicated resistance awaited.

Southdown in Colour

Prior to World War II photographic images in colour of British buses were rare indeed. They might occasionally be found lurking in the background of Kodachromes featured in the American *National Geographical Magazine*, but there were mostly the red buses of London. Colour photography, even then, had been available for over twenty years but, principally because of the price, pioneers of bus photography worked in black and white. The tradition stuck, and only now is colour beginning to oust the monochrome print. Colour slides of Southdown vehicles generally date from the founding of the Southdown Enthusiasts Club whose members, appropriately, have provided the majority of these illustrations. Fortunately there were some splendid surviving vehicles from earlier times still around at that time, but this volume offers a selection of the better-known types from then until 1990. A more comprehensive range of variations in colour and detail will be featured within the contents of Volume II.

Below: One hundred Guy Arab utilities were acquired by Southdown in the latter stages of World War II; so many that the Southdown Enthusiasts Club published a special booklet devoted solely to the type. Number 417 (GUF 117) seen largely unaltered at Worthing Pier.

Above: Offering a pleasant mix of pre-war bass notes and smart post-war replacement bodies were numerous Leyland Titans new in the later 'thirties. Number 248 (GCD 48) was a Leyland TD5 new in 1939 but with replacement Park Royal body dating from 1950.

Representing a range of post-war coaches with widely differing body styles is Leyland PS1 of 1948, No. 1303 (HUF 303) with Park Royal coachwork. Sister vehicles entered service with bodywork by ECW, Harrington, Windover, Beadle – and twelve others also by Park Royal.

Looking somewhat similar to the earlier PD1 model is a PD2/1 all-Leyland double-decker of 1948. Number 329 (JCD 29) crosses Broadwater Bridge on a Worthing and Lancing local service in November 1962.

Offering increased passenger protection from the elements is Leyland PD2/12 No. 808 (RUF 208) dating from 1957 with Southlancs sliding doors. It is pictured at Brighton. Earlier examples had doors fitted at Southdown's Portslade works.

Originally delivered as straightforward saloon buses in 1952 this pair of Royal Tigers were among those reclassified for dual-purpose duties in 1956. Number 1508 (LUF 508) and 1528 (MCD 528) are in Kingston Lane on the last day of service of route No. 21 to Brighton in April 1963.

Representative of the classic Southdown coach of the 'fifties is Leyland Royal Tiger PSU 1/16 NUF 74 (originally No. 1674) of 1954. It is fitted with Duple 'Ambassador' coachwork and pictured at Chichester in September 1962.

Just when Leyland may have thought they were enjoying a Southdown monopoly, the company placed a 'free-choice' order for Guy Arab III models with far from utility Northern Counties bodywork. Delivered in 1948, No. 503 (JCD 503) is on service in Pavilion Parade in May 1963.

Guys again! This time Mark IV with Park Royal bodywork which entered service in 1955-6. Number 513 (OUF 513) at Pool Valley, Brighton in November 1962 was one of 48 fitted with platform doors, which now became standard on Southdown vehicles.

With its distinctive purr echoing across Ladies Mile, No. 973 (973 CUF), a Leyland PD3/4 departs South Parade, Southsea bound for Horndean in the spring of 1964. First delivered in 1958 – and all of them with Northern Counties bodywork – the type became the most numerous and best loved of Southdown's buses.

The classic Harrington 'Cavalier', mounted on Leyland Leopard chassis, brought new levels of style and comfort for coach cruise work. A bow-tie was *de rigeur* to drive one: No. 1743 (8743 CD) at Royal Parade in July 1963.

Mackenzie script fleetnames were not uncommon on saloon buses and some open-toppers. Bristol RE No. 446 (NUF 446G) with Marshall bodywork wears a full set at Old Steine in 1969. The choice of chassis marks the onset of the NBC era.

'Southdown-BH&D' – another manifestation of NBC: Bristol Lodekka No. 2011 (RPN 11) ex-Brighton Hove & District repainted into full Southdown livery. This type reintroduced the sunken lower gangway floor pioneered in 1907 – and then forgotten– by the All British Car Co Ltd of Glasgow.

Originally earmarked for delivery to BH&D, No. 383 (TCD 383J), a Daimler Fleetline with Northern Counties bodywork, was instead painted in green and primrose and delivered to Southdown with traditional block fleetname, and Mackenzie script at the front. It is at rest in North Street, Brighton.

A transitional vehicle if ever there was one! Looking very much like a close relative to a Bristol VRT, because of its ECW bodywork, is Daimler Fleetline CRL6 No. 394 (XUF 394K). At Pool Valley on a limited stop duty for Arundel, the vehicle wears NBC style fleetname and 'Double N' logo.

What might have been! In full NBC leaf green and white livery and carrying Brighton-Portsmouth 'Coastliner' logos is 729 (in pale blue), SCD 729N, a Leyland Atlantean AN68 with Park Royal bodywork. But for nationalisation this type would probably have become a Southdown standard.

Independent Southdown made a return to traditional apple green and primrose, with one or two additional embellishments. A dark green skirt, reduced size NBC style fleetname with, in this instance, 'West Sussex' divisional identity beneath and 'Hissing Sid' logo are all displayed in August 1986 by Leyland National No. 81 (YCD 81T).

Looking a whole lot better in National Express white than earlier Southdown coaches repainted into that livery is No. 1329 (GWV 929V), a Leyland Leopard PSU3E/4 with Plaxton 'Supreme' coachwork. It is at Golden Cross en route to Eastbourne in April 1987.

With cherished number 401 DCD, pinched from a PD3 two years previously, is No. 1001, a Leyland Tiger with Plaxton Paramount body, at Uckfield on a National Express working on 27 March 1989. It wears the later version of the red, white and blue 'Venetian blind' logo.

Top Line livery – one could hardly fail to see it coming – is worn by MOD 822P, a Leyland National at St. Helens Hospital on 27th May 1989. Top Line was a joint Southdown/Eastbourne Buses operation.

In Stagecoach ownership on 23rd February 1990, but still decked out in full independent Southdown livery, is Volvo B10M No. 303 (F303 MYJ), at Cornfield Road roundabout, Eastbourne. It was among the last to be delivered in traditional livery.

Wearing Stagecoach colours and labelled 'Southdown' in blue is No. 710 (G710 TCD), a Leyland Olympian with 85-seat Alexander bodywork with places for 12 standees. It is at Uckfield bus station on 31st July 1990.

In the city centre of Portsmouth on 4th August 1990 stands No. 957 (D936 EBP), an Iveco Turbo Daily 49-10 with Robin Hood 19+6 bodywork; transferred in full Stagecoach livery from Magicbus (Scotland) Ltd for 'Southdown Portsmouth' duties.

Chapter Five: BET's Southdown

For many, 1942 was the turning point of World War II. It was at least the year that a formal alliance of Britain, the United States and the Soviet Union was made against Germany. At home, in the bus world, it was also the year that an alliance was undone. The fourteen-year-old marriage of Tilling and British Electric Traction interests in the United Kingdom – Tilling & British Automobile Traction Ltd – was disparted into its two original components. Southdown was one of the 21 bus companies which found themselves in the British Electric Traction Co Ltd group – and in Southdown's case it was a return to the fold. The secretary of BET, Raymond Beddow, joined the Southdown board of directors and Tilling's Thomas Wolsey departed.

Although the company was obliged to withdraw its remaining express services that September, the absence of holiday visitors was being compensated for by wartime traffic on its stage-carriage services and contract work. Thanks to the high standards achieved by its staff, Southdown had begun its wartime task with rolling stock and buildings in excellent condition. Accordingly, despite being short of both vehicles and personnel – particularly in the maintenance sector – the company was fulfilling its obligations to the national effort with comparatively few hitches. The strain upon its resources was eased somewhat after 1st January 1943 when a 9.30pm curfew was placed upon bus services by the Regional Transport Officer in order to secure economies of fuel and rubber and relieve the drivers. On Sundays, no buses ran before 1pm.

That month, as though in retaliation for Lt Col Alexander Burman's OBE award, six of the Luftwaffe's new Focke-Wulf 190 fighter aircraft dived in from the sea at an altitude of 50 feet and proceeded to set about a Southdown bus. Midst a fusillade of cannon and machine-gun fire, driver E. J. Hoskin calmly pulled his loaded vehicle up beside a 10ft bank and frustrated the attack. Curiously and despite a heavy transfer of traffic to the buses as private car owners were forced to give up 'for the duration' such attacks were rare. In 1943, some vehicles serving flat terrain ran on producer gas, brewed up in two-wheeled trailers, as a contribution to liquid fuel economy. It proved difficult to maintain the schedules with such buses, however, and the attempt was abandoned in the summer of 1944. In 1943, the first of 100 Guy Arab utility vehicles arrived to relieve the overworked and intensively repaired Southdown fleet. Many of the early ones had wooden seats which made them seem hard-sprung – but no-one appeared to mind. The hygienic varnished woodwork and the general sparkle of the interiors made a brave effort to retain the Southdown image. When stage-carriage services in Worthing were drastically reduced, several local drivers took their new Guys over to Portsmouth to help with the preparations for D-Day – the allied invasion of Normandy.

The transfer of Southdown from Tilling to BET occurred in the middle of World War II. Fear for the continuity of oil supplies led the Government to demand that all larger bus companies were to convert a proportion of their fleet to producer-gas. Number 952 (UF 8852), a Leyland Titan TD2 dating from 1933 trundles its gas-producing trailer past an AEC Regent of BH&D and sets off in pursuit of a trolleybus. It ran in this form, together with other vehicles, until reversion to petrol was permitted in 1944. The Short Brothers body had received the wartime dark green roof, hooded headlights, white three-quarter disc and lower skirt to help mark its presence in the black-out.

Wartime austerity extended to the manufacture of buses also. In recognition of Southdown's good work along Britain's coastal 'front-line', the company was allotted 100 Guy Utility double-deckers, delivered between 1943-5. The bodywork was angular and the early examples had wooden slatted seats. Four different bodybuilders were involved and the liveries in which they arrived were varied, as though no-one was quite clear whether raids by the Luftwaffe had yet ceased. Number 420 (GUF 120), a Northern Counties 56-seater, takes a prudent line in green and grey on service from Brighton to Eastbourne.

Van Johnson is the star in the film showing at the cinema next to Brighton's Pool Valley as No. 260 (GCD 360), a Leyland Titan TD5 of 1940 with 57-seat Park Royal bodywork rolls to a halt beside the Palace Pier Hotel. The bus is en route for Pulborough and Petworth, still in its wartime livery: apple green to the waistline, grey above with a green band under the upper deck windows. The general appearance of the vehicle reflects a time when all Britain seemed very much in need of a nice new coat of paint.

In July 1946, Southdown entered into an agreement with the City of Portsmouth Passenger Transport Department in which mileage and receipts were pooled within an area bounded by Fareham, Petersfield and Emsworth – the Portsmouth Area Joint Transport Services; an arrangement which would last in modified form for 40 years. Whilst corporation buses might turn up at Fareham, Southdown buses worked municipal routes in the city. Southdown Guy Arab II No. 481 (GUF 181), a Weymann-bodied 56-seater is at work on Portsmouth's service F. To reach Alexandra Park from Milton, it would have crossed Copnor Bridge, positively foreign territory for a company bus, and wears an 'on-hire to CPPT' notice in the front window to show it is about its proper business. In Portsmouth Corporation usage, motor (rather than trolleybus) services were lettered instead of numbered.

The PAJTS agreement facilitated the hire by Southdown of CPPT Bedford utility saloons as a stop-gap before the new Hayling Bridge was opened. Portsmouth's 162 operates Southdown's service 47 from Havant Station to Hayling Island on 8 September 1956 as part of a ten-day hire whilst Southdown's light-weight Cubs were withdrawn for sale. The Bedford pulls away from the stop at Southdown's office in Havant High Street, where excursions are advertised to Fontwell Park Races, the Farnborough Air Show, to Chelsea for a Portsmouth FC away match, and for the express service to London.

During World War II, the Brush-bodied 51-seat Leyland Titans of 1929 had been fitted with temporary stretched-canvas roofs. By 1948, they had been removed and the vehicles were pressed into service at the seaside, and to the Devil's Dyke, to cope with the demand for local travel at a time when petrol was still rationed and cars were still difficult to come-by. Number 803 (UF 4803) looks in its element as it provides a service along Hayling Island's southern shore. The vehicle was withdrawn from passenger service in 1950.

Sadly, the whistling, gear-crashing Guys proved to be the last new vehicles Douglas Mackenzie saw enter the fleet. He died, aged 74, in December 1944, when victory in Europe was well in sight. His beloved company had come through its severest test with style. Damage to premises had been relatively light. In hard-hit Eastbourne and Portsmouth they seemed to have a charmed life. From its total staff of 2,500, 987 had joined the armed services. Thirty-one had been killed and sixteen taken prisoner. Many of the remainder had driven 88,717 passengers around gaps blasted in the Southern Railway network by enemy air activity in addition to the other wartime transport provided by the company, added to in 1944 by the acquisition of the Bognor-Slindon route of the Silver Queen Bus Service.

Sidney Garcke resigned his chairmanship of Southdown in favour of Raymond Beddow in May 1946, but remained a director until his comparatively early death in October 1948. The imposing, courteous Beddow was to remain chairman of the company until the Transport Holding Company assumed control in March 1968 – a record unlikely to be broken. The long overdue co-ordination agreement with the City of Portsmouth Passenger Transport

Department came into effect on 1st July 1946. It embraced operations within the city and the surrounding areas served by Southdown as far afield as Fareham in the west, Petersfield in the north and Emsworth in the east. Mileage and receipts were pooled on a 57 : 43 per cent division, with the Corporation enjoying the larger share. Originally a 20-year agreement, negotiations later extended the 'Portsmouth Area Joint Transport Services' in modified form.

Alfred Cannon, a local legend in his lifetime, retired as managing director on 13th June 1947, but retained his seat on the board until his death in June 1952, when a commemorative plaque to his memory was commissioned for display at Southdown headquarters. Area manager at Portsmouth in the difficult years of the war, A. F. R. (Michael) Carling was appointed general manager following Alfred Cannon's resignation. The man who shepherded his depot through the nightly rigours of the blitz was now to guide Southdown into full peacetime operation and the buoyant years of the early 'fifties. The company came through a brief period of gloom when severe fuel rationing placed dust sheets over many of its coaches, but put in train plans for new building work at Haywards Heath,

The withdrawal of the 1929-vintage Titans saw a replacement in 1951 by utility-bodied Guy 'Arabs' neatly converted to permanent open-top configuration. Service 97, Eastbourne-Beachy Head, had been a 'single-deck only' operation, but Eastbourne Corporation had recently relaxed the restriction to include licences for open-toppers to operate to the headland. Taking advantage of the dispensation is No. 412 (GUF 72), a Park Royal example.

The introduction of Guy 'Arab' open-topped double-deckers on the Eastbourne Pier to Beachy Head route led to the withdrawal of the quartet of three-axle Leyland Tigers specially purchased for the service in 1934 and 1935. Originally No. 51, then 551 (AUF 851) was one of the first pair, the TS6T model: the next pair were TS7T. The bodywork, built to a coach-style specification was by Short Brothers and, indeed, looked much like the contemporary express vehicles of the company. The end for these rather special 39-seaters came at the close of the 1952 season.

In the early 'fifties, unemployment in Portsmouth and the reverse in the Southampton area saw a period of co-operation between Southdown and neighbouring Hants & Dorset to move the necessary work forces. Service 136, Portsmouth to Swaythling, north of Southampton, where Briggs Motor Bodies were enjoying a boom, was one such joint service. Number 964 (AUF 664) is a Titan TD3 of 1934, with Beadle bodywork dating from fifteen years later, having been part of a large rebodying programme carried out by Southdown at that time. Hants & Dorset's contribution was likely to be an all-Leyland TD1 enjoying its last few weeks of service. The 'Setright' ticket system was used by both operators on these journeys.

Changing crews at Southdown's Hilsea garage is No. 223 (FUF 233), a Leyland Titan TD5 of 1939 with Park Royal bodywork replacing that by the same manufacturer as originally fitted. Heavy wartime use was largely responsible for the comparatively short life of Southdown's pre-war double-decker bodywork, but the replacement designs remained in harmony; this Park Royal example particularly so. The bus is running into Portsmouth from Fareham on the 45 service, much preferred by through passengers to the 45A, which went 'all around the houses' at Portchester. The 45B was even better: it missed out Cosham.

Southdown in repose: No. 149 (CCD 949) a Leyland Titan TD4 of 1936. Its original Beadle body had been replaced in 1950 by an East Lancs 54-seat unit. The style remains decidedly Southdown, however, right down to the illuminated red 'stop' sign in the rear waistband. A rustic waiting room and woodlands at The Green terminus in Rowlands Castle represent a considerable contrast with the seafront setting which awaits the vehicle at the South Parade Pier end of its journey.

Although based on a 1939 design, Leyland launched its impressive Titan PD range of double-deckers in 1946. Southdown's first examples were bodied by Park Royal: the second batch, the following year, was comprised of the classic all-Leyland mass-produced, metal-framed product. It had the singular capacity to look at home in any operator's livery. Number 309 (HCD 909) succeeds in looking very much a Southdown and brightening up a winter's day en route from Hastings to Eastbourne.

The photographer photographed! On a private hire duty from Hilsea in 1961, Southdown driver Alan Lambert is caught by the camera of Eric Surfleet at Petersfield, Hants. William of Orange, with transport of his own, turns his back on the historic moment. Number 331 (JCD 31) is a Titan PD2, distinguishable at a glance from the PD1 model by the shortened dash below the windscreen, though the important difference was the use of a 9.3-litre O.600 engine rather than the 7.5-litre E181.

Littlehampton, Hassocks and Chichester, together with extensions to the works at Portslade. This was the period when, following nationalisation of the railway companies – including the Southern's one third share in Southdown – the Thomas Tilling organisation relinquished its United Kingdom bus interests to the state. Arthur Greenwood's 'thirties dream of a common drive towards the social good, now urged on by Herbert Morrison, met stern resistance from BET – and Southdown remained two-thirds un-nationalised.

During the late 'forties several of the old open-top Leyland Titans had the wartime covers (fitted to allow them to remain in all-year round service) removed and ran newly-painted and topless along the seaside routes. In 1950, Portslade Works began lopping tops from wartime Guys and they re-entered service on the scenic run to the Devil's Dyke. Similar vehicles were sent to Eastbourne for the Beachy Head run and to other locations on the coast, until they were replaced by Leyland convertible double-deckers. There was unusual stage-carriage work from Portsmouth in the early 'fifties as a combination of high unemployment in the city coincided with the development of Esso's refinery at Fawley, a boom in car body-building at Swaythling, and of aircraft production at Eastleigh in the Southampton area. At one stage Southdown had a bus and its crew based at Hants & Dorset's Eastleigh garage. Back in its own area, the company purchased the goodwill of Mrs M. Hay-Wills' stage-carriage service from Arundel to Burpham.

There was also increased co-operation with another

As this conductor's eye view of the lower saloon in No. 777 (RUF 177) discloses, the Southdown 'sparkle' was not restricted to the polished exteriors of the vehicles. Although the varnished woodwork has gone in this the metal-framed era, the 1956 interior retains the usual Southdown characteristics of high-gloss ivory ceiling and attractive brown, orange and fawn moquette seat covers – long a company standard. The vehicle is a Titan PD2/12 with Beadle 59-seat bodywork.

bus-operating neighbour, Maidstone & District Motor Services Ltd. In 1948, an incredibly long run between Brighton and Gravesend was introduced and run jointly with double-deckers. Following the acquisition of the stage-carriage services of Beacon Motor Services (Crowborough) Ltd, controlled by Southdown from 16th September 1949 and fully absorbed in the spring of 1954, and company control of three services operated by Sargents of East Grinstead, achieved in March 1951, there was further inter-company activity. Maidstone & District gained ground in East Grinstead, but the two companies began to plan a co-ordination scheme which led – on 2nd June 1957 – to the establishment of a joint-operation called the 'Heathfield Cycle'. This made all routes in the area – save an infrequent Southdown working – a joint affair, which doubled the number of services operated with Maidstone & District and actually reduced some of the fares. At the other end of its area, Southdown acquired the Petersfield-Buriton service when Percy Lambert ceased trading.

Whereas it had been Michael Carling who co-ordinated the detail work for Southdown's running agreement with Portsmouth Corporation, it fell to his successor Arthur Woodgate – appointed general manager in 1954 – to supervise a mileage agreement with the London Transport Executive in 1958, dealing with through services at Crawley New Town and, more importantly, the negotiations which led to the establishment of the 'Brighton Area Transport Services'. Discussions between Brighton Corporation, Brighton Hove & District and Southdown had been taking place for a number of years and agreement in principle was reached in February 1960. An area had been mapped out which included the whole of Brighton, Hove, Portslade, Southwick and Shoreham, including Shoreham Beach. All

June 1957 had seen the establishment of the 'Heathfield Cycle', a co-ordination scheme with Maidstone & District Motor Services Ltd, which reduced fares and doubled the number of services operated in the area. All-Leyland PD2/12 No. 735 (LUF 235) of 1952 departs from Brighton's Pool Valley on service 180 to Heathfield, Battle and Hastings – one of the pooled routes. The bus carries an advertisement for 'Beacon Tours', a coach-cruising banner adopted by Southdown in 1953.

Resting in Chichester Bus Station on 29 June 1958, No. 739 (LUF 239) shows off the platform-doors fitted at Portslade works to all PD2/12 models delivered without them. The bus had made the long attractive run in from Petersfield via Midhurst en route for Bognor Regis and the seaside – and if the young lady with the child can find any room left inside she will be lucky. The twenty year lineage of the basic Leyland body design is evident in this unusual view. Chichester Bus Station itself was a legacy of Southdown expansion in the 'fifties.

In 1958, Portsmouth City Council decided that the cost of renewing its overhead trolleybus equipment had become too great. Trolleybuses were abandoned in favour of diesel powered vehicles from 1960-63. The PAJTS agreement meant that Southdown were on hand to help with the replacement services after conversion. On 24th February 1962, Titan PD2 No. 317 (JCD 17) wears trolleybus route number 3 as a tired pole in the background tries to support the remaining wires. The driver demonstrates the hand and footholds for changing the front screen.

revenues from stage-carriage services operating within BATS orbit were pooled in the proportion:

Brighton Hove & District   50½%
Southdown Motor Services Ltd 29%
Brighton Corporation Transport 20½%

Part of the revenue from Southdown's cross-boundary routes into Brighton was also accountable and provision was made for services operated wholly within the BATS area to be reallocated between the three concerns, to give each a fair share of costly services with slower scheduled speeds.

The post-war building programme had been pursued with considerable vigour during the 'fifties. There were major additions to the garages at Eastbourne and Hilsea, new ones at Crawley, Seaford and Moulsecoomb and, in addition to Chichester getting its long-discussed bus station, there were also new ones at Haywards Heath and Lewes. Major contribution to the company of its architect H. A. F. Spooner, however, was the design and construction-supervision of 'Southdown House' in Freshfield Road, Brighton, the new head office completed in 1964. Southdown also updated its facilities at Hailsham the following year.

Sadly, Arthur Woodgate met an untimely death in 1961, only months after that of his wife. Southdown's unexpected loss was expressed in a beautifully-written tribute by chairman Raymond Beddow, which appeared in the *Southdown Chronicle*, the updated version of the company's journal. Created, like several other Southdown directors, a CBE in 1956 for his service to the bus industry,

Beddow had represented Southdown in the negotiations which led to the area agreements in Portsmouth and Brighton, had taken a personal interest in every aspect of the business, and attended as many Southdown social functions as his numerous commitments would allow. Chairman of the Executive Committee of the BET Federation and for many years a member of the National Council for the Omnibus Industry, he retired in March 1968, still very much a BET man, as the Transport Holding Company assumed control.

Meanwhile, Jim Skyrme was general manager from 1961-66, returned as a director in 1968 and, at the end of the year, succeeded Wilfred Dravers, who had been chairman for nine months. Traffic manager Gerald Duckworth was promoted to general manager in 1966 – a creditable performance for, despite being a Lancastrian and in some respects an 'outsider', he had risen to that rank from a relatively humble position within the company. As government pressure upon BET to sell its bus interests to the state mounted, it became clear that Southdown's days as a public company were at last numbered. In January 1968, BET finally agreed to sell its holdings in British bus companies to the Transport Holding Company, set up pending the formation of the National Bus Company. The NBC's reorganisation programme included the transfer to Southdown of the Brighton Hove & District Omnibus Co Ltd in 1969, and Gerald Duckworth became director and general manager of that company also. The initial organisation of the National Bus Company in the Southdown orbit is described in TPC's *Regional History of British Bus services: South East England*, and the history of BH&D in TPC's *British Bus & Trolleybus Systems, No. 4. Brighton Hove & District* by Southdown's own John Roberts, for many years a BH&D man himself.

To the surprise of some, Southdown took further deliveries of Guy Arab double-deckers – Mark IIIs in 1948-49, Mark IVs in 1955-56. The latter were fitted with 8ft-wide Park Royal bodywork which, although now standard, looked even wider on the Guys because of that manufacturer's comparatively narrow radiator. Number 518 (OUF 518) is at Haywards Heath bus station on 28 May 1961, a busy commuter point for local passengers by train on the Victoria line. The economy of the Gardner 6LW engine enhanced what was by now a very good chassis.

The post-war successes of the rugged Leyland Titan PD2s in most parts of the company area ensured a continuing patronage for the marque. For its first 30ft-long double-decker, Southdown chose the PD3/4 model with Northern Counties bodywork. With it came the full front, front entrance and stair case, and a seating capacity up to 69 passengers. Southdown took delivery of the first in 1958 and liked them so much that they purchased a total of 285 – the largest single group of double-deckers ever owned by the company. It thus became the quintessential Southdown bus. Number 857 (XUF 857), built in 1959, is at Market Parade, Havant on the 46A service to Leigh Park on 3 October 1962.

Chapter Six: Excursions, Tours and Private Hire

When, between March and July 1908, the Sussex Motor Road Car Company provided journeys to Ascot races from the Gloucester Hotel, Brighton, and the Sussex Hotel, Hove at 10/6 (52½p) return, it set in motion the process by which Southdown was to build its reputation as a purveyor of coach facilities without peer. It was carried further by such private hire work as the military 'motor-dash' to Newhaven Fort undertaken by Worthing Motor Services the following year.

Once installed at 23 Marine Parade, Worthing, Cannon began to build up day, afternoon and evening excursion traffic from the sea front, whilst Mackenzie set about realising his long-felt desire to take members of the public touring to far-off places. The setting up of Sussex Tourist Coaches' initially for working excursion traffic from Brighton, together with the delivery of the first 'Silent Knight'-engined Daimler CC chassis gave him the combination for which he had waited. Soon, the Sussex Tourist slogan 'Green Cars Run Everywhere' would have real substance.

There was at first, however, some scepticism. If Mackenzie was sure he now had a reliable vehicle, the potential customers were not. When, in May 1913, he advertised a proposed fortnight's tour from Worthing to the Lake District, he could not get a single booking. It was thought too much of a risk. A group of ladies who listened to his chin-rubbing account of this failure suggested that if he provided a shorter tour lasting 'say seven days' they'd provide a nucleus of seven friends – and 'the rest is up to you'. Several years later, one of those ladies was to become Mrs Eva Mackenzie.

So started the well-documented Devon and Cornwall tour with a full complement of 24 passengers, including Mackenzie, his father and his future wife, in a Daimler CC coach with slipper bodywork of his own design. The journey, which began on 14th June 1913, was full of incident, but each was safely overcome: passengers had to walk up some steep hills; the coach jammed under the entrance arch of the Bude Hotel, Exeter. When the passengers got out, the springs went up and lifted the floor of two ladies' bedrooms above. The rivers Dart and Tamar were crossed by ferry and barge; planks placed over a shingle beach were used to get the coach safely ashore; the brakes failed on Paracombe Hill, but only Mackenzie and the driver noticed; the old-oak scotch was used more than once to stop roll-back; eighteen Lynmouth fishermen were recruited to lift the back end around an impossible corner; when the coach was being driven empty up Combe Hill, a stake protruding from the hedge smashed a side window; and on a narrow road in North Somerset it had to wait half an hour for the daily coach drawn by six horses to come safely through in the opposite direction. "Well, what can they expect: said a small West Country lad, if they goes about in a bloomin 'ouse?"

By any standards it was a triumph, and one of the passengers wrote an article for the *Worthing Gazette*

Above: Where it all began – Alfred Cannon (leaning against the front-wheel arch), has come out to see off the well-documented tour of Devon and Cornwall in 1913. Douglas Mackenzie is already aboard the 'bloomin' 'ouse', as a small West Country lad was to call it, and his father and future wife Eva are safely tucked away inside among the 24 excited passengers. The vehicle is DL 701, a Daimler CC with body by Worthing Motor Services. The vehicle's chassis is believed to be one of those which was commandeered for military use the following year.

Right: In that following year, Mackenzie was again in his 'engineer's position' beside the engine, when sister vehicle DL 705, with body built by Hora to WMS design, took another 'Sussex Tourist Coaches' party to the Lake District, this time with Alfred Cannon and Percy Lephard aboard (co-founders with Mackenzie of the reconstituted Wilts & Dorset Motor Services Ltd the following year). In 1960 Percy Lephard's son, R. Lephard, was Area Manager at Worthing. The main stop-over was made at the Keswick Hotel. The DL registrations of these vehicles were taken out through Mackenzie's Ryde, Isle of Wight office which he had kept open for his consultancy work.

The only excursion work possible during the second half of World War I was the special allowance local authorities were able to make for operators engaged by military forces wishing to provide recreational facilities for their personnel. At Queen Victoria's feet on the Hove seafront are a platoon of military men born part of her overseas Empire of India. The Tilling-Stevens TS3 charabanc, (LH 8926), was purchased from Thomas Tilling Ltd, in whose service it is seen here, by Southdown in 1919, when it became No. 54.

Daimler CB charabanc No. 3 (IB 703) with 27-seat Harrington bodywork was new in 1915 and is pictured soon after WWI restrictions on private hire work were lifted. The passengers gained their seats via the tiered running boards or, if they were less able, by means of the ladder moved along by the driver; and the doors clump, clumped shut like those of a commuter train. The picture was taken no later than 1919, for that year the Mackenzie-acquired Armagh registration was changed to CD 5003 (see below).

Above: What Cannon would have called, with the candour acceptable at the time, people not of the 'tripper class' have hired a Southdown charabanc for a private party in 1922. They look well-dressed, quite affluent, and the kind of folk who, a few years later, would have made the trip in a convoy of their own motorcars. Tilling Stevens TS3 No. 63 (CD 4863) looks in good condition also, having just been refitted with a new Harrington body in place of its 1919 original.

Above left: After World War I, Southdown restricted its coaching activity to private hire and local excursions until 1925, whilst it built up a solid series of stage carriage services. Many of these started at Marine Parade, Worthing, with Mackenzie's office overlooking the stand – a nervous moment for any driver as he hopes he can start his vehicle. The amount of effort required is conveyed by the driver's stance and the need to remove his dust coat. The charabanc is IB 703 renumbered CD 5003 in 1919.

Left: Number 106 (CD 3536), a Leyland N of 1919 with 32-seat charabanc body, again by Harrington the local firm with whom Southdown became closely identified, has arrived on Brighton seafront and set up shop for a local excursion. The departure for Newhaven and Seaford will be at 2.45pm and the return fare 4 shillings (20p). The driver wears a white dust coat with green collar and cuffs and, like his naval counterparts of those days, a white cover for his cap worn only from May to September. His badge is of the original long rectangular type.

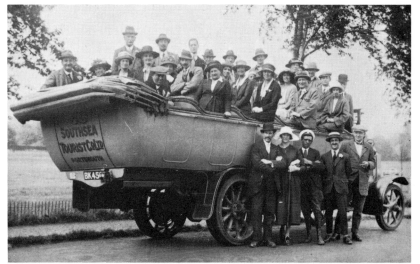

It was the purchase of Frank Plater's Southsea Tourist Co Ltd in 1925, together with its well-established tour arrangements, which encouraged Mackenzie to re-establish his long-distance coach cruising programme. Plater's Portsmouth fleet was comprised entirely of Dennis vehicles. And they seem to have been very successful on the coach front: this charabanc (BK 4502), nominally a 28-seater, has 31 passengers displaying a sense of belonging around the driver. It became number 364 in the Southdown fleet, was rebodied by Harrington the following year and gained pneumatic tyres

called Seven Counties in Seven Days' which finished by paraphrasing Macaulay; "...The tales repeated still, How the big Worthing motor drove, Up Countisbury Hill!"

There followed a three-day tour to the New Forest in July 1913 with two nights spent at the Stag Hotel, Lyndhurst, and, in September, two coaches labelled Aberystwyth' left on a tour to Mid-Wales with a total of 34 passengers and only Duncton Hill in home territory causing any trouble – with the possible exception of a Welsh goose who spread his wings and refused to permit the leading coach to pass. As a result of these successful tours, the 1914 programme started with an 11th May departure for the Lake District, with Mackenzie, Cannon and Percy Lephard among the passengers. This coach sank to its rear wheel hubs on a soft road surface at Ennerdale and in trying to push a projecting stone, Mackenzie brought down at a run an entire dry-stone wall-to the amusement of the owner. When this party returned all available vehicles at Worthing were sent loaded to the Derby. In June two coaches went to Devon and came back in time for Ascot, whilst a Welsh tour returned in July as vehicles were prepared for Goodwood races. There were also 3-day tours to the New Forest and to Kent. Further tours were planned, but the outbreak of war in August 1914 put paid to them. After the Armistice, what vehicles the three-year-old Southdown company could acquire were needed for stage-carriage work. Additionally, the board of directors did not prove too keen to restart holiday tours. Southdown's first coach cruise as they came to be known throughout the company's area, was run as an experiment in September 1922 when a Daimler CB charabanc left on a not uneventful trip to North Wales. No tours were run in 1923 or 1924, although a tour to the Lakes was advertised in May and again in July 1923, but did not secure sufficient bookings.

Meanwhile, the acquisition of Arthur Davies' excursion licences at Bognor in 1915 proved to be the first of a long and on-going series of take-overs designed to consolidate and protect Southdown's interest in the field set up by Alfred Cannon. The Southdown coach fleet in the early twenties consisted of 36-40hp Tilling-Stevens and Leyland chassis with open canvas-roofed charabanc bodies, relieved from time to time by acquired vehicles of various makes. As early as 1922, experiments included arm-chair type seats with central gangway, thus removing the need for a battery of doors down the nearside. Of the 130 vehicles then owned by Southdown, 50 were charabancs and coaches, and the proportion was increasing rapidly. In the west of the prescribed Southdown area, tours work was considerably strengthened by the purchase of Frank

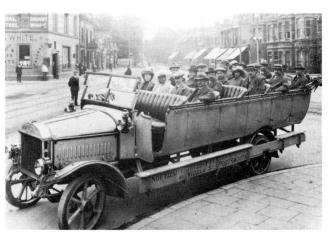

The oldest Plater vehicle to enter the Southdown fleet was BK 2211 (348) of 1919. It is parked beside the Southsea Tourist office in London Road North End. This had been erected by Plater and sported a carved STCo at the top of the facade: it became a booking office for Southdown. The '49 Middle St' address on the charabanc formed the basis for Southdown's Hyde Park Rd garage.

Demonstrating an early example of the Southdown shine (what reflections!) on its torpedo bodied sides is No. 240 (CD 9641), one of a pair of Tilling Stevens TS3A charabancs with 26-seat Harrington bodywork delivered in 1925. One of the main reasons why the charabanc was gradually replaced by the enclosed coach was the marked deterioration of the long hot English summer during the 'twenties. First acknowledgment that a problem existed was the provision of the diagonal side screens to give added protection from spray.

Experiments were made with older charabancs, by fitting them with clip-on transparent side-screens made from stiff celluloid. These provided nearly complete protection when the hood was up, but then proved extremely draughty and liable to jump smartly inward with a loud 'crack' if hit by a sudden on-shore breeze – and there were plenty of those in Southdown territory. Number 98 (CD 6898), new in 1922 with Harrington body, tried its best until withdrawn in 1929.

Plater's two companies, South Coast Tourist of Littlehampton and Southsea Tourist Co Ltd in 1924 and 1925 respectively. It was the purchase of the latter, as described in Chapter 4, together with its already established tour organisation which gave Mackenzie his opportunity to re-start his coach-cruises and a few were worked to Devon and the Wye Valley in 1925. The following year, a comprehensive programme of three, seven, ten and fourteen-day tours, booking at Brighton, Worthing and Portsmouth was launched with complete success.

Among the large rival coach concerns bought out by Southdown were J. Poole's 'Royal Red Coaches' of Hove, whose proprietor was placed in charge of Southdown's Hove office in 1930, and Potts Coaches of Brighton. In 1932 came the largest purchase of all, the entire coach business of Chapman & Sons (Eastbourne) Ltd. Ironically, one of the horse-brakes which William Chapman had run to the top of Beachy Head had been called 'The Southdown'. He and his sons had turned to motors in 1912 and built up the largest fleet of charabancs in Eastbourne. In World War I, one of their coaches was the first gas-powered vehicle to be seen in Brighton. The family's pioneering spirit flourished after the Armistice and by 1920, tours to Scotland and Wales – and even to France and Switzerland were on the programme. George and William Chapman Jnr continued to expand the business and, by the Easter of 1925, the fleet consisted of 37 Dennis charabancs; tours to Italy and the north and west of Ireland had been added, and over 100,000 passengers were being carried each year.

In 1931, however, coach proprietors everywhere suffered the worst weather for a quarter of a century. It is difficult to understand how one wet summer could have such an effect, but Chapman's, in any case lacking sufficient capital to modernise its fleet, decided to wind up the business. Yet, to a certain extent, a coach company was obliged to hibernate during the winter, whilst those with stage-carriage services had a steady all-year-round return, which supported the tours section during a poor season. Southdown, of course, enjoyed such insurance and, in 1932, a combination of this factor, rising costs, and – above all – the stultifying after-effects of the Road Traffic Act 1930 sealed the fate of Chapmans fifty coaches, 44 of which entered the Southdown fleet. The goodwill of the business and certain leasehold premises were sold to the company, who thereafter enjoyed a patronage built up in Eastbourne over a period of fifty years.

Southdown's coach-cruises now covered the country from Lands End to John O'Groats. Included in their cost was accommodation in first-class hotels and all gratuities. In many instances the more exclusive hotels rejected all coach traffic save that of Southdown – a trend which reached its climax when it became a mark of distinction for an hotel to have a Southdown touring coach parked upon its forecourt. By 1934, the company had become the largest operator of long-distance tours in Great Britain,

Centre: The next logical stop was to provide rigid frames at the sides fitted with plate glass wind-down windows. Harrington had already provided Southdown with several like that by the time No. 490 (MO 9313) entered the fleet in 1932. It was one of 50 vehicles acquired by Southdown, together with the business of Chapman & Sons (Eastbourne) Ltd, and was one of six similar Tilling-Stevens B9B coaches which that firm, in turn, had acquired from Thames Valley. Accompanied by another of the batch, it is on a private hire job – and the driver is looking anxiously for his missing passengers.

Lower: Just acquired from Potts' Luxury Coaches of Brighton, together with five other Dennis coaches, is what would become No. 395 (UF 4925), a Dennis F with 30-seat Duple coachwork. The vehicle is still dressed in Potts' livery and fleetnames, but is about to be driven off by a Southdown crewman on a 'Grand Coastal Drive' – to Worthing for 2 shillings (10p). This is 1930, and the drivers are wearing the first of the famous Mackenzie cursive script cap badges.

One of six Leyland Lioness LTB1 coaches with 20-seat Harrington bodywork, No. 302 (UF 5850), specially designed for long range coach cruising. It was delivered in 1930 during that brief spell when Leyland products emerged from the works with beautiful enamelled badges displayed on the head of the radiator. This one sports an impressive full-frontal furry face of a Lioness. A further six (without the feline head) were delivered in 1933, and one of these is an exhibit in a Southdown marquee, hired from the NAAFI, at an agricultural show. It is impressively marked 'Scottish Highlands' on the slipboard.

Above: The year 1933 marked the last attempt by the company to preserve the 'completely open to the elements' feel given, on long-distance work, by the fold-back canvas roof. Thereafter, touring coach roofs would incorporate sliding sections and, in some cases, glass quarter-lights to retain the upward view. Still not fully enclosed is No. 2 (ACD 102), a Leyland Cub KP2A with Harrington 14-seat coachwork, one of a pair delivered in that year.

using finely tuned Leyland Lioness and Cub coaches with Harrington bodywork built to Southdown's own specification. In 1936, they were joined by six beautiful Burlingham-bodied Leyland Tigresses, which became popular with American tourists who booked the tours in advance in the United States or at one of the company's booking offices opened in London. The drivers were selected from among the best of the long-serving employees and wore chauffeur's uniform with no badges. On their first trips they were taken around the routes by Mackenzie himself, such was his concern that their numerous and diversified duties should be carried out with the utmost professionalism. Relatively high charges were made for the cruises, so that only passengers of good standing were attracted. Speaking of this with delightful candour in 1934, Cannon opined that 'reasonable profits can only accrue when the entire organisation is conceived with the object of catering for luxury coaching as distinct from popular motor tours arranged for passengers belonging to what is commonly known as the tripper class.' Fortunately for the company, a considerable number of the populace reached the acceptable plateau of sophistication as the 'thirties progressed and by the end of the decade the coach cruises were so popular that petrol tankers were out-stationed at the more remote spots to refuel the cars. Cruise diaries were introduced and all passengers names entered therein so that there could be immediate communication with them. The coaches cruised at a leisurely average speed of 22 mph and covered no more than 100 miles per day, with no driving undertaken at night, in order that the vehicles were not excessively stressed. The high standards achieved by and with these coaches gradually encompassed all the operations of the company, including the more prosaic stage-carriage services.

Meanwhile, back on the seafronts from Southsea to Eastbourne, the tripper-class excursions, each carefully advertised by beautifully written advertisements in coloured chalks on blackboards placed beside the appropriate vehicle, continued steadily to build up the destinations and departures. From Southsea, trips to Southampton Docks, the New Forest and Meon Valley were the most popular, whilst farther east, the Devil's Dyke, Winchelsea and Rye attracted considerable custom In the years prior to World War II, traffic became so heavy that the favoured places

Left: The 'airiness' of a coach fitted with quarter lights is evident in this interior view of a 1936 Leyland Tigress RLTB3 with Burlingham coachwork. The armchair seats are so generously spaced in this sizeable coach that only 20 passengers were carried on what was considered the ultimate long-distance touring vehicle. Southdown referred to the drivers of their six examples, which cruised at 22 mph and looked like outsize luxury limousines, as chauffeurs. Once on the open road the purr of the Tigress was barely audible.

upon the stands were allocated on rotation to each proprietor according to the relative size of its fleet. Such was the success of the company in this quarter, some smaller rivals began labelling their vehicles with fleetnames done in Mackenzie-style script and in a similar colour scheme-until requested to stop by the Traffic Commissioners.

Some signs of a trade recession in hotels nationwide in 1938 had its effect upon bookings that year but, as tension rose in continental Europe thereafter, many travellers used to foreign travel switched to coach cruising in Britain during 1939, and thus provided Southdown with its best year to that point. Even the booking office established at inland East Grinstead the previous year had practically more work than it could handle.

The following summer was a different matter; with the Germans on the French coast opposite. Britain slammed shut its front door, the barbed wire went up on the seafronts, piers were breached to stop unwelcome visitors by steamship and what appeared to be an excursion booking office was much more likely to be a concrete pillbox. Military requisitioning of Southdown coaches had started already in the autumn of 1939, and some soldiers evacuated from Dunkirk and landed at Portsmouth declared that they had been living in Southdown coaches in France for the last six weeks – the records suggest that this is not likely, but some 24 were converted to ambulances. Others were drafted into the 'Southdown Home Guard: or utilised for carrying munitions workers, troops or ENSA parties far from the leafy lanes of Sussex. At least one Tilling-Stevens became home for a searchlight crew on the cliff-top, somewhere in Southern England: and others contributed to putting our armies back onto mainland Europe during D-Day preparations in 1944. Thereafter, the company's coaches provided transport for German prisoners of war working upon road construction and the land.

With the resumption of peace in Europe in May 1945, came the lifting of restrictions upon visitors to the coast. With the barbed wire, if not the larger obstacles removed, waves breaking upon the beach were now met in the opposite direction by hordes of trippers anxious to make up for lost time. With a sadly depleted fleet – thus leading to some mildly unsuitable vehicles being pressed into service – great efforts were made to cope with the weight of traffic. The 1946 service of excursions and tours was thus greatly extended to a proportion well in excess of prewar figures, and Southdown went back to the Derby and Ascot. Only difficulties in finding adequate hotel accommodation delayed the restart of the coach-cruising programme which actually got going again in time for the 1947 season – 20 passengers leaving, fittingly perhaps, for a tour of Devon and Cornwall on 1st May.

Fuel rationing remained, however, and as late as 1948 a government directive led to considerable curtailment of this growing area of business, which in turn presented the company with manpower problems. It was not until 'rationed' petrol, stained red to prevent its misuse In private cars, entered the history books, that the upward trend continued. By 1950, however, the year that Southdown started its tours to the continent, some 7,500 passengers per annum were booking on the company's tours. In 1953 Southdown began to use the 'Beacon Tours' style to cover a series of tours using 37-seat coaches rather than the 28-seaters of the 'Coach Cruise' programme. Effectively the opportunity to accommodate nine extra passengers (33 per cent larger

As with World War I, the second (1939-1945) brought coaching to a virtual standstill, save for military purposes. From 1939 onward many were requisitioned by the military or became ambulances, whilst the remainder turned upon stage-carriage work. One of those taken by the War Department, No. 1169 (DUF 169), a 32-seat Harrington coach was among those never returned. It remained close to home, however, being numbered first M8033 and then 50 YP 14 in the post-war army series. It is seen here in khaki livery, with Headquarters Depot Battalion flash in blue, red and yellow on the nearside wing, passing by Southdown's Hilsea depot en route for Hilsea Barracks, home of the Royal Army Ordnance Corps a few hundred yards to the south. It served the RAOC until 1959.

payload) enabled these tours to be sold in a lower priced sector of the market. Similarly, in 1958, the 'Triumph Tours' style was adopted to cover certain activities in the Portsmouth area, notably forces leave services and private hire. In 1964, almost 22,000 passengers travelled by Southdown extended tours to many parts of Britain, Ireland and most countries in western Europe. Under contract between 1958 and 1960, Southdown coaches went even farther than that – to Moscow. Large numbers of the passengers carried on these long-distance tours were visitors from America, Australia, Canada, New Zealand and South Africa .

The founding of the National Bus Company led, of course, to the transfer of control of the coach-cruising programme from Southdown to NBC's Central Activities Group; the vehicles involved being repainted in an all-white livery with red and blue lettering. For the best part of ten years, the block letters **SOUTHDOWN**, in red, marked the company's nominal ownership of these vehicles. Then, from 1980, the spirit of Mackenzie rose up once more, and into service came a coach bedecked in traditional Southdown green, script fleetname and all – and promptly won a class award at that year's British Coach Rally It was soon joined by others.

In March 1981, in the aftermath of coach deregulation, the 'Southdown Excursion Club' was introduced to expand considerably the company s coaching activities. Through a combination of personal service, repeat orders, priority bookings, loyalty discounts and demand-based excursions and mini-tours programmes, the company set out to increase its excursion and private-hire carryings. The club met with an overwhelming response: the demand for

The seven year gap in coach deliveries, caused by World War II, ended at last in 1947. By this time the technology gained under military conditions had been incorporated within the robust-looking Leyland Tiger PS1 with 7.4-litre Leyland diesel engine and the new-fangled self-starter. The first batch of these excursion coaches was based upon Harrington's new fin-tailed design (on the rear of the roof), with chrome strakes on the rear wings. Southdown accepted the strakes, but turned down the fin as 'definitely not our class, darling!' The finless No. 1265 (HUF 5) is on a West Sussex excursion for 7s. 6d.

War production and other military duties had severely affected manufacturers' ability to get back into their stride to deal with work which now flooded their way. Not surprisingly, Southdown found it necessary to share out the orders for full-size coach bodywork to six different coachbuilders. A surprise choice for the second batch of private hire, excursion and tour coaches was Windover, in common with other BET companies, hitherto builders of luxury car bodywork. The resultant design with pointed wings and half canopy was most unusual for Southdown. The vehicle is No. 1273 (HUF 273).

In addition to Beadle of Dartford and Park Royal, Duple provided sizeable numbers of coaches for Southdown in 1948. Number 1335 (HUF 935) is painted in original livery, with seating reduced from 32 to 27 for extended tours; this one to 'Scotland and the English Lakes'. This batch represented Southdown's introduction to Duple coachwork from new yet, together with the Beadle product, Duple more closely followed Southdown's ideas of how a coach should look than other contemporary coachbuilders. The production of this one-off design was a recognition of Southdown's importance by Duple.

The Leyland Lioness and Tigress coaches were retired when a radical alternative became available. This was Southdown's first purchase of the new underfloor-engined 30ft coach, the Leyland Royal Tiger PSU1/15, specially designed for long-distance coach cruising with only 26 seats, arranged 'two and one' in Duple 'Ambassador' coachwork. Number 1806 (originally 806: LCD 206) was delivered in 1951 but gained its front dome glass and had its destination boxes lowered in 1954. It is on private hire duty for the Royal Naval Association, Worthing branch, on 28th July 1963.

Standing outside the Edinburgh Road, Portsmouth, office of Triumph Coaches on 31st May 1962 is Southdown Leyland Tiger Cub No. T1101 (SUF 901). The firm was acquired in 1957 and had been largely concerned with express work, but private hire also featured and this was kept on by Southdown, its own vehicles being repainted in the blue and cream Triumph livery in sufficient numbers to reflect the degree of goodwill that firm had built up in Portsmouth and Southsea.

Another Southdown coach in blue livery was No. 1129 (UCD 129), dating from January 1958, which was painted in the colours of the Linje Buss International concern and used exclusively for that Swedish operator's tours of Britain, as far afield as the Lake District and Scotland. The vehicle was a Leyland Tiger Cub with 32-seat bodywork by Beadle: it remained on this duty until the end of the 1963 season.

'Southdown-style' coaching was still there. The summer of 1983 saw a new recruit for such activity enter service; the 'Southdown Diplomat', a twelve-year old coach refitted as a luxury palace on wheels, came away from that years British Coach Rally with four major awards and a great deal of press coverage Said coaching officer Christine Watts, 'It's ideal for business use – whether as a mobile hospitality suite or a conference and dining facility for parties of executives travelling between factories and offices – and it's far more flexible than any executive jet.'

Such imaginative use of the company's resources came at a time when a local upturn in the public use of coach facilities was gaining momentum. For instance, 12,000 passengers travelled in the company's vehicles to see the various away football matches in Brighton's cup run to the final at Wembley. Cricket was not forgotten either, and a 'Sussex-Link' coach was made available to the Sussex County Cricket team for its Easter tour that year. Not without a sense of humour, the management gained further publicity in the grand manner when a Southdown Leyland Tiger coach was hired for a trip which set a new world record for the Guinness Book of Records. Driven by Ted Elms, the vehicle travelled 320ft – from Nobles Bar in New Road, Brighton, to the Theatre Royal – with a stop at 'The Volunteer' pub on the way. Each of these differing examples of the coaching section's activities epitomised its watchwords: reliability, quality and flexibility – words which added up to the good name of Southdown.

The upturn was to be short-lived, however – the last bright flame before the fire goes out. Even if Brighton's and Portsmouth's FCs stay in the top flight of football had been longer-lived, the traffic generated would have been insufficient to redress the general decline in coaching, particularly in the south of England.

In part, this had been hastened on by latter-day NBC policy. Not only had its subsidiaries in the south, by and large, received no new double-decked service buses since 1981, new coaches too had been few and far between. The reliability and quality aspects of Southdown's image thus came under threat from an ageing coach fleet – not a helpful situation when competition in the market place for a diminishing customer demand required the very best equipment. Given less, the potential customer was much more likely to go and see Mackenzie's clapper bridge in Cornwall in his family saloon.

Southdown attempted to address this problem – as did numerous other operators – by hiding their age of their coaches with re-registrations. Elderly Leyland PD3 double-deckers awaiting disposal provided a ready source of registration numbers free of a tell-tale 'year' letter. In the brelief that one can fool some of the people all of the time, they began to be divested of them. After the reorganisation of Southdown on 1st January 1986 and the dissolution of the coaching division, this process was increased as the geographical bus divisions were each allotted a share of the coach fleet. 'Hampshire' division at Portsmouth was particularly active in this respect.

Among the 'few and far between' in 1985 was the one-off Hestair Duple 425 integral 57-seat coach, decked out in silver and green and labelled 'SOUTHDOWN COACHES'.

This Leyland Leopard PSU3B/4R with Plaxton 32-seat coachwork was delivered in 1971, in a batch originally decked out in traditional Southdown green. They became the first to be painted in National white coaching livery; but several sneaked back into their old colours under such banners as '65 Years of Southdown' and, as in this case, as 'The Southdown Diplomat' for executive hire. Southdown's Christine Watts toasts its success in the 1983 Brighton Rally. Number 1829 (UUF 329J) did, however, sport a gold waistband in this guise. The vehicle had only 21 seats, but boasted tables and a fully equipped galley etc.

Freedom to choose certain liveries returned by 1982/3 and Southdown which had always managed to maintain some connection with the past, took up the offer quickly. In dark green and gold is No. 1002 (XUF 532Y), a Leyland Tiger TRCTL11/3R of 1983 with Plaxton Paramount 50-seat coachwork beginning to collect passengers for a Southdown-controlled excursion on 20th July 1984.

In 1985, one of the more remarkable vehicles to enter the Southdown fleet was the one-off Hestair-Duple 425 integral 57-seat coach No. 1185 (C716 NYJ). It too had green stripes at the rear, but its body colour was silver. Seen here undertaking a private hire job from its initial Portsmouth depot on 12th April 1986, the 'plastic pig', as it was unkindly dubbed, received mixed notices despite its futuristic image, and was passed on into National Express work.

It was initially allocated to the Portsmouth depot, but despite its aerodynamic design and advanced features, like its electronic destination display, it was promptly dubbed – as only busmen can – 'the Plastic Pig' by those who worked with it. Four rather more conventional coaches, Leyland Tigers with Duple Carribean bodywork, were earmarked for limited stop stage carriage duties rather than tours. That design had much in common with the earlier 'Southdown Statesman' which had itself created a small sensation upon its arrival in the fleet. Both the 'Statesman' and the 'Southdown Diplomat' were on active service across the company area during Southdown's 70th anniversary 'road-show' in 1985.

Throughout the following year there were several attempts to produce an acceptable standard Southdown coach livery. It was the Hampshire division which, in the spring of 1986, came up with a white coach with black window surrounds, and 'SOUTHDOWN COACHES' and trim in green. This followed the basis for a short-lived coaching corporate-image, yet variations were still to be found among coaches with the 'National Holidays' logo on a white ground.

By early 1987, coaching was under serious threat. The National Holidays programme, successor to NBC's Central Activities Group's work in this field – was suffering from a reduction in bookings, late cancellations and a consequent patchy utilisation of Southdown vehicles, frequently leaving the coach and its driver with nothing to do. And the rules meant that non-use was not paid for.

The inevitable on-going effect was that the coaches were not returning a sufficient revenue, so that the company – already hard pressed in the competitive stage-carriage market – could not look to replace its touring coaches. In the previous decade, bus-grant coaches would have been made available as replacements, but those days had gone. The downward spiral gained momentum.

After a considerable amount of thought, the management decided to withdraw from the arrangement with National Holidays. In March 1987, Southdown instead entered into an agreement with the famous coach touring and holiday firm, Wallace Arnold of Leeds. That company's holiday programme was at the time managed by a team which had transferred en bloc from National Holidays and with whom Southdown enjoyed good working relations, We were also satisfied with the quality of the Wallace Arnold product which would go out. The deal went something like this: "We will let you have a coach and driver for a fixed period, say 210 days, for a fixed price; if you cannot use it for tours, you can use it for what you like." It gave the company a bit more stability at a time when it was needed.'

Four Leyland Tigers, with Plaxton coachwork, went north to Leeds, where they were repainted in Wallace Arnold livery; although the Southdown fleetname was retained at the rear and each carried the legend 'operated by Southdown for Wallace Arnold'. In the event, this enterprise came to an end when Wallace Arnold found that even they were not able to use the coaches for that length of time. The fall-off in tours was becoming nationwide.

Thus the 'Southdown Holidays' programme was the first aspect of coaching to cease. In October 1987 the company's Portsmouth depot instead provided coaches and booking facilities for Weypac Tours of Southampton. This venture too came to an end at Easter 1988 when

Weypac ceased to trade. Southdown's last connection with such work was as booking agents in Portsmouth for Vernon Maitland's Excelsior coach holidays.

Southdown's active involvement with local excursions (the last link with those beautifully and lovingly prepared itineraries done in coloured chalks and displayed beside the sea-fronts from Southsea to Eastbourne) and with private hire ceased on 31st January 1989. In that quarter, Southdown became agents for Hellyer/Byngs excursions from Portsmouth and Southsea. An historically nice point about that is that old man Byng used to take passengers from Portsmouth Hard to Fratton Park in horse-drawn carts before 'Southdown' meant buses rather than sheep.

So the classic apple green Southdown coach, Mackenzie's cursive fleetname included, passed into history. It was not that the management were without soul; simply that people's travel habits had eventually changed so much that customer demand was no longer there.

Above: 'Operated by Southdown for Wallace Arnold' reads the legend on the side of this Southdown coach painted in the livery of that well-known coach tour operator of Leeds. One of four Leyland Tigers with Plaxton coachwork, No. 1004 (XUF 534Y) which went north as part of a deal designed to keep both vehicles and drivers busy, as custom for coach tours, excursions and private hire bookings on the south coast began to plummet in the late 'eighties.

Below: One of the last duties performed by a Southdown excursion coach was carried out by No. 1017 (JPU 817), a Tiger with Plaxton bodywork, on 19th November 1988. Appropriately perhaps, it was a private excursion party booked by *The News*: Portsmouth Newsreaders' Club – a newspaper which had reported the doings of Southdown since it first arrived in Portsmouth under the watchful eye of Frank Bartlett. Sadly, *The News* now had to report the end of Southdown's once-proud private hire, excursion and coach cruising activity.

Chapter Seven: Express Coach Operations

Whilst Douglas Mackenzie was largely responsible for launching Southdown's tours and developing its stage carriage network, if not its local excursions business, credit for seeing the opening for express coach operations must surely go to Alfred Cannon. Indeed, in some quarters it was said that the cautious Mackenzie was positively sceptical about what, in effect, was a motorised revival of the long-striding stage-coaches of Chaplin and his rivals – particularly since most of the likely routes would offer a direct challenge to the railways.

When in September 1919 the National Union of Railwaymen, under the energetic leadership of James Thomas, took on Lloyd George's government and went on strike against the threat of a wage reduction, several bus companies within range of London saw their opportunity both to make some unexpected extra money and to put notions of such services to the test. Anxious to satisfy the railwaymen before they called upon their alliance with the miners, the government acceded to their terms. What seemed at the time a total victory for the NUR, however, was in one sense hard-won for the bus companies found just how easy it was to run limited-stop services to London and, when the strike was over, that there was sufficient demand from the travelling public for them to be set up and expanded upon a permanent basis

Alfred Cannon had watched with interest the earlier efforts of such operators as Len Turnham of Victoria and William Chapman & Sons of Eastbourne and, in that autumn of 1919, was quick to come to the aid of holidaymakers stranded at the coast, sending several charabanc loads to the capital during the eleven days of the strike. Thereafter, Southdown could ill-afford to ignore the increasingly successful operations of other companies such as Pickfords Ltd, who joined Turnham and Chapman on the Brighton or Eastbourne roads. In 1920, nine companies interested in such activity pooled their express coaching interests and formed London & Coastal Coaches. Among them was Southdown Motor Services Ltd.

Southdown's contribution to the co-ordinated service was actually regularised in 1923 at a time when several other competitors appeared on the Brighton road. This was to lead to the establishment, in April 1925, of London Coastal Coaches Ltd, an organisation specifically designed to apportion mileage, charges and departures, and get the coaches at the London end off their congested roadside stands and into a specially provided coach park. Alfred Cannon was one of the five directors selected to represent the interests of the constituent companies which now included United Automobile Services Ltd and the National Omnibus & Transport Co Ltd. By 1925 Southdown was sending regular departures from Portsmouth, Bognor, Worthing and Brighton to various roadside stands in and around London Victoria.

In 1919, during the national railway strike, Southdown was one of several companies which grasped the opportunity to run stranded passengers to London. The idea stuck, and the company became one of nine which formed London Coastal Coaches in 1920. For several years departures were made from various roadside stands in the capital: No. 111 (CD 5111) a 32-seat Harrington-bodied Leyland N charabanc is having its canvas hood raised prior to taking on board passengers for Brighton.

It was not until 1928 that a site in Lupus Street near Vauxhall Bridge was made available to LCC and the visiting coaches left the streets. The crowded and temporary nature of the site, with its wooden 'cloak rooms' and general air of do-it-yourself organisation, is evident as another Southdown coach for London rolls out carefully at the statutory 4 mph. The vehicle, No. 427 (UF 2027), is a Tilling-Stevens B9B with 30-seat Harrington sunsaloon body, built in 1927.

Finding a site for a coach park was not so easy as expected, and It was not until April 1928 that, as a temporary measure, a two-acre site near Vauxhall Bridge, in Lupus Street. was allocated to the London company by another LCC – the London County Council. In this overcrowded marshalling yard, largely unprotected from the elements. Southdown boasted the tallest noticeboard, clearly visible both over charabancs and sprayed mud. By the late twenties, competition with operators outside the group had brought the fares from Brighton to London down

to 5/- (25p) for a day and 8/6 (42½p) for a period return and. by 1933, there were eleven departures per day on this route alone.

Although a complete 'inverted-fan' of routes to the capital would be established from this framework, from Warsash in the west to Eastbourne, there was to be one route which drew a firm line along the coast itself. In May 1929, Southdown began running between Margate and Bournemouth in conjunction with East Kent and Wilts & Dorset Motor Services Ltd, from whose board Mackenzie had just retired. This was something of a reflexive action, for Elliott Brothers' Royal Blue of Bournemouth had pioneered the route, which now saw sharp competitive running between the 'joint-three' and Royal Blue. However, in March 1932, an agreement was reached between the contestants, whereby Portsmouth would be the dividing place common to them all, the passengers transferring at Southdown's Hyde Park Road depot. Southdown's agreement with Wilts & Dorset was adjusted to give Royal Blue a free reign west of a line from Southampton-Salisbury-Bristol. From 9th May 1932, Royal Blue, Southdown and East Kent launched their joint service between Bournemouth, Southampton, Portsmouth, Brighton and Margate under the title 'South Coast Express' a name warmingly close to that denied the directors by the Registrar of Companies back in 1915. In fact, all three operators vehicles were to run through 'on hire' to the 'foreign' sections.

When Chapman & Sons (Eastbourne) Ltd, together with Southern Glideway Coaches Ltd, also of Eastbourne, transferred their licences and vehicles to Southdown in 1932, it represented the company's first direct acquisition of competitors' express routes. Whereas Chapman's large

Right: London-based operator, Fairway Coaches Ltd, was another firm which was persuaded to give up its south coast express work. It had run from London to Worthing via Leatherhead with a fleet of Maudslay and Dennis coaches. Eight were handed over to Southdown, and one of a pair of Maudslay ML4 is seen in Worthing garage after purchase in December 1933. The ML4s were numbered 345/6 by Southdown, but were soon withdrawn.

Southdown began running an express route between Margate and Bournemouth in 1929, in conjunction with East Kent and Wilts & Dorset in competition with Elliott Bros 'Royal Blue' of Bournemouth. In May 1932, Wilts & Dorset withdrew, leaving the other two companies to form an alliance with Royal Blue to run jointly between Margate-Brighton-Portsmouth-Southampton-Bournemouth under the title 'South Coast Express'. Going west to Bournemouth, in the early competitive days, is RU 8819 an AEC Reliance/Duple 32-seater of Royal Blue, which pioneered the route. It is picking its way through the winding streets of Arundel – deep in Southdown country.

Above: Chapman & Sons (Eastbourne) Ltd and Southern Glideway Coaches Ltd, also of Eastbourne, transferred their operations to Southdown in March 1932, representing the company's first direct purchase of a competitor's express services. Ten coaches from Southern Glideway's very mixed express fleet joined the Southdown ranks, including this Tiger TS2/Duple 28-seater (JK 1098) which became No. 1000 in the Southdown ranks.

fleet of worthy Dennis coaches had been engaged on tours and excursions in addition to the London express traffic, Southern Glideway's ten coaches (of six different makes) were concerned solely with its express work. That same year, competition on the Worthing and Brighton services to London eased with the acquisition of the licences held by G. B. Motor Tours Ltd of London and G. F. Wood & Sons Ltd of Steyning—and again in July 1933 when H. J. Sargent's 'East Grinstead Motor Coaches' express interests were merged with those of Southdown. Then, in time for Christmas, another London-based operator was persuaded to give up its express service into Southdown territory: Fairway Coaches Ltd, who'd been sending their Maudslays and Dennis Lancets down to Worthing, handing eight of them over to the company for disposal the following year.

Meanwhile, on the roads to London from the Portsmouth area Southdown's Portsea Island-based rivals, North End Motor Coaches (Portsmouth) Ltd, Alexandra Motor Coaches Ltd, T. S. Bruce's 'Imperial Saloon Coaches' and Underwood Express Services Ltd transferred their licences for the London express route to the company in a flurry of selling which was complete by June 1935. The well-known London-based firm, A. Timpson & Sons Ltd, gave up just its Portsmouth express licences to Southdown during this period, and area manager Chevallier was able to round off a remarkable expansion of express coach working by actually extending operations into Hants & Dorset Motor Services Ltd territory to the west of Portsmouth Harbour. Although Hants & Dorset had established itself at Gosport as early as 1924, it had that same year entered into an agreement with Royal Blue in which it promised not to run any express services. So when G. A. Cross of Gosport wanted to sell his 'Perseverance Coaches' express licence for his service to the capital he had to turn to Southdown. Thus the company gained a route which went from Gosport and Fareham to London up the beautiful Meon Valley. The same applied to Fuger's 'Fareham & Warsash Coaches' licence for similar work, although Warsash passengers for London were later expected to travel to Fareham on the 45 stage-carriage bus and meet Southdown's London coach coming up from Gosport at Hants & Dorset's Fareham bus station.

These acquisitions enhanced the work of the excursion and private hire department also. For instance, when Portsmouth FC reached the cup Final at Wembley in April 1934, Southdown and five other local coach companies asked the Traffic Commissioners for permission to run additional coaches to the stadium. Bruce, Cross and Southdown were granted licences at the expense of the others 'because they ran a regular service to London'. Now that these had been absorbed, proportionally more excursion traffic would come Southdown's way relative to its share of such work. There were now eleven journeys to London each day from Portsmouth alone, some via Putney and Fulham, others via Richmond and Hammersmith, to Victoria Coach Station at 6/-(30p) single, 7/6 (37½p) period return. Certain journeys went beyond Victoria to Kings Cross Coach Station, a short-lived terminus in Euston Road, closed later on the outbreak of World War II.

Stops for refreshment on the London routes had been established at licensed premises on the roads from Portsmouth, Bognor and Eastbourne. So, too, had they at the White Lion on the Worthing route and The Chequers

Strachan & Brown, London Lorries and Harrington all built dual-door low-line coaches of a very similar pattern around 1930, right down to the curved front panel and window glass. Southdown purchased examples from the latter two firms, constructed upon Leyland Tiger chassis. Number 1021 (UF 6621) is a TS2 model with 26-seat Harrington body, and is operating on the London service acquired from Chapman & Sons (Eastbourne) Ltd.

Gosport was in the territory of Southdown's sister company Hants & Dorset Motor Services Ltd, but because the latter had entered into a 1924 agreement with Royal Blue, whereby H&D promised not to run express services, Southdown were able to move in when G. A. Cross of Gosport wanted to sell his 'Perseverance Motors' service to London. Despite Southern Railway representation upon the board, that meant some additional competition – this time along SR's Meon Valley line. There is no record of complaint however. Cross' Thornycroft TP7286 did not join the Southdown fleet

Below: By now operating from Victoria Coach Station, the TS4 Tiger/Harrington 32-seat coach, No. 1072 (UF 8842) of 1932, sports a route-description board not too dissimilar from the Perseverance version.

from Brighton. By 1931, however, traffic on the confluent Worthing and Brighton routes had reached such proportion that Southdown erected a half-way-house coach station at County Oak, one mile north of Crawley. at a cost of £10,000. Within four years over a million passengers had used the premises during their break of some ten minutes in the 2½-hour journey. Finding that many of the passengers were asking for alcoholic drinks to go with their snacks, Southdown applied for a liquor licence – a procedure hastened on by the fact that considerably more ladies than men were doing the asking. The first application in 1934, was opposed by the police, the next by a formidable combination of Tamplin's, Portsmouth United and several other breweries with interests on the London road: the Temperance Church, the Congregational Church, the Baptist Church, the Salvation Army and the ultimate in self-denial 'The British Women's Total Abstinence Union' – a not altogether holy alliance. The matter went to court at Horsham in February 1937 when the justices overturned the refusal made twelve months previously to award a 3½-year licence. This, in turn, brought down from the High Court a call for the confirming authority to show cause why a writ of *certiorari* should not issue. Those who eventually enjoyed one for the road in the restaurant and lounge thereafter had little inkling of the complicated and technical legal wrangling which made it possible. Meanwhile this little piece of Southdown history became part of the legal casebook.

Stopping off at the County Oak coach station in the middle 'thirties were fifteen journeys per day each way during the summer on the Brighton run and three on the Worthing with eleven and two respectively in the winter months. Up to 1,080 passengers per day were being carried on these routes. As the Southern Railway Company's electrification of the lines to the Sussex coast was stepped up there had been a slight drop in the traffic which, since the arrangement whereby Southern became a one-third owner of the Southdown shares, had now been stabilised by the inter-availability of rail and coach tickets In contrast, during this period several sections of the South Coast Express route were unremunerative for the best part of the year.

The acquisition of C. R. Shorter's express licence for the Brighton to Robertsbridge service in 1939 proved to be the last step in the consolidation of such services in the uneasy days before World War II. The war brought difficulties of driving in the blackout and, initially, a rush of mums visiting their evacuated children – until the worst winter for years, followed by war in earnest. began to reduce the programme to a pale shadow of its former self. Requisition of vehicles, fuel rationing and air-raids, together with the slogan "Is Your Journey Really Necessary?" convinced many people that it was not. Finally, in September 1942, an order issued by the Minister of Transport brought most express services to a halt, and Victoria Coach Station was taken over by the War Office and the National Fire Service, Southdown did its best to compensate with the introduction of limited-stop stage-carriage workings on some sections.

Express coaching began in earnest once again on 22nd March 1946. Armed with 48-hour passes, reluctant heroes – National Servicemen – helped restore the numbers of passengers to healthy levels; a factor which was to lead to 'forces-leave' express services at weekends. Southdown's express service fleet was not allowed to reappear in the somewhat battered state sometimes found elsewhere after the war years. Even the oldest Leyland Tigers were, by exceptional effort, restored to the usual spotless condition. The process was aided by the delivery, from 1947 onwards, of new Leyland coaches with engines which owed much to the technology learned in World War II. Such traffic extended several journeys from Worthing, Brighton and Eastbourne beyond London to Birmingham, particularly during the summer months. There were now services to London from Hayling Island – with a pair of Bedford OB coaches purchased in 1948 to augment the pre-war lightweight Leyland Cheetah models – Littlehampton and Rotherfield, together with summer departures from Brighton to London-Oxford-Worcester and to Southampton-Exeter-Torquay-Totnes. There was also some extra work generated by Southdown's link up with Channel Airways' London traffic from Portsmouth Airport. Southdown's interests in such traffic were enhanced in 1954, when the company's chairman Raymond Beddow became chairman also of London Coastal Coaches Ltd and perhaps even more effectively in 1956 when the latter post was taken up by Southdown's ex-general manager Michael Carling.

In 1931, Southdown created a 'half-way house' refreshment and rest stop for its passenger on London Express services from Brighton and Worthing, at County Oak, just north of Crawley. It was the subject of a lengthy and well-publicised legal battle, in which the High Court, no less, was involved, before alcohol could be served to the customers. Over a million passengers had used its facilities within four years of its opening. The advertisement dates from 1957.

Southdown **Crawley station**

SHOWING REFRESHMENT ROOM & FULLY LICENSED BAR

FOR THE EXCLUSIVE USE OF PASSENGERS ON ....

London Express Services

TO **BRIGHTON·WORTHING LITTLEHAMPTON·EASTBOURNE**

Right: Even Hayling Island enjoyed an express service to London, at weekends in the summer. Because of restrictions on the bridge to the island, lightweight vehicles had to be employed until it was replaced in 1956. Leyland LZ3 Cheetah No. 501 (EUF 501) with 25-seat Park Royal coachwork was one of five purchased in 1938 for this work and for local excursions in the area. They were joined by six more Cheetahs the following year.

Centre: In 1948, the Cheetahs were joined by two Bedford OB/Duple 27-seat coaches – the only two in the Southdown fleet – numbered 70 and 71. Their work on the Hayling Island-London service came to a close with the opening of the new bridge. Number 70 was then downgraded to act as a bus at East Grinstead for the two remaining years of its service with Southdown.

Below: Sitting in a side street near London's Victoria Coach Station is No. 1135 (CCD 715) a Leyland Tiger TS7 with 32-seat Beadle coachwork, a firm now beginning a long association with Southdown – although this one and its sisters were built to a Southdown pattern devised with Harrington. Number 1135 is operating on the London-Uckfield-Eastbourne service: it served with the company until 1953. Several of the batch served as ambulances in World War II.

An innovation on the Eastbourne-London road on 17th January 1951 had been the introduction of a Leyland Titan double-decked coach. Overweight and upstaged by the large new under-floor-engined saloon coaches, it was relegated to private-hire work after one season. A longer-lasting peculiarity was the retention by Southdown of 'Triumph Coaches' livery. Once part of the Hants & Sussex group, its week-end forces leave express services went as far afield as Liverpool and Leeds. A total of eighteen of the company's Leyland Tiger Cub and three Leopard coaches were painted in Triumph's cobalt blue and cream livery first applied by

Left: Marked up for service from London-Hindhead-Portsmouth-Isle of Wight, is No. 1157 (CUF 157) with Blackpool-built Burlingham bodywork. Passengers were expected to make the last part of their journey on a paddle steamer, but Southdown did later make its own journeys to the Island! As newer coaches became available post World War II, the 1936 Tigers found employment on excursion work, like 1157 at rest outside the local Maidstone & District office at Bexhill. This vehicle represents another example of a bodybuilder adapting his standard product to Southdown ideas.

Centre: Most express work came to a halt in World War II and didn't get going again in earnest until March 1946. Available from the spring of the following year were 25 new Leyland PS1/1 Tiger coaches with bodywork previously unknown in the Southdown ranks – Eastern Coach Works of Lowestoft, more usually associated with Tilling-controlled companies. Nominally, but not in fact, the first vehicle in the batch was No. 1227 (GUF 727), it provided seats for 31 passengers, and raised Southdown's image further with its power and purposeful appearance.

Foot of page: Shining at Oxford: at Gloucester Green bus station in the summer of 1949. A new joint express service with South Midland Motor Services Ltd had commenced between Worcester-Oxford-London-Brighton in May of the previous year. Leyland PS1 Tiger saloons had continued to come on stream, the majority fitted with updated versions of Southdown's pre-war coach style bodywork by Park Royal, Beadle and, like No. 1336 (HUF 936), by Duple. Lingering wartime restrictions at Leyland meant that some of its vehicles were still being delivered with dark green painted, rather than chromium-plated radiators.

an intermediate owner. As well as this Portsmouth-based traffic, Southdown picked up similar work from ex-Hants & Sussex territory at Lee-on-the-Solent, whilst two further, and last, acquisitions of express licences from rival operators consolidated the series; Unity Coaches of Portsmouth in 1959 and G. F. Graves & Sons (Redhill) Ltd. in 1962.

All the services were given a considerable boost in their competition with the growing threat, the private motor car, in 1961 by the raising of the speed limit for public service vehicles to 40 mph. The 'sixties were noteworthy for the considerable improvements made in the design, construction and performance of the vehicles, together with the high standard of maintenance lavished upon them at regular intervals, in particular by Portslade's craftsmen. Noteworthy too for a most unusual experiment

With the more subtle curves for which its products were noted, Beadle's interpretation of the basic design is displayed at Hants & Dorset's Grosvenor Square bus station and garage, Southampton. PS1 No. 1297 (HUF 297), on South Coast Express duty for Brighton, is double parked beside ETA 998, a Southern National 'Royal Blue' AEC Regal on the shorter run to Southdown's Hyde Park Road garage in Portsmouth – not part of the joint agreement with Southdown.

With the benefit of hindsight, looking rather more Australian than British, this Leyland PD2/12 was specially designed and was equipped with luxury double-decked coachwork by Northern Counties, specially for express working on the lucrative Eastbourne-London route. Prior to entering service No. 700 (KUF 700) had been exhibited at the 1950 Commercial Motor Show. Unfortunately the winding roads between the two destinations caused discomfort to the upper deck passengers, and the coach was downgraded to excursion work from Bognor Regis in 1952.

If it hadn't been No. 700's own fashionable rock and roll which caused its rapid exit from express work, the arrival of the first underfloor-engined coaches would have done the trick. Leyland PSU1/15 Royal Tiger coaches with Duple 'Ambassador' bodywork led the way. Number 1614 (LUF 614) was in the second batch, which arrived in 1952. The coach is operating on a through service which was in existence between 1953-5 and ran jointly with Ribble's subsidiary W. C. Standerwick Ltd along a route: Worthing-Brighton-London-Blackpool.

Number 1626 (LUF 626), a Leyland Royal Tiger PSU1/15 coach of 1952 with bodywork by Leyland also, is earmarked at Pool Valley, Brighton, for a working on the special hospital service express to Robertsbridge, acquired from C. R. Shorter in 1939. there were 25 of these 41-seaters and they remained an unusual buy for Southdown in one respect: for a company which ordered so many different types of Leyland chassis, many fitted with double-deck bodywork by Leyland, they proved to be the only single-deck vehicles with bodywork by that manufacturer purchased by Southdown.

Awaiting naval personnel from shore-bases at Fareham, Gosport and Lee-on-the-Solent, Leyland Tiger Cub SUF 900 wears the blue and cream 'Triumph Coaches' livery acquired with the business in 1957. On forces leave express duty, the vehicle is standing at Fareham Creek on a parking space first allotted to Basil Williams' Hants & Sussex vehicles on Fawley Refinery contract work, some ten years previously. Triumph Coaches Ltd had at that time formed part of his business interests.

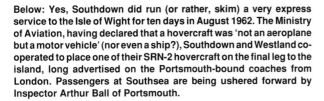

Top left: Also destined for Leeds in Triumph livery is No. 1158 (8158 CD), a 49-seat Weymann-bodied Leyland Leopard PSU3/3RT coach, one of the first 36ft vehicles in the Southdown fleet. Triumph had built up an extensive group of weekend leave services during National Service days, prior to being taken over by Southdown, for which reason the trading name was retained. Newly washed and polished, No. 1158 awaits the call in Hyde Park Road Garage, Portsmouth on 31st October 1962.

Top right: On 18th May 1958, Commer/Beadle TS3 No. 13 (TCD 13) has paused for a tea break and a rest at Huts Hotel, Hindhead, Surrey, on route from London to Portsmouth and Southsea. It was one of 20 fitted with 41-seat Beadle 'Rochester' bodies, which spent their entire Southdown service on London express routes. The driver is not looking for comparative peace and quiet: the noise normally associated with Commer vehicles was not so pronounced on these coaches.

Centre left: Back on the ground, No. 1197 (EUF 1970), a Leyland Leopard PSU3/3RT coach with Plaxton 49-seat bodywork returns from a nearby parking lot to the Victoria Coach Station stand for the Chichester and Bognor Regis service. The curved waistline, until then very much in vogue, was perceptibly flattened from the middle 'sixties; since when it has become parallel with the road – and stayed that way. Gone were all the boards, detailing the route, from this time onward, also.

Below: Yes, Southdown did run (or rather, skim) a very express service to the Isle of Wight for ten days in August 1962. The Ministry of Aviation, having declared that a hovercraft was 'not an aeroplane but a motor vehicle' (nor even a ship?), Southdown and Westland co-operated to place one of their SRN-2 hovercraft on the final leg to the island, long advertised on the Portsmouth-bound coaches from London. Passengers at Southsea are being ushered forward by Inspector Arthur Ball of Portsmouth.

Nearly half a century after Mackenzie closed his Ryde, Isle of Wight office, the company has another – of sorts – upon the island. Not very large, and there for only ten days, the Southdown-Westland Hovercraft Terminal booking office forms the backdrop for a commemorative photograph of the official Southdown party. S. J. B. Skyrme (General Manager) second left; W. G. A. Hall (Chief Engineer) second right; Gerald Duckworth (Traffic Manager) extreme right; and Inspector Ball and his colleagues await a return journey to the mainland aboard the only twin-engined vehicle to carry the 'Southdown' fleetname.

carried out by the company in conjunction with Westland Hovercraft. In what might be called the bravest use of the more abstruse parts of its Articles of Association ever carried out by a bus company, Southdown actually operated an express service across Spithead from Southsea to the Isle of Wight. Not entirely sure how to go about setting the spray in motion, the company first applied for licences to operate hovercraft' from the Air Transport Licensing Board. The Ministry of Aviation, however, had already ruled that a hovercraft 'was not an aeroplane but a motor vehicle'. This came as something of a surprise for the South Eastern Traffic Commissioners, but from 13th-22nd August 1962, a Westland SRN2 hovercraft bearing the fleetname 'Southdown' skimmed back and forth across the waves – ten days which fluttered the dovecotes of the omnibus world. In the event, such services were left to Hovertravel and British Rail 'Seaspeed', but Southdown's reputation for bold innovation had been done no harm.

The late 'sixties proved to be the last years of Southdown's direct control of its old-style express services. Boosted by a further increase of permissible speed to 50 mph, the scurrying green coaches' days were numbered. However, although the National Bus Company was formed

in 1968, it was not until 1972 that London Coastal Coaches Ltd changed its name to National Travel (NBC) Ltd. All the constituent companies' express services were placed under the control of NBC's Central Activities Group and standard white National livery was applied to Southdown's coaches.

Throughout the 'seventies, Southdown, of course, provided vehicles for operation upon the routes which it had established, although service provision was determined in liason with National Travel until, in July 1979 and as a sign of things to come, Southdown beat British Rail to a

In 1972, London Coastal Coaches Ltd became National Travel (NBC) Ltd. Together with the other constituent companies' express services, Southdown's were placed under the control of NBC. Standard white NATIONAL livery was then applied to Southdown's coaches, with SOUTHDOWN in red over the front wheelarch and red and blue alternate letters in the 'National' logo at the rear. Number 1250 (CUF 250L), a Leopard PSU3B/4RT with Duple Dominant livery is at Brighton on 17th January 1977.

Right: 'Sussex Link' routes were basically those which National Express had abandoned and the Southdown management had decided to operate commercially. The livery was an attractive white with dark green skirt, leaf green waistband bisected with a double yellow and black stripe; lettering was in white. On 29th June 1984 Leopard No. 1325 (GWV 925V) is taking a rest at Chichester Bus Station after performing on 567 to Littlehampton and Bognor Regis from Victoria.

Below right: Following its disappearance under the National Express regime, the South Coast Express was revived in October 1984 and a handful of Leopard coaches had eponymous vinyls applied direct to the bodywork; as on No. 1293 (VCD 293S). The route, however, was a pale shadow of its previous self, running only between Brighton and Portsmouth – and that over a longer route to the north of the previous track.

contract to operate the London-Brighton part of a new cross-channel hydrofoil link to Paris. This was awarded to the company by Jetlink Ferries and its success was all the sweeter when it was learned that the land section to Paris was to be run by SNCF (French Railways). The complete route was London-Gatwick Airport-Brighton operated by the Plaxton-bodied Leyland Leopards painted by Central Workshops, Portslade, in Seajet white to blue livery: Boeing 'Seajet' hydrofoil Brighton-Dieppe and SNCF express Dieppe-Paris.

'Sussex Link'

Then following the enactment, on 6th October, of the Transport Act 1980, National Travel found itself challenged on its express routes by some swashbuckling rivals. Although in the Southdown area it was not as strongly threatened as elsewhere, there was a brief period of independent activity on the London roads from Brighton and Portsmouth but this withered comparatively quickly. However, both economic and political considerations caused National Express to reappraise its operations in the area. Its own Worthing and Eastbourne routes were now pulled inwards to Brighton whence an hourly non-stop service to London was established. Southdown was now able to provide a series of stopping coach services on what National Travel perceived to be the less strategic routes. Testing the market carefully the company introduced a three journey 'Solent Link' service on the Southsea to London via Guildford route, but combined most of this service with its S76 'Sussex Link' route from Chichester in 1984. The 'Sussex Link' series of routes, a pleasant reminder of the 'Sussex Tourist, Green Cars Run Everywhere' days of 70 years before, provided green and white liveried coaches running on a number of services with widely differing headways. From Eastbourne, Lewes, Brighton, Worthing, Selsey, Littlehampton, Chichester, Hayling and Bracklesham Bay, 'Sussex Link' coaches linked the South Coast with London, whilst at the weekends another ran along the old 'South Coast Express' route from Eastbourne as far west as Havant, where it took off for Salisbury, Taunton, Exeter and Torquay.

Specially posed for its portrait, this Leyland Leopard was a one-off special. Delivered in 1981, its original body was destroyed by fire and replaced in 1984 with this new Plaxton Paramount 3200 example. Number 1358 (LPN 358W) became a 'Southdown Express', wearing an eye-catching livery derived from the 'Sussex Link' – dark green skirt, white, apple green waistband and diagonal, black window surrounds, with yellow and black stripes, and yellow lettering; yet still an NBC derivative arrangement.

This time-honoured title was officially revived on 28th October 1984, however, when a new limited stop service with an hourly headway commenced running between

With the closure of Steine Street Coach Station, all express services from Brighton were transferred to Pool Valley where, in October 1985, this green and white dual-purpose Leopard/Duple coach No. 1260 (CUF 260L) waits to go out on London service 064 as a relief vehicle. Stage carriage buses had moved out to Churchill Square.

Originally delivered with logos for the National Holidays programme during 1984, Southdown's withdrawal from that activity saw No. 1006 (A806 CCD) transferred to National Express duties. It is a Leyland Tiger TRC TL11/3R 50-seat coach with Duple Laser bodywork. En route for Chichester on 15th August 1987, it was soon thereafter re-registered as 416 DCD.

The general run down of coaching also chased the Duple 425 into National Express duties. Number 1185, previously C716 NYJ, was re-registered 420 DCD in 1988 and is seen here on 7th September of that year engaged upon one of its new duties from The Hard interchange at Portsmouth. A twinkling message deep within the windscreen announces that it is going to London – vinyls across the tops of the windows disclose the route; a welcome return to Southdown's earlier 'route-board' style. In 1990, the vehicle became the property of Hastings & District.

Brighton and Portsmouth – the centre section of its predecessors. At its peak, the 'Sussex Link' operations numbered fifteen separate services. Most of these were summer season routes which were operated from May to October each year. A notable exception was the S67 which kept pegging away after the rest had stopped, taking in Selsey, Chichester, Bognor Regis, Littlehampton and Worthing before setting off north for Dorking, Kingston and Victoria.

Numerous route adjustments and extensions to the 'Sussex Link' services were tried over the following three years as Southdown supplemented its contribution to the

National Express network. At the London end some involved an extension beyond Victoria Coach Station to Oxford Circus via Marble Arch outward and Upper Regent Street on the inward journeys. A service which owed nominal allegiance to neither ran from Peacehaven to Brighton before setting off for Victoria, for the first time, since 28th April 1985. Unusually, but sensibly, it was called the 'Earlybird' on the early morning outward departure and the 'Night Owl' on its late evening departure from Victoria.

Those routes which National Express deemed worth holding on to numbered nine in the Southdown area and to which the company contributed vehicles for operation. Apart from those operating from Portsmouth and Brighton to Victoria Coach Station, once the core of Southdown's express network, Southdown coaches in National Express livery were to be found *en route* to Margate, to Coventry, Leicester, Sheffield, Leeds, Bradford, to Plymouth and Penzance, to Cheltenham, to Bristol, and to Oxford and Birmingham.

The only Southdown coaching activity engaged in under Stagecoach management was the commitment to National Express workings from Portsmouth, for which a small fleet was retained, initially at Eastney. Number 1016 (C474 CAP), a Tiger with Plaxton 'Paramount' coachwork, has just arrived from London on 2nd February 1991 with only the legal address block to show that it is a Southdown vehicle.

To so Few

By the end of the 1987 season, the 'Sussex Link' series of services were deemed by the newly independent management to have served their purpose and were gradually phased out. Those Southdown coaches allocated for express work were now painted in white National Express livery only and, by 1989, following the company's decision to pull out of touring holidays, excursions and private hire with coaches, those which remained on the active list in Southdown Coaches and Wallace Arnold livery emerged afresh in the latest 'Welcome Aboard' logo of National Express. Among them was ex-'Southdown Coaches' only Hestair Duple 425 integral coach. At this stage, the coach fleet totalled something like 20 vehicles.

When, in 1989, Stagecoach Holdings acquired Southdown Motor Services Ltd, coach operations had ceased, with the exception of National Express contract work from Portsmouth – for which nine coaches remained in the city.

The honouring of this contract would represent the only express coaching activity in which Stagecoach's Southdown would remain involved. Although officially a Southdown subsidiary by then, Hastings Coaches small fleet of blue and yellow vehicles could scarcely be counted as 'Southdown' – and the same goes for Portsmouth City Bus's brace of Leyland Leopards which went in 1991.

So those few National Express workings, reduced even further to Plymouth and London journeys only, from Portsmouth, were to prove the last link with the once-proud Southdown coaching fleet of some 350 vehicles.

Chapter Eight: NBC's Southdown

Squeezing out of Titchfield's East Street, en route for Fareham and Southsea on service 45, ex-Warsash, on 29th August 1974 is 1971 Bristol VRT WCD 524K . The wall on the right still bears evidence of the cyclone which hit the village in 1945, leaving all surrounding areas unscathed, including Warsash – for over 50 years Southdown's most westerly terminus. Despite the setting up of the National Bus Company in 1969, the vehicle remained in Southdown colours with only the cream fleetname and NBC 'double N' symbol to announce its holding company. It took Southdown some considerable time to paint its fleet in NBC's comparatively lifeless leaf green and white livery. The supply of Bristol chassis and ECW bodywork now extended rapidly to ex-BET companies. Southdown had already ordered vehicles from these companies in the late 'sixties prior to Nationalisation.

Despite diminishing profits, the British Electric Traction Co Ltd retained its British bus holdings until, under pressure, it agreed to their sale on 22nd November 1967. Completion was set for March 1968 with the Transport Holding Company the formal buyer. The National Bus Company, incorporated by the Transport Act 1968 thus gathered under state control the remainder of the territorial companies, including Southdown Motor Services Ltd.

From 1st April 1972 Southdown was located in NBC's Southern Region. The chief executive of National Bus was S. J. B Skyrme who had left his general managership of Southdown in 1966 to join the executive staff of BET.

When Freddie Wood became chairman of the Group, one of the first changes wrought was the adoption of a corporate image. Designer Norman Wilson's package was to include an NBC 'Double N' symbol to be carried on all vehicles and publicity, sales offices, garages and depots, uniforms, badges and flags, bus stops, signs and printed matter, which were themselves to take on a characteristic 'new look'. Stage-carriage buses were to be either red or green with one white band: the treasured Southdown apple green and butter yellow and ornate lettering, including Mackenzie's cursive script, was to go. Southdown buses would be a flat leaf green with white lettering.

Almost as though it had seen it coming, the management had pulled out of retirement a 1929 Leyland Titan open-topper, refurbished it in the traditional livery and placed it on a seafront service. The official opening was performed by the Mayors of Brighton and of Hove on 5th July 1971 and the vehicle was crewed by staff in period uniform and the passengers got tickets issued with the aid of a Williamson Bell-Punch machine. The following year, a 1922 Leyland N open-topper retained by Provincial, now also in the NBC fold, was also presented to an admiring public in traditional livery – and one way or another that, and the Mackenzie script, never quite disappeared from the Southdown scene.

In January 1971, David Deacon had replaced Jim Skyrme as chairman of the company and of BH&D.

One of 23 similar vehicles delivered in 1929, Leyland Titan TD1 with Brush open-topped bodywork, No. 813 (UF 4813) remained with Southdown throughout its life and was restored, save its radiator, to original condition and livery in 1970. It was placed on a special 'Veteran Bus Service' between Brighton and Hove from 5th July 1971, crewed by staff in period uniform. It was fully licensed to undertake similar duties wherever the management chooses.

Above right: Preserved vehicles kept the traditional livery in use during the early 'strict' years of the NBC corporate image era. Leyland N, No. 135 (CD 7045) with chassis dating from 1922 and Short Bros 51-seat open-top body fitted in 1928, owed its survival to having been purchased in 1934 by Provincial's Gosport and Fareham Omnibus Co where Orme White had it partially restored for publicity appearances at Gosport and Titchfield Carnivals and the like. Recovered by Southdown in 1970, it was superbly rebuilt to 1928 condition. It is seen here momentarily devoid of slip boards and advertisements at a rally in August 1972.

Repainting a fleet of the size that Southdown's was at the time was not something which could be done overnight – even if there had been a will to put the task in train. This Leyland Titan PD3/4 sets out for Goodwood Races from Chichester garage on a special duty on 20th May 1975. It is still clad in apple green and primrose and with only the white NBC style logo and lettering.

February 1972 saw general manager Gerald Duckworth, after 35 years with Southdown, leave to become director of manpower for NBC. He was succeeded briefly by Leonard S. Higgins father of Roland Higgins – later Southdown's commercial director – who in April 1972, became chief general manager of the so-called 'Channel Coast Companies' (Southdown, Maidstone & District and East Kent) as NBC commenced a revised management structure. Just two months later, Len Higgins went east to become general manager of Maidstone & District and, in preparation for what proved to be a short-lived adjustment to the areas of responsibility for chief general managers, Geoffrey C. Smith replaced him at Brighton in a new grouping which put Southdown and BH&D together with the Isle of Wight operator Southern Vectis.

The standardisation of livery for the now combined fleet of BH&D and Southdown commenced in 1971. Southdown began transferring some of its Leylands to BH&D, new Daimler Fleetlines were shared and some BH&D Bristol VRTs were diverted to the Southdown fleet. Bristol Lodekkas appeared in Southdown green and cream, marked SOUTHDOWN-BH&D. NBC's green and white livery, which first appeared on new Leyland Nationals at Bognor that year was adopted for both fleets in 1973. The letters BH&D were removed from the buses in the summer of 1974. Curiously, it was one of the ex-BH&D Lodekkas – a far from typical Southdown vehicle – which was the last double-decker on regular NBC stage-carriage service in the old green and cream of Southdown, some four years later. Two similarly-painted Lodekkas with open tops remained in stock and were brought out in June for the Derby and occasional trips to the Devil's Dyke.

With the absorption of BH&D, Southdown at last turned front-to-back. Belatedly, compared with most sister companies, it now adopted rear-engined double-deckers as standard. First came the Bristol VRT and then the Leyland Atlantean AN68, the latter

NBC had decided that single-deck buses were to carry the individual fleetname and NBC logo towards the front of the vehicle and above the windows. These were applied long before much of an impact had been made in the drive toward a corporate NBC image. Leyland Leopard No. 132 (BUF 132C) of 1965, with Marshall bodywork to BET Federation design, is en route to Pool Valley, Brighton from Durrington.

Under NBC, having identified Southdown as a 'green' company, leaf green was specified, to be relieved by one white band. At once it was clear how much the traditional livery had contributed toward the renowned Southdown sparkle. Anonymity was now the order. Ex-coach Leyland Leopard No. 480 (EUF 224D), now with Willowbrook bus body, demonstrates at Haywards Heath.

In January 1971, David Deacon became chairman of both Southdown and Brighton Hove & District Omnibus Co Ltd. The standardisation of livery for the now combined fleets commenced that year in line with NBC policy generally. BH&D's GPM 902 became No. 2442 in the Southdown list and was among the more elderly of the buses transferred. Its 'togetherness' displayed in a standard NBC advert, it was relegated to driver training duties and became the last Bristol KSW6G/ECW vehicle to remain on the books.

Originally delivered in full BH&D livery, this Daimler Fleetline CRG6LX with Northern Counties 71-seat bodywork, No. 2105 (PUF 205H), was repainted into NBC leaf green and given SOUTHDOWN-BH&D logos prior to the total absorption of the latter company. It continues to operate as before on a service within the Brighton Area Transport Services area.

It was a Bristol Lodekka with ECW body, ex-BH&D, like this one (No. 2008, OPN 808) which in 1977 became the last bus of the NBC era on regular stage-carriage service in traditional Southdown apple green and primrose – a doubtful honour for a far from typical vehicle for the company. The message on the destination screen of 2008 – RELIEF BUS – is pure BH&D.

BH&D's open-top cream and black livery lends itself very nicely to an easy reading of the now extended joint fleetname – an interim measure. The lettering style was also in brief use by Southdown alone, before NBC decided to go the whole hog with its corporate image. The vehicle, a Bristol FS6G convertible 60-seater, XPM 43, became 2043 in the Southdown fleet.

Above:Very few of the ex-BH&D vehicles wandered far from their BATS area home ground. An exception was No. 2051 (AAP 51B) a Bristol FS6B convertible 60-seater of 1964. In 1975 it was to be found on what became the *Ferrylink* service between Eastoke, Beachlands and the ferry across fast-running Langstone Channel to Eastney, Portsmouth, between June and September each year.

Top right:Southdown took delivery of the remainder of the 1970 Daimler Fleetline order in traditional green and cream livery and original style, but simplified, fleetname. Number 381 (TCD 381J) heads for Pool Valley through desirable real estate on the northern outskirts of Brighton.

Centre right:Looking somewhat better than some other types in NBC livery is No. 350 (HCD 350E), one of the Leyland PD3/4 vehicles fitted with Northern Counties bodywork which incorporated extra-wide side windows and BET style upper deck front screens. Such 'panoramic' designs were considered ultra-modern at the time of their introduction in 1965. The vehicle is on its way to South Parade Pier, Southsea from Bognor Bus Station.

Lower right: One potential passenger seems somewhat confused by the shape of the destination box on this Bristol VRT/ECW double-decker at Pool Valley in April 1974. Number 544 (LFS 296F) came south from Scottish Omnibuses Ltd together with four others. It seems that the Scottish Bus Group became disenchanted with VRTs in a way less evident south of the border and Southdown exchanged 1967-vintage Bristol Lodekkas in their stead. To its chagrin much money needed to be expended in modifying these VRTs to the Mark 2 standard in the pursuit of acceptable reliability. In order to meet trade union demands they were also down-seated.

to a body design much like that evolved for London Country buses.

During the 'seventies the company adopted the public relations policy of opening its Central Works at Portslade for a day's demonstration of the skills of the various departments and the sale of any memorabilia it could lay its hands upon. In 1974. 4,000 people visited the works; on the workshop's 50th anniversary in 1978 the figure was 7,000. An annual event of no mean proportion had been established.

Following some homework by operations manager Brian Hirst, the old 31 route – the 51-mile Brighton to Portsmouth service – got a new number (700) and a complete face-lift. Launched in January 1975 with its identity writ-large along the length of the vehicles. the 'Coastliner' as it was now called, was a speeded-up limited-stop service of rear-engined double-deckers. The first vehicle carried a message of goodwill from the Mayor of Brighton to the Lord Mayor of Portsmouth who sent a reply in the return vehicle. The theme and introductory mayorial salutations were continued with the 'Solenteer: a through limited-stop service from Portsmouth to

Southampton via Fareham, in conjunction with Hants & Dorset, which started on 7th March 1976 – the first time that such a public stage-carriage exchange had taken place in 50 years. The following spring 'The Regency Route' in harness with Maidstone & District from Brighton to Tunbridge Wells further extended Hirst's distinctly railway-flavoured idea. Several other innovations took place at this time. including the 'Timesaver' limited stop services from the suburbs into Brighton town centre. services from Kirdford to Brighton and to Chichester, a Lewes and district circular and 'Midbus' a new Seaford town service.

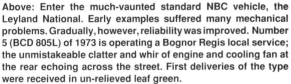

Above: Enter the much-vaunted standard NBC vehicle, the Leyland National. Early examples suffered many mechanical problems. Gradually, however, reliability was improved. Number 5 (BCD 805L) of 1973 is operating a Bognor Regis local service; the unmistakeable clatter and whir of engine and cooling fan at the rear echoing across the street. First deliveries of the type were received in un-relieved leaf green.

Upper right: In January 1975, the old-established service 31, from Brighton to Portsmouth, received a new image. It was renumbered 700 and the name 'Coastliner' adopted, unwittingly providing a forecast of things to come, some seventeen years later (see Chapter 10). At the same time a limited stop status was bestowed upon the route, considerably speeding up the journey between termini. Leyland Atlantean No. 736 (SCD 736N) with Park Royal/ Roe bodywork was among the vehicles chosen to launch the new service.

Centre: After an absence from the city of some 50 years, Southdown re-entered Southampton on a stage-carriage service, with the launch of 'Solenteer' – a joint effort in conjunction with Hants & Dorset Motor Services Ltd (later re-numbered X16) on an hourly headway. The only unfortunate thing about the title is that Southampton is not on the Solent, but perhaps 'Southampton Waterer' has an unsuitable ring. Bristol VRT/ECW 564 (GNJ 564N) is taking a break from that journey on 13th November 1976.

Lower centre: Looking considerably rather more BET than Tilling, as a result of the choice of coachbuilder, No. 436 (NUF 436G), a Bristol RE/Marshall saloon of 1969 is about to set out on a local run to Findon. The bus is at the stop opposite Mackenzie's original Worthing office, overlooking the sea front, in May 1976.

Foot: Southdown's 'midibus' era arrived in 1976 with the entry into service of two Ford A-Series vehicles with Alexander 27-seat bodywork. Delivered at the insistence of NBC, the company experimented variously and gamely on several difficult routes – and passed them on to Western National after a couple of years' service. Number 651 (LWV 651P) is one of the unloved pair.

The 'Channel Coast' division was restored In July 1975, when Geoffrey Smith followed Gerald Duckworth to NBC headquarters. Len Higgins resumed the responsibilities he held three years previously and John Birks became general manager. Throughout this period there were numerous changes of management as NBC strove to establish a happy balance at national and local level. In January 1977, John Birks returned to Midland Red as general manager of that firm and was replaced by Michael Sedgley whose appointment was to prove considerably more indelible than had those of his NBC predecessors. On the same day, Irwin Dalton became regional director in place of Frank Pointon who was now promoted to deputy chief executive NBC and, following a September 1977 reorganisation which placed Southdown together with seven other operating

companies in the newly-created South Eastern Region of NBC, under Irwin Dalton, previous divisional director Len Higgins was promoted to the post of Group Executive for consultancy services. Jim Skyrme had retired at the end of December 1976 and singled out Southdown for a memorable farewell one-liner on the standards and courtesy set by its personnel: "It had to be seen to be believed" – enough said!

One of the excuses found for giving its traditional livery another airing was Southdown's participation in a Community Bus Scheme devised by NBC and supported by East Sussex County Council and the Sussex Rural Community Council. The Cuckmere Community Bus project was launched in the winter of 1976-77 with two Ford Transit 15-seaters on a self-help basis. Under the scheme, Southdown provided professional guidance in driver training to PSV standard, advice on licensing, marketing and publicity, vehicle maintenance – and green and cream livery. The villagers, meanwhile, were to do the driving and collect the money over some 340 miles per week. Southdown's own fleet in 1977 was to be enhanced by the latest addition to the open-topped stable – Bristol VR double-deckers, which would eventually replace the Leyland Titan PD3s on such time-honoured services as that from Rottingdean to the Devils Dyke. Meanwhile, entering the world of aesthetics and enthusiasts at one stroke, the SMS publicity and public relations officer got together with the draftsmen at Portslade Works to produce an annual trophy – a polished piston and con-rod – to be presented for 'best road vehicle' at the Bluebell Railway Vintage Day.

That summer, Southdown staff at Portsmouth acted as hosts for the crews of 100 additional buses from NBC subsidiaries drafted into the city as part of the local municipality's arrangements for a park-and-ride scheme during the week of the Queen's Silver Jubilee fleet review. Rain considerably dampened the proceedings, but Southdown organisational ability was well demonstrated. The following April at Hove, devotion beyond the call of duty was much in evidence when Southdown staff braved 40ft flames to drive

Top left: Still running around Brighton on ex BH&D routes in 1976 was Titan PD3 No. 251 (BUF 251C), on what is clearly a hot July afternoon. Doors, vents and windscreen are open, the latter a feature much appreciated by drivers, and now vanished. The vehicle was one of a total of 45 PD3s allotted to services acquired with BH&D.

Top right: NBC's dual-purpose saloon livery is suitably demonstrated by No. 455 (NUF 455G), a Leyland Leopard with Northern Counties bodywork. For these vehicles the fleetname and logo was green. The bus is putting down passengers beside Chichester Post Office on service 266, which in June 1976 meant a journey to Arundel Bus Station. Note the very tall bodywork of these vehicles.

Below: 'Good pay, good times, good jobs on the Buses' says the advertisement. Legislation on psv drivers' hours had created healthy employment opportunities in that era. Number 371 (TCD 371J), a Daimler Fleetline of 1970, is running on limited stop service 701 from Arundel to Brighton's Pool Valley on 30th July 1976.

blackened and charred buses to safety from a blazing Conway Street garage in the early hours of the morning. Nine buses were completely destroyed and five badly burned in the smoke-filled interior. Among those driving the buses out, despite the dangers of explosion and hidden inspection pits, were the men who were to take their buses out on time from 5.50am onwards. Whilst company officials contemplated the smoking ruins, some passengers out of range of the garage wondered why they were travelling to

Above: Taking a rest at South Parade Pier, Southsea, prior to setting out for Havant and Westbourne, is No. 2097 (OCD 767G) an early flat-fronted Bristol VRT/ECW 70-seater. It had begun its operating career as No. 97 with Brighton Hove & District, where it had been one of ten delivered to that company in 1969. It was originally destined for the Bristol Omnibus Company.

Above right: Another vehicle which had previously operated in the red and straw yellow of BH&D was Bristol RESL6G saloon No. 2208 (PPM 208G) with dual-door ECW bodywork and room for 35 seated and 27 standing passengers. Having been repainted in NBC green the whole batch of ten was reallocated to the Portsmouth area, where 2208 has been placed upon Havant local services.

Below: A real tongue-in-cheek effort: this half-and-half liveried Daimler Fleetline/ECW 74-seater of 1972, No. 396 (XUF 396K) had been a special exhibit at Southdown's Portslade works during an open day in 1978. With NBC 'new' livery at the rear and the traditional green and cream at the front, it had there depicted the efficiency of the ongoing repaint programme, now all-but complete. In yet another nostalgic outburst, the vehicle somehow escaped onto the streets, far from Portslade. It is seen at Chichester Cross on 20th September of that year.

work on open-toppers meant for scenic work, and relief vehicles were coming in from as far afield as Portsmouth and Eastbourne. All those who helped that day received a personal letter of thanks from the company.

Another kind of letter introduced that year stemmed from an idea which traffic manager David Bending got from his parish magazine. Local organisations were given the facility to produce their own newsletters or information bulletins inside personalised front covers. The back cover carried bus service news and timetables relevant to the area in which the organisation was based, throughout the company's 2,500 square mile operating area. Within six months some groups were using as many as 6,000 copies. Further steps to bring Southdown's services to the notice of the community were to involve the local divisional manager for the Brighton area, and members of his staff in taking display material into local factory canteens. The factories also began to relay to their employees the service bulletins by Southdown on Radio Brighton.

In order to test just what it was that the average citizen wanted from his local bus company. Southdown was one of a number of NBC companies which undertook surveys of its area for the 'Market Analysis Project'. Its participation was launched by Southern Television coverage.

Southdown responded to its newly-gathered information by either adding to, speeding up or reducing its headways in various localities, rather than dividing up its territory into separately identified semi-entities, which many NBC subsidiaries were obliged to do, and which in turn led them to be sold off in parts eventually; in some cases resulting in a complete loss of identity. At Midhurst, which actually saw a reduction in the number of buses provided, an interesting result was the provision of a bus owned by that seasoned contestant Basil Williams, which donned a label marked 'On Hire to Southdown'.

Two of Southdown's own employees could claim to be well-seasoned in 1978-79 when both joined that very special roll of employees with 50 years service. Harold Gill started as a parcel-boy at Hyde Park Road garage, Portsmouth, and Central Divisional engineer Bob Mustchin who had started as a store-boy at Worthing and saw service also at Bognor and Chichester. Senior citizens outside the company were not forgotten either, when from 1st June 1979 every man over 65 and woman over 60 were given access to a half-fare pass covering almost the entire company area. Southdown had already established its annual event for the young: at Christmas 1977 the first of its 'Santa Claus Special' buses went on the road and become an established feature. The company's own loyal band of enthusiasts were not ignored either. Founded in 1954 as the 'Southdown Spotters Club', the Southdown Enthusiasts Club celebrated its silver jubilee, courtesy of the company, in some style. Its 25th anniversary

management committee meeting was held in the boardroom at Southdown House, the company provided a souvenir cover for the club's monthly news-sheet, and a Portslade Works-prepared headboard to go on any coach which they hired in the future. On its own account, the company reflexes proved up to the moment when the unfortunate vessel *Athena B* ran aground near Brighton's Palace Pier. Out popped the posters 'SHIPWRECK EMERGENCY! The best way to see the 'Athena B' is from a Southdown bus...' TO BRIGHTON. There then followed a list of the eight services to use. Other peoples misfortunes: the tumbrils were well patronised – well, why not?

A personalised version of NBC's employee newspaper called *Southdown Bus News* appeared in December 1980. Disclosing that there were nearly 2,500 people employed by the company in one capacity or another, they were referred to for the first time by the newly-coined name 'Southdowners'. Also, "More conscious consideration of the needs of *customers* (was necessary) "as opposed to the needs of Southdown to attract more *passengers* opined traffic manager Philip Ayers: and everyone did their best to call them that for a considerable period afterward. It might not last as long as Mackenzie's *cars* for *buses*, but time would tell. Meanwhile, the editor made the irrefragable comment. "Southdown have done a great deal to be proud about".

In June the following year, the paper was able to announce that Derek Fytche had replaced Irwin Dalton as South East regional director and had thus joined the Southdown board of directors. Irwin Dalton, a director of Southdown since 1977, had been its chairman since August 1979. There now followed a period of considerable rationalisation: diminishing financial support from County Councils in real terms, together with a reduced level of new bus grants from central government and less money generally in customers pockets, made it necessary for Southdown to cut its costs accordingly. Apart from the non-replacement of some personnel and the transfer of others at Crowborough to Maidstone & District Motor Services Ltd, the most noticable savings involved the sale of some historic property. The Bognor bus station and depot closed lock, stock and barrel, all vehicles and operations being transferred to Chichester which fairly burst at the seams in an effort to accommodate the newcomers. The old Beacon garage at Crowborough was sold: activities previously based on Emsworth garage were transferred to the new bus station at Havant; Uckfield garage and bus station were closed, whilst Haywards Heath bus and coach station became headquarters for a church. Such measures were to help stabilize the 1982 trading figures and provide a springboard for the operating surplus which was to follow. Doubtless the press. radio and television coverage also helped when, in 1982 consumerist and authoress Elizabeth Gundrey came to Brighton as part of the publicity scheme for her book *England by Bus* . The Company's marketing officer took part in the interviews on BBC Radio Brighton and Southern Television's 'Day by Day' programme, and the occasion was used to launch Southdown's 'Explorer' bus travel scheme – part of a nationwide effort to get people out and about with some of the new, fast services now being introduced by NBC subsidiaries.

Following the enactment of the Transport Act 1980, which deregularised the issue of licences for many stage-carriage activities and placed the onus of proof upon objectors rather than applicants, Southdown began to offer its customers – and those who had yet to acquire that title – a whole new range of limited stop services in the 700 range. Some island-hopped over existing routes, others broke completely new ground. One which deserves special mention here is that which scurried along from Brighton through time-honoured Storrington and Pulborough all the way to Winchester (after over half a century's absence) and on to the later centre of Mackenzie and Cannon's other 1915 venture – Salisbury in Wiltshire. This was service 710 which operated all the year round: it was joined in the summer by 720 which took in Worthing, Bognor and Chichester before rejoining the 710 route at Petersfield.

The Chairman's Award

The first charabanc, the first buses on pneumatic tyres, the first long-distance tours, the first bus company to involve itself in hovercraft services are some of the claims made, with varying degrees of truth, on behalf of Southdown and its predecessors. There can be no shadow of doubt

Following the Transport Act 1980 which abolished Road Service licences for express services, a new range of '700' services was introduced. What would have been impossible beforehand was the 'Flightline 777' service operated jointly between Green Line and Southdown. In order that Southdown could continue to participate on a route which ran Crawley-Gatwick Airport-London, Victoria, a reciprocal facility for London Country Bus Services Ltd was made south of Gatwick Airport on joint service 'Sealine 773' in May 1982. This ran hourly between the airport and Brighton and Hove. Number 1343 (MAP 343W), a Leyland Leopard with Plaxton coachwork, in gold, green and white with yellow and white lettering; and No. 1289 (RYJ 889R), another Leopard, but with Duple bodywork in green and turquoise livery are representative of Southdown's contribution to the enterprise. Joint operation of the 777 service ceased on deregulation in October 1986, but was continued by London Country.

whatsoever though about its major triumph in 1981. That year, NBC chairman Lord Shepherd announced the introduction of his scheme for giving recognition to new ideas and practices – the Chairman's Award for Innovation. And, for the successful production of bus drivers fare chart by computer, that first award went to Southdown Motor Services Ltd – the best of 33 entries. By enabling the company to respond more quickly to market conditions the microcomputer involved had more than repaid its purchase price within a year. Thereafter, instead of the usual 'doubleN' logo, Southdown's buses were decorated with a special commemorative badge somewhat reminiscent of the Citroen trademark.

Rather more extensive decoration was now applied to selected buses. The company's contribution to the English Tourist Board's 'Maritime England: ageing open-topped Leyland Titan 409 DCD was relaunched at Newhaven Fort as a brightly painted grandstand-cum-hospitality suite. A sister vehicle saw service in Bognor Regis as part of the British Tourist Authority's 'Beautiful Britain' campaign, whilst a Bristol VRT in a yellow, red and blue disguise became the '1066 Bus'. This one took visitors from Eastbourne to the historic castle country of Herstmonceux and Camber, and to the site of that quarrel which decided who would be our upper and middle classes – the Battle of Hastings. Early in 1983, this bus went to Dieppe and Rouen and did its best to get more Normans to come across the Channel. In recognition of the company's contribution to the economic well-being of East Sussex "with particular reference to the advancement of tourism", Southdown was subsequently presented with East Sussex's 'Europe Flag' by Euro-MP Sir Jack Stewart-Clark.

The Portslade paint-shop artists were also at work applying a contemporary white, yellow and orange livery to eight Bristol VRTs from the Conway Street garage for the 'Mile Oak Shuttle' – the first service in Britain run on a 'total-

Top: Left to right: Philip Ayers, traffic manager; Martin Harris, coaching manager; Michael Sedgley, general manager; and Simon Brown, chief engineer of Southdown, unfold the European flag presented to the company by Euro-MP Sir Jack Stewart-Clark in 1983. The red, yellow and blue-painted '1066 Bus', No. 621 (UWV 621S) had been to Dieppe and Rouen to publicise East Sussex. Over the wheel arch, the vehicle also displays the NBC Chairman's Award (1981) badge presented to Southdown for the production of a fare-chart by computer.

Centre: In a 'total planning' exercise with East Sussex County Council and Brighton Borough Transport, Southdown painted eight VRTs in a white, yellow and orange livery for 'Mile Oak Shuttle' services. Passengers became eligible for discounts in local shops.

In 1984, after a brief spell in the English League's First Division, Brighton & Hove Albion Football Club reached the FA Cup Final at Wembley. In order to provide celebratory transport, whatever the outcome, Southdown repainted VRT convertible UWV 619S in the team's colours. The club's 'Seagull' badge looks well on the panelling.

planning' basis. Together with East Sussex County Council and Brighton Borough Transport, Southdown had engaged in extensive research to discover the principal travelling requirements of residents in Mile Oak and Hollingdean. Shuttle bus customers became eligible for discount facilities at certain shops along the routes selling items ranging from fish and chips to antiques. Southdown launched the Mile Oak route, and Leyland Nationals of Brighton Borough Transport followed with the Hollingdean service, with an average ten minute headway. In the 1983-84 football season, another Bristol VRT reflected the local euphoria when the tide of hope came up the beach at Brighton & Hove Albion FC. As part of the fairytale which almost came true, Portslade labelled this one 'Southdown Backs the Seagulls Home and Away', when the local team fought its way through to Wembley and the FA Cup Final. The fact that it was a convertible open-topper shows both what duty it was expected to undertake and who was going to get the job. In September 1983, Southdown introduced its 32-page 'Good Bus Guide' in answer to those potential customers who claimed that their lack of use of the buses was because they didn't know where to find out about them. The six-part booklet was graphically of a good standard, the right size for the job and had sections on "which bus to catch", and "where they go"; maps showing where they operated in fourteen major towns; how to make use of 'Busranger' (joint with neighbouring Kent and Sussex operators) and 'Explorer' facilities, half fare passes and travel-cards; information on how to obtain timetables; on where to obtain details of all the facilities offered; and a note on Express services, coach hire and excursions. It was one of those rare publications which seemed to get bigger as one looked through its pages, so filled was it with just the right kind of information. There was, as the company claimed, "no excuse for missing the bus" after that.

That summer saw the introduction of a practical outcome of the co-operation between East Sussex County Council and SMS. By happy chance, the title 'East Sussex Co-ordinated Rural Transport' lent itself to the emergence of the acronym ESCORT, and the Escort Country Rider came upon the scene. This combined the duties of a country bus with an added ability to carry disabled people. Specially designed Reeve Burgess bodywork on Leyland Cub chassis was fitted with tailboard lift for wheelchairs at the rear-door position, thereby adopting the function of Social Services vehicles.

The first such service, 823 – Lewes-Newhaven-Peacehaven, began in July, gained access to villages long reserved by buses and thanks to the caring and friendly 'Southdown' attitude of the drivers, records John Allpress, was an immediate success. 'So much so that birthday cards adorned the inside of the vehicle on its first anniversary'.

A second service, also running two-hourly on Mondays to Fridays, 825 – Lewes-Glynde-Firle, followed with similar social success. So much so, that the following autumn of 1984 saw the purchase of three additional Cubs equipped likewise and the introduction of similar facilities on the 836 – Seaford-Denton; the 820 Seaford Town service; 843 Uckfield-Buxted; 849 Uckfield-Fairwarp; 850 Uckfield-Claremont Rise and 869 Uckfield-Newick, each based upon previously extant routes in the 100 series.

With vehicle intake severely restricted, some interest focused upon the loan of Southdown buses to other NBC subsidiaries. The most far-flung was the six-week sojourn in York of Bristol VR, 598, on loan to West Yorkshire Road Car

Upper: In 1983 and in conjunction with East Sussex County Council, Southdown introduced the ESCORT County Rider, which combined the work of a country bus with an ability to carry disabled people, by means of a tailboard lift. Number 800 (KJK 800Y), in turquoise with fashionable shaded vinyls applied, was the prototype for a small fleet of such vehicles. It was a Leyland Cub with specially-designed Reeve-Burgess bodywork and was an immediate success.

Left: An event not too frequently recorded by camera: a Southdown stage-carriage vehicle in Southampton (on 14th April 1984). Bristol VRT No. 266 (JWV 266W) is at rest, ex-Portsmouth and Southsea, in Southampton Bus Station on service X16 – and even its advertisements are concerned with Southampton. Hants & Dorset, the erstwhile owners of the bus station, had been divided up in latter-day NBC reorganisation, the service was now run jointly with Provincial, and the days of the station itself were numbered. Note the unusual rear service number display.

Company where, in open-top configuration, it operated the service 50 city tour during July and August 1984.

Back home, efforts to preserve the buoyancy of services continued with the provision of NBC's 'Explorer' tickets which on some trips reduced the price of admission to stately homes and other places of interest; 'Travel Cards' which provided unlimited travel for either one or four weeks on most Southdown and other local operators' buses or second class rail services in Brighton, Portsmouth, Worthing and Eastbourne areas; 'Bargainride'; an off-peak cheap day return which could be bought on the bus when the round trip would be more than six miles; 'Busranger' which enabled the passenger to use his ticket also on neighbouring NBC subsidiaries' vehicles and Brighton and Maidstone Borough Councils' as well; and of course the 'Half Fare Pass' for pensionable and disabled folk.

On the coach front, similar endeavours were made with 'Southdown Holidays', which were short tours of up to seven days to a selection of destinations in Britain and upon the Continent. These still operated throughout the year and lauded the advantages of 'duty-free' shopping on those journeys which crossed the channel; 'coach excursions' which were offered as short half-day, day and long-day trips from many tours and resorts in the company area; and the 'Southdown Excursion Club', which provided its members with a discount of up to 20p in the pound on normal fares. The promotional drive for these accompanied the company's stage-carriage service publicity.

Came the spring of 1985, and travellers were able to use the 'Master Rider' ticket on five new 'Stagecoach' services in the 700 range. These long-ranged from Brighton to Southend-on-Sea (715), to Cambridge (719), to Reading (736), to Oxford (738), and to Oxford via Midhurst and Petersfield (739), all on selected days of the week. With the exception of 738, these were summer-season services only.

70 Years of Southdown

Southdown celebrated its 70th anniversary in some style. A special logo replaced the NBC Chairman's Award badge on the vehicles; reproduction 1915 time-tables were issued, together with celebratory mugs, pens, badges, beer mats and stickers; and a 'birthday road-show' was launched which visited sixteen locations in the company area and concluded with an 'Anniversary Run' between Worthing and Brighton. Just in case anyone hadn't heard about the birthday, 36 Southdown vehicles, old and new, came from far and near and, in glorious sunshine on the actual Sunday of the anniversary, caused a goodly, but good-natured traffic jam on their way to Madeira Drive.

Less energetic celebrants had already attended an Anniversary Luncheon at the Old Ship Hotel, Brighton on 19 April 1985. The guest list of 137 included Southdown stalwarts like John Birks, J. M. Bodger, A. F. R. Carling, F. E. Dark, David Deacon, John Hargreaves, Frank Pointon, B. C. Sellars and P. H. Wyke Smith, together with

In 1985, Southdown celebrated its 70th Anniversary. A considerable publicity effort was made to promote the company on the occasion – all the more necessary with privatisation looming. A special logo appeared on the vehicles – as shown on VRT No. 276 (JWV 976W) on service duty between Midhurst and Petersfield. Table mats, lapel badges and stickers which replicated it were distributed to the public.

representatives of the current Southdown staff, of local government, the media, vehicle manufacturing industry, tourism, other operators, trade unions, support services, local members of parliament, publishing and various relevant societies including, as a nice touch, John Allpress, chairman of the Southdown Enthusiasts Club. The event included a top-table speech by the Lord Teviot and the launch of a celebratory book – *British Bus Systems – Southdown*. It had been supported by Don International, Esso, Gulf Oil, Hestair Duple, Leyland Bus, Lucas CAV, Michelin, Plaxtons, Texaco, Tinsley Bridge and, of course, the Old Ship Hotel. The Lord Teviot was there as he had worked as conductor for BH & D earlier in his life.

Nothing more could have been done to promote the good name of a long-lived public service. Yet, as the old saying goes, 'what central government finds, central government alters'!

Decentralisation

In addition to the ramifications of the Road Traffic Act 1930, there have been three periods of considerable change in the British omnibus industry. Those in 1948 and 1968 represented the two-step acquisition by the state of the territorial Tilling and BET interests. The third, better described as an upheaval, marked the Conservative government's determination to unpick the weft and weave of socialism. The painstaking process had begun with the Transport Act 1980.

By the summer of 1984, the National Bus Company's response to the drive towards its undoing was to seek from its remaining unreformed subsidiaries plans for increased localised accountability. This would be activated in readiness for a deregulated and privatised environment where there would be no revenue support except that won by competitive tender.

Regional director John B. Hargreaves (also chairman of Southdown) had already supervised the splitting up of such operators as Hants & Dorset and Bristol into separate companies. In the south of England, Alder Valley and Southdown were now earmarked for similar treatment. Thus far, earlier in the year, only Southdown Engineering Services (based upon the Central Workshops at Portslade) had been created as a separately accountable unit.

However, the Southdown management believed there was only limited evidence to support a division into separate companies. They considered there was a strong case for the company to remain as an overall entity. Accordingly, they opted to recommend 'decentralisation', to achieve maximum flexibility in the future marketplace and to cope with possible changes affecting the municipal undertakings in Brighton, Eastbourne and Portsmouth. Such a 'decentralisation' would be achieved by partitioning the company, which would remain 'Southdown Motor Services

In preparation for the forthcoming demise of the National Bus Company and as the likely division of the Southdown interests became clearer, the dormant Brighton Hove & District Omnibus Company began to reassert itself. Bristol VRT No. 606 (UWV 606S) emerged from the paintshops in 1985 with its 'Brighton & Hove' divisional title considerably larger than 'Southdown' on the sides – and standing boldly alone at the front. The cream and red livery was already far removed from NBC standard also. A BBT Leyland National 'shuttle' en route for Churchill Square follows.

As the NBC era drew to its final close, there were six core long-distance services in the 700 range running under the marketing name 'Stagecoach'. The hourly 'Stagecoach 727' running between Southsea and Southampton, jointly with Hampshire Bus ran on a route, more direct than the Solenteer, which utilised the M27 motorway (Leopard No. 1284 labelled for this service). Among the others, the 'Stagecoach' label applied to the 'Coastliner' was to prove the most remarkable (VRT No. 256 on this duty, going west at Littlehampton) with the company deeply involved in its own preparations for future privatisation, thoughts of Stagecoach Holdings of Perth entered no-one's head. Yet, even that 'Coastliner' title would assume almost equal, if not greater, significance for the Southdown company, some seven years hence.

Ltd', into five more, separately accountable units.

Thus the Hampshire, West Sussex, East & Mid Sussex and Brighton & Hove bus divisions and a 69-vehicle coach division were fully established by 1st March 1985, on which date three of the four geographical bus division managers were appointed (to be followed by S. L. Noble for the West Sussex Division on 27 April), each responsible to Michael Sedgley, the general manager, and having an approximately equal slice of the 481-strong bus and express coach fleet.

Restructuring

Pressure for rather more evidence of moves towards completely independent units continued to be applied nevertheless. On the one hand anxious to attempt the preservation of the 'big four' subsidiaries (Crosville, London Country, Ribble and United), yet on the other wishing to demonstrate to the minister that it was doing his bidding with the rest of its operators, NBC did not let the dust settle on Southdown's 'decentralisation'. Nothing short of 'restructuring' into independent companies would do; and each had to saleable.

Indeed, in May 1985, following publication of the government's white paper, NBC actually decided to convert the Southdown 'divisions' into six separate companies. If that had been carried out, Southdown – as an identifiable unit – would have disappeared there and then. That it was not, is one of the more fascinating outcomes of NBC's farewell: there would be no immediate sea-change at Brighton.

Convinced that some of the 'divisions' could not support themselves in the marketplace as separate companies competing with each other, Michael Sedgley offered a range of options reflecting this view at a meeting of the Southdown Board – and this notion prevailed. Yet there was, perhaps, more to it than that; old loyalties and codes of honour may have placed their part: key NBC officers Robert Brook and John Hargreaves were ex-Tilling men, Southdown's general manager Michael Sedgley had risen through the British Electric Traction ranks and, in this matter, was surely seen to be defending a cherished entity steeped in BET tradition. Magnanimity was not universal in the business world of the 'eighties, but a gentlemanly view was probably taken here.

However, government intransigence over the future of NBC pensions caused NBC to reconsider its plans and for two months nothing more was done. Then, in mid-July, it was decided to make Southdown Engineering Services into a separate limited company as part of NBC's arrangements for reorganising engineering facilities throughout the group (Ex-SMS chief engineer Simon Brown was to become manager of SES).

In early August, Michael Sedgley was informed that the remainder of Southdown would be divided into two companies – on the lines of his preferred option at the May board-meeting. The Brighton & Hove division would be reactivated as a separate company under its old title, and the rest of the bus operations would continue to function as 'Southdown Motor Services Ltd'. The coach division would be dissolved and split between Southdown and BH&D. The two companies would trade 'at arm's length' with Southdown Engineering Services. Southdown's fairly recently acquired Bognor Travel Agency Ltd would go (eventually) to National Travelworld.

Personnel, premises, rolling stock and other property were to be divided simply according to existing nominal allocation – with one notable exception. Given the choice, Michael Sedgley elected to remain at the seaside and take charge of the revived Brighton & Hove undertaking – a decision which may well have surprised the ex-Tilling senior officers at NBC. It was agreed that he should become *managing director* of Brighton & Hove, an office previously only extant, within the NBC operating orbit, at London Country.

This arrangement cleared the way for Philip Ayers, traffic manager of Southdown Motor Services Ltd, to become its general manager designate – an appointment eventually confirmed on 24 October 1985.

A joint headquarters, feasible under the old order, would not be possible in the forthcoming competitive environment. To demonstrate that a genuine opportunity for rival concerns existed, two ex-NBC companies would not be permitted to compete in the same geographical area (not at this, the planning stage at least). Since Brighton & Hove, with its headquarters at Conway Street, would provide services largely within that conurbation, Southdown would be reduced to 'running-in' from its own areas, west, north and east of Hove and Brighton. Its headquarters would have to be set up elsewhere.

The Estate Divided

Given the opportunity to choose the location of the HQ, Ayers chose Lewes, and this was approved by 19 September. 'Southdown House' in Freshfield Road, barely come-of-age, was declared 'surplus to future requirements' and reverted to National Bus Properties during 1986, together with the adjoining Vicarage Garage. The existing headquarters staff were split between companies: some agreed to redundancy arrangements, whilst others declared themselves willing to go with SMS to Lewes. The Freshfield Road, Vicarage, Whitehawk, Conway Street and Moulsecoomb garages were to be retained by Brighton & Hove which also acquired Southdown's Shoreham office (since it was in the BATS area) and Steyning outstation. Southdown Engineering Services took the Portslade Works in Victoria Road, together with all employed there.

Initially, it was expected that these arrangements would be approved at NBC's forthcoming main board meeting on 10 October 1985. But NBC had already decided that the SMS proposals were acceptable, and Michael Sedgley wanted the changes given the longest opportunity to become effective prior to the forthcoming deregulation of the bus industry. There was also the need for him to negotiate the termination of the Brighton Area Transport Services joint agreement with representatives of Brighton Council.

Thus, the basic *de facto* outline was made public in a press release on 19 September and was confirmed at NBC's October meeting.

The official parting of the ways came on 31 December 1985, on which date, after a quarter of a century in place, the Brighton Area Transport Services agreement ceased to function. From 1 January 1986, Brighton & Hove, Southdown Motor Services and Southdown Engineering Services became *de jure* separate companies.

An interesting sidelight on Michael Sedgley's decisive

past in these discussions is that, having appointed him *managing director* of the revived Brighton, Hove & District company, NBC later decided that each of its subsidiaries' general managers should be similarly retitled.

The plaque on the wall of Southdown House declaring it to be the registered office of Brighton Hove & District Omnibus Co Ltd was now removed to that company's old home in Conway Street, Hove, where Michael Sedgley set up office, with Roger French responsible for general management.

Transferred to BH&D from Southdown Motor Services Ltd as its initial fleet were 46 Leyland National saloons, 25 Leyland Leopard/Plaxton coaches, 14 Leopard/Duple coaches, 8 Leyland Tiger/Duple coaches, 13 Mercedes Benz/Alexander minibuses, 115 Bristol VRT double-deckers, 20 Leyland Atlantean AN68 double-deckers, and 4 Bristol Lodekka double-deckers; a total of 245 buses. When Southdown had absorbed the BH&D fleet at the formation of the National Bus Company, only 153 buses had been forthcoming. Being subsumed under Southdown for best part of two decades had not turned out too badly for the fortunes of BH&D in the long run.

Those extra vehicles were to come in handy as BH&D prepared to trade as the 'Brighton & Hove Bus & Coach Company Ltd' and to step outside its traditional confines, both functional and geographical.

Southdown Engineering Services Ltd was destined to become the first 'Southdown' company to be sold by NBC when, on 5 March 1987, it was acquired by Frontsource Ltd, a Robert Beattie firm. Seven other former bus company engineering departments were included in the sale, among them the neighbouring 'Hants & Dorset Distribution Ltd'.

'Find us, keep us'. An overall advertisement in red and blue on white for Portsmouth's local 'Radio Victory' – a useful ally for Southdown in its NBC days with its travel bulletins and updates. Bristol VRT/ECW double-decker No. 660 (AAP 660T) soldiered on and, under new management in 1989, would be rebuilt to front entrance only, and increased capacity, for further use with Southdown.

Chapter Nine: Independent Southdown

The choice of Lewes as the headquarters of what was to become a fully independent Southdown was not arrived at without some considerable thought. The removal of the Brighton, Hove, Portslade and Shoreham-by-Sea conurbation left comparative 'outposts' at Eastbourne, along the northern Sussex fringes and at Worthing, Chichester and Portsmouth in the west. It was felt that to push the HQ west of Brighton would isolate the East Sussex operations. In the view of Philip Ayers and his team, there was some evidence that proximity to a county hall could be helpful. Chichester (for West Sussex) was, it had already been decided, too far west. Lewes, the county town of East Sussex, was on that basis much closer to the previous centre of company administration, and to choose it would give staff the option of an eastern, central or western location for themselves.

Philip Ayers and his fellow officers had looked at Worthing – but no farther west – and compared the price of offices per square foot in Worthing with those at Lewes, and the cost of potential administrative staff, since one of these 'marketplaces' was from whence they would be drawn. Lewes, a county town, was traditionally a place well endowed with office staff – and county councils are not renowned for paying salaries which compare too well with the private sector. On the other hand, Worthing was a very big centre for banks, building societies and the like, so the prices of offices and staff in that town would, perforce, be higher. For a company which would clearly need to mind every penny, this was a decider.

The team looked initially at the top floor accommodation of the company's existing bus station premises in Eastgate Street, Lewes but, to the relief of those who enjoyed the use of the cafeteria and the snooker room, decided that the space would be insufficient. Instead, they chose to rent from the local district council premises in Walwers Lane which had lain vacant for some two years. At that stage, no-one could not have guessed how the choice of Lewes would, some six years later, result in quite so many service buses in the southern half of England declaring the town to be their parental home.

Divisions

Faced with a potentially vulnerable company spread across a considerable area of the south coast, the managing director's first concern was how to ensure that such a far-flung empire would pull together. Expected predatory forces in the coming competitive world would require consistent responses to challenges as they arose. Paradoxically, the 'divisions', to whose setting up just ten months previously the company owed its very existence as a holistic unit, were quickly seen to be not entirely appropriate for such a task. 'Divisions' are, by nature, just that. Their days would be numbered.

Settling into its new headquarters at Lewes, and preparing for privatisation, Southdown inherited vehicles carrying several variations of NBC logo, indications of use and travel concessions. It took some little time to sort these out and adopt a suitable image. Still in leaf green and white, and sporting both double 'N' and 70th Anniversary logos, Bristol VRT No. 608 (UWV 608S) is operating a local Havant circular to Waterlooville and Lovedean. Despite the fact that 'Stagecoach 900' had been diverted through Waterlooville in 1985, all the rest of the information on the bus was no longer appropriate.

Below: Also inherited were the divisions, which proved to be something of a mixed blessing. 'East & Mid Sussex' had been first off the mark in repainting its vehicles in near traditional colours and identifying the vehicles as 'its own'. One of 16 Mercedes L608D delivered in 1986, No. 913 (C593 SHC) has 20-seat bodywork converted by PMT, apple green and yellow livery, 'East & Mid Sussex' logo at the front and pleasant combination of old and new graphics at the sides incorporating Mackenzie's 'Southdown' signature. It is operating on a Haywards Heath local service, and was one of the last 'Southdown' vehicles based in the town.

Nevertheless, on 1st January 1986, the Hampshire division had as its manager Roland Higgins with Michael (Mike) Gooch as engineer, the West Sussex division was managed by Stephen Noble with Richard Alexander, and the East & Mid Sussex: Ian McAllister and Brian Juffs. Together with the managing director, company secretary Alan Ritchie (albeit briefly) completed the management. They comprised a very new team. Three engineers, only one of whom had previous experience of Southdown practice, commendably set out to ensure the best standards for their division.

Compared with many other NBC companies, however, whose post-nationalisation format had been finalised previously, some as early as 1983, Southdown had precious little time in which to prepare itself for the rigours of a deregulated arena, now some few months away. Much midnight oil was burned behind the scenes.

Apple Green and Primrose

Up front, Southdown had begun the process of removing the NBC livery and logo months previously. It had adopted the NBC Chairman's Award logo with alacrity, then another lauding the company's 70 years of service; it had brought back into use the traditional livery at the least excuse and had generally challenged the corporate identity more frequently than some other NBC subsidiaries.

Premises, vehicles, stationery and general presentation took on a more recognisable traditional Southdown flavour. All divisions were to revert to apple green and primrose livery throughout the forthcoming year, although each demonstrated its own degree of independence by experimenting with several variations in application. In the case of the West Sussex division, this involved the different positioning of dark green to the lower panels of service buses. The policy of contracting out by the divisions to various local paintshops contributed toward the differences. East & Mid Sussex division had been displaying its sub-title on its stage-carriage vehicles since 1985, to be followed by West Sussex; but Hampshire declined to identify itself in this way.

One of the greater dissimilarities in divisional approach was in the public information sector, which had become the individual responsibility of each division during 'decentralisation' days in 1985. The timetables issued by Hampshire and West Sussex continued to utilise the 24-hour clock system, introduced to United Kingdom passengers in the 'sixties by most territorial bus companies, airlines, shipping and British Rail to bring the country into line with what, in those days, was called 'the Continent'. East and Mid Sussex (together with the now separate Brighton & Hove company) decided to go back to good old British am/pm times – a move welcomed by more senior citizens for whom the clock had previously only seemed correct in the mornings.

As the standardised 'Freshfield Road' publicity material ran out in 1986 – a difficult act to follow since it had only recently been given an award by the 'Plain English Campaign' – so each division presented itself in differing styles. Sizes, layouts and degree of information were at variance; so too were graphic presentations of route maps or diagrams and town plans. Inevitably, there were one or two discrepancies in areas of overlap.

'Hissing Sid'

Only three days into his his new role, Philip Ayers learned that he'd lost a Bristol VRT double-decker in a fire over an inspection pit at Eastbourne depot. His quest for a replacement was met by an NBC response of 'you can have any vehicle you want as long as it's a minibus'. Few NBC subsidiaries in the south had received new double-deckers since 1981, as the parent company pursued its miniaturisation policy and Southdown was no exception. Mercedes Benz L608D minibuses with Reeve Burgess and PMT-converted bodywork seating twenty passengers apiece were made available to the company. It was not, however, a policy with which the reshaping Southdown readily agreed. When it came down to the employment of the 'Southdown Mini Bus', the East & Mid Sussex Division found that its allocation for the proposed operation on service 41 from Eastbourne to Willingdon and Polegate had not arrived, and four Mercedes borrowed from

Below : Whilst Hampshire division declined to identify itself upon the vehicles, 'West Sussex' set about promoting its image in this way. Veteran Leyland Titan PD3/4 No. 3215 (415 DCD), originally a convertible open-topper delivered in 1964, stoically continues to promote Southdown's flagging coaching activity in August 1986, with a new 'West Sussex' logo beside its NBC badge. The traditional livery is a small wickedness from the Sedgley era under NBC.

Below right: The summer of 1986 saw the introduction of 'Hissing Sid' – as the crews irreverently dubbed it – a new logo specially designed for Southdown to replace that of NBC. A white rolling road crossing the green Southdown Hills formed a lazy 'S'. Leyland National No. 45 (RUF 45R) of the East & Mid Sussex division displays it on sides and front, whilst en route from Hayward's Heath to Brighton in August of that year.

National 81 (YCD 81T), displaying its membership of the West Sussex division, is a Worthing-based saloon preparing to depart on the hourly 700 service to Portsmouth. This vehicle heralds the company's return to traditional livery, but demonstrate also the divisional variation in evidence during the 1986 repaints. Number 45, seen on the previous page, has dark green wheels and a black front bumper, whereas No. 81, seen here, has deep dark green skirt rising with the panelling over the wheel arches.

Centre: Hampshire division demonstrated its preference for a corporate company image on Bristol VRT No. 686 (EAP 986V). Its locally-modified screen up-date, however, displays a curiously eccentric message from the California of the 'seventies. Since the British tend not to like being ordered about, it was thankfully not adopted. Service 326 was a new service which operated a Havant-Leigh Park circular on week days and resulted from the rationalisation of existing routes to the north east of Portsmouth. Beside 686 is an AEC 'Swift' of Basil Williams' resurgent 'Hants & Sussex' of Emsworth – a fleetname not used by him for over 32 years, but reintroduced on de-regulation day, 1986. Notice the ungainly electronic digital destination display.

Lower: The double-decker version of the 'new' traditional livery saw the cream paint restricted to the lower deck, rather than over the roof and around the top windows as in days of yore. Allowing the existing lower panelling to dictate design, the 'West Sussex' double-decks received a narrow dark green skirt. The white vinyl legal-owner label on these vehicles reflects the need to re-address the whole fleet at once upon the company's removal to Lewes. Number 682 (EAP 982V), a Bristol VRT of 1979 waits on Midhurst Bus Stand.

Eastern National were temporarily substituted. Southdown's 1986 deliveries of minibuses, dressed in a predominantly yellow and apple green, eventually comprised seven PMT conversions and nine by Reeve Burgess, plus another provided as a replacement Cuckmere Community Bus. The arrival of the PMT batch from June 1986, led to the establishment of minibus services in and around Haywards Heath – an introduction hampered initially by a shortage of personnel to drive them at the prevailing lower wage rate.

If minibuses were not then too popular at Lewes, Harry Blundred, an ex-assistant traffic manager with Southdown and now in charge at Devon General, positively loved them. Having led his management team into the first buy-out of an NBC subsidiary, he now purchased a large fleet of Ford Transit-based minibuses for use on considerably increased headways around Exeter and Torbay. This meant he had a surplus fleet of conventionally-sized vehicles, and Southdown was among six large companies who moved in to acquire some. Twelve Bristol VR double-deckers of various configurations, several already second-hand, together with seven Leyland National saloons, were earmarked for Southdown. For a while, some poppy-red 'Southdowns' were to be seen on service at both ends of the company's operating area. Those Leyland Nationals which went to the East & Mid Sussex division were joined by another acquired from Western National.

The ownership of all the variously decorated stage carriage vehicles was made plain, however, following the adoption in the summer of 1986 of a new Southdown logo to be displayed in proximity to the fleetname. It comprised a portayal in white of a road going away in winding perspective across the green Southdown Hills, in an unmistakable 'S'. Influenced by television, company employees irreverently dubbed it 'Hissing Sid'.

111

Advertising Lord Montagu's abbey home and National Motor Museum, No. 648 (AAP 648T), a Bristol VRT/ECW double-decker cruises south through Hilsea, en route for The Hard, Portsmouth on 8th November 1986. The vehicle sports the Hampshire division's red 'SOUTHDOWN BUSES: PROUD TO BE LOCAL' logos with 'O's filled in with hearts. This out-of-date valentine proved short-lived.

The stepped waistrail and high lower-saloon window-line on this Bristol VRT/SL3 74-seater with ECW bodywork discloses its 14ft. 6in. height. The vehicle is an ex-Ribble Motor Services purchase still in its NBC poppy red livery, running in from Petersfield to South Parade Pier. It is passing The News Centre and Southdown's Hilsea garage.

En route to North End, Portsmouth, but with no suitable screen to say so (how standards were slipping!), is No. 624 (UTO 834S) a standard Bristol VRT/SL3 ECW double-decker. Purchased in 1986 from Devon General Ltd, it was built originally for Trent of Derby. It carries an outside 'Southdown' logo on the front to aid identification because the livery is still the NBC poppy red of its previous owner.

Chichester-based in April 1988, yet showing evidence of duties much farther east, is Bristol/ECW No. 285 (PTT 91R), another Southdown purchase from Devon General. In its second year after purchase, the vehicle is still in its NBC poppy red livery with 'Hissing Sid' looking somewhat embarrassed beside the Southdown fleetname on its daubed background and dented panelling.

The 1986 'Love you' message flanks the destination screen of Leyland AN68 Atlantean No. 709 (PUF 139M). Dating from 1974, this was one of forty-one 73-seat Park Royal double-deckers delivered to Southdown. Although the vehicle has a distinct 'London' look about it, the design was in fact a product of NBC Engineering. Number 709 is running from Lovedean to Havant on 30th August 1986.

Still in NBC leaf green livery on 4th October 1986, when it was on duty at Leigh Park, operating a local circular service, AN68 Atlantean No. 720 (PUF 720M) advertises the 28-day travel-card facility (as well as the warning that smoking can cause heart-disease). The vehicle was later sold to Ribble Motor Services Ltd with whom it lent its weight and capacity to the support of that firm's brief provision of services wholly within Greater Manchester.

De-Regulation 1986

Throughout a long academic career, Professor John Hibbs of the University of Central England had waged a lonely campaign for the regulatory reform of British bus services. Heard at last, he was awarded an OBE for his efforts. I mention this, not because of a degree of irony therein, but in order that praise or blame may be laid according to our affiliations. What, by rights, should have been called "Hibbs' Day", but the government and industry preferred to call Deregulation Day, arrived at last on 26th October 1986. Like footballers shuffling their feet before the kick-off in the face of an untried opposition, Southdown had made a number of adjustments to those services which it wished particularly to preserve.

Philip Ayers' assessment of the company's fortunes was necessarily cautious. Under the NBC regime, armed as it was with local government subsidies, Southdown had become an extremely successful company, enjoying a near 100 per cent monopoly of passenger custom throughout its operating area outside Portsmouth, Brighton and Eastbourne – and had done well in those places also.

In concert with other territorial companies, one of the harsh facts of life that Southdown had to face in 1986 was that in the newly-created world of competitive tendering, there could be only one direction in which its share of the existing market would move – for the immediate future at least. The policy was 'to tell the staff and face them up to that fact'. As elsewhere, expansion could only come at someone else's expense or by finding hitherto unrealised sources of income.

During the early part of 1986 any operator was able to 'register' any service it wished to run commercially from 26th October of that year. Southdown was no exception but any mileage not so registered was liable to be competitively tendered by the respective county council if it felt that the journeys were socially necessary. In many ways this 'D' Day was an anti-climax as few other operators saw the early opportunities to both attack Southdown and simultaneously to benefit from the comparatively high tender prices in the early days of deregulation.

Brighton & Hove's one bus per day on the 700 route from Brighton to Portsmouth (as against six by Southdown) and four buses per day on the 712 to Eastbourne (against Southdown's three), as well as other jointly-operated

services, were already an established fact: what came as a surprise was Brighton & Hove's appearance on what, for them, was a totally detached route along Southdown's northern fringe – the road between Horsham and Haywards Heath. West Sussex division, in whose territory John Belson's 'Sussex Bus' had already established itself on the Henfield road, also lost a local Horsham service to Tillingbourne (Sussex) Ltd and another to Alder Valley South. A restricted service northwest from Chichester went to Yellowline Tours and Blue Lake of Chichester found a toe-hold in the area. At Worthing, traditionally a Southdown stronghold, C. J. Chatfield placed the first of his 'Cedar Travel' minibuses on service, under the trading name 'Cedarbus'; and Access Cars commenced running commercial services from Worthing to Shoreham-by-sea and Southwick. Chatfield would go on to develop a series of minibus services in and around Worthing which, by and large, tended to complement, rather than compete with, those of Southdown. In so doing, he gathered quite a little following.

London Country South-West found some extra work in the northern edge of the West and East & Mid Sussex areas, and the latter found itself sharing the road with newcomers like Autopoint Coaches of Herstmonceux, Arthur J. Chapman's 'Lewes Coach Company' of South Chailey, which added two new services to the one it had gained in April 1985, Plumpton Motor Coaches and RDH Services. West Sussex division counter-attacked London Country deep in Surrey with a service from Redhill and another at Epsom in October 1986.

There was give and take at Eastbourne as Southdown's East & Mid Sussex division gained local services in the town, whilst Eastbourne Buses, the municipally-owned company, captured the road to Jevington. This operator remained on good terms with the company, however, and was to become an ally in a joint expansion at the eastern edge of Southdown territory.

Hampshire division made some notable inroads in the west, in the face of minor incursions from White Heather Coaches of Southsea, Priory Coaches of Gosport and Basil Williams' Hants & Sussex Motor Services Ltd.

Give and Take

Portsmouth was a location where Southdown had worked very closely with the city council. The Portsmouth Area Joint Transport Services (PAJT) agreement, now ended, had always worked particularly smoothly and the company had enjoyed very good and friendly relations with the city councillors previously concerned. Consequently, Southdown did not set out to compete with Portsmouth City Transport Ltd – indeed it was already running a joint circular service with that operator on Portsea Island and out to Cosham and Farlington.

Yet, by the time D-Day arrived, it had become very obvious that PCT was encountering serious operating difficulties. In accordance with its options, Portsmouth decided not to register Sunday services – some were then registered commercially by others, whilst others were put out to tender. Southdown simply tendered to replace them and was successful in its bid. Whereas their municipal counterparts now took an enforced day-of-rest, Southdown staff at Portsmouth found themselves working an increased number of Sundays in their rotas, but did so willingly in the knowledge of what was at stake. Even so, PCT's nautical fighting spirit carried it outward to claim ground in the former PAJTs area at Lovedean and Waterlooville, in competition with its former ally.

As soon as the three month hiatus had come to an end Southdown were able to consolidate their position in Portsmouth. In February 1987, operating difficulties were ironed out, contract workings on evening journeys were gained on a long term basis from Hampshire County Council, and one-month contracts were obtained to operate two PCT circulars on the island. What used to be the old 45 route from South Parade Pier to Fareham (now 347)

Above left: This Leyland Leopard PSU3E/4R with Plaxton Supreme IV Express coachwork, No. 1318, was previously BYJ 918T. It was one of 16 vehicles of the Hampshire Division to receive 'cherished' registration numbers in 1987; this one (422 DCD) from a Leyland Titan PD3. It is here among those relegated to dual-purpose configuration following the run down of the coaching fleet.

Above right: More prosaic duties for the downgraded Leyland Leopard No. 1284 (RYJ 884R) included the 326 Leigh Park circular from Havant Bus Station, on which service the vehicle is operating on 8th September 1987. Engaged on such work, the growling Leopards lent an added degree of comfort and style to an otherwise run of the mill journey, although they were not ideal for the purpose.

At Clarence Pier on 13th June 1987, is Leopard No. 1284 (RYJ 884R) with 49-seat Duple Dominant Express I coachwork. Pressed into service from its more usual stage-carriage work, it lacks the necessary 'Southampton' on its screen. The Bus Station terminus in Southampton, already in the hands of Stagecoach, was to be sold the following month, when service 727 would instead terminate at the mediaeval Bargate in that city.

In 1987, two Leyland Titan PD3/4 convertible open-toppers went from Southdown to the Provincial Bus Company at Hoeford; and from Provincial to Southdown came four Iveco A49-10 minibuses with Robin Hood coachwork – a most unusual company acquisition. Although painted in full Southdown livery, No. 918 (D128 DRV) and its sisters saw little use with the company, save the provision of that summer's 'park & ride' services at Chichester, before being sold to West Yorkshire Road Car Co Ltd.

was diverted via Paulsgrove in the evenings to pick up more passengers and had its headway doubled to half-hourly. On 1st September 1987 this diverted route became the familiar-sounding 345, in its own right and ran throughout weekdays. Meanwhile, Provincial Bus Company Ltd was beginning to make its presence felt in the city which its ancestor quit 52 years previously.

Elsewhere, however, mixed fortunes had been encountered. The West Sussex division's incursion into Redhill and Epsom proved a short-lived affair of three months: both services were deregistered on 23rd January 1987 and were re-tendered by Surrey County Council. Not unlike some military campaigns of the past, the expeditionary force fell back upon its depot, only to find that this too would be in retreat only two days later. Horsham depot, where Southdown had been represented since 1919, closed its doors as a result of the company's need to reduce with rising overhead costs. Released from the imposed three months' pause, Sussex Bus came in to pick up some of the ex-Southdown services. Tillingbourne appeared on the Oakhill service briefly and London Country moved in with half a dozen 16-seat 'Horsham Minis', and other services with full-size vehicles. Southdown's presence in Horsham was then restricted to services from elsewhere and the gradual rundown of the best part of 50 of its redundant vehicles kept there for inspection by potential customers, Eastbourne Buses, amongst other contending buyers, went away with six Leyland National saloons.

Southdown's Mercedes minibuses, in contrast, soldiered on, despite being 'imposed' upon the management in 1986. Local authority contract work became their speciality. Some worked on East Sussex County Council service 727 at Eastbourne (but were then sent to work commercially in Burgess Hill during 1988), whilst others, including No. 911 (C591 SHC), saw service on a new series of West Sussex County Council contract services at Haywards Heath, where the Southdown depot was now under threat of closure.

Top Line

It was to be the latter operator which provided the key for an expansion of Southdown activity in the east. This was at Hastings, which development came about two ways. First, the Southdown management felt that the town of Hastings had more affinity to Sussex than to Kent, and its bus services had been separated out from Maidstone & District by NBC in 1983, destined for sale, under the familiar-sounding title Hastings & District Transport Ltd.

Initially, this company had looked to Southdown House for much of its administrative backup, including wages and accounts. That had soon ceased, but seen through Southdown eyes, Hastings & District operations seemed commercially to have an affinity with those of its eastern extremity.

Secondly, Eastbourne Buses, in keeping with its own expansionist policy, had won some school contract work along the coast at Hastings in March 1987 and was now looking for further work in the middle of the day at that location. This was primarily to occupy drivers and vehicles or, at least, to eliminate dead mileage. Eastbourne Buses approached Southdown to suggest the launch of a joint operation in Hastings. So was born 'Top Line'.

Southdown gave up its share of the Eastbourne to Hastings service, joint with Hastings & District Transport Ltd, together with the 799 limited-stop service between Brighton, Hastings and Rye; demonstrated its new solidarity with Eastbourne Buses by entering into a new open-top joint service to Beachy Head; and prepared to provide seven green and cream Leyland Nationals to travel over to Hastings each day from Eastbourne garage to join a similar number of Eastbourne Buses Atlantean double-deckers, based there in a haulier's yard.

Whilst both operators' vehicles remained in their owner's liveries, they sported the new 'Top Line' logo in black on

This Bristol VRT open-topper, No. 621 (UWV 621S), seen operating in full Stagecoach livery in the summer of 1991 at Eastbourne on service 3B, is doing so as a direct legacy of a new understanding forged between Philip Ayers' management team and Eastbourne Buses in the spring of 1987. The new service, operated jointly with the municipal operator, ran from Eastbourne's Leisure Pool to the top of Beachy Head with effect from the 24th May 1987.

Right: Having eyed Hastings as a possible place for expansion, Southdown entered into an agreement with Eastbourne Buses, who already enjoyed a toe-hold in the town, to set up a joint operation to be called Top Line. It commenced on 25th May 1987, in competition with Hastings & District Transport Ltd; both Southdown and Eastbourne buses contributing their own vehicles adorned with 'Top Line' slip-boards. Southdown's Leyland National No. 118 (ENJ 918V) was one of seven of the type allotted for Top Line service by the company at the outset: it is on the main Hastings town route at Churchwood Drive, Hollington.

Centre: Despite the route-order suggested on the slip-board Leyland National 110 (ENJ 910V) is running to Eastbourne on Top Line service via Bexhill, Sidley, Herstmonceux and Hailsham, approximating what in earlier times would have been Southdown's route 15. The vehicle, one of the originals dedicated to Top Line by Southdown, is climbing Montgomery Road, Ore – and showing signs of battle damage – on 2nd July 1987. Service 98 (and the more direct 99), from Eastbourne, utilised the same King's Head, Ore terminous as the Hastings local service 53.

Lower: Typical of Southdown's search for additional revenue was the contract from Havant Hypermarket to provide a weekday free bus service to the store. Painted in the appropriate overall livery is Southdown No. 631 (UTO 831S), a Bristol VRTSL3/501 with ECW 74-seat bodywork purchased from Harry Blundred's Devon General in 1986. Having a change from its advertised service, it is seen on a Saturday in June 1988 in Portsmouth, running on service 343 from Wecock Farm to South Parade Pier, Southsea. On this occasion the passengers were expected to pay.

yellow with an arrow beneath, pointing to the 'politically-appropriate' right. The joint services commenced on 25th May 1987, three in Hastings with two more linking that town with Eastbourne.

Stung by the defection of some of its own drivers, the jilted Hastings & District hurled minibuses at the intrusion, and continued to provide frequencies at almost saturation level for the best part of that summer. But, by and large, young mothers with pushchairs led the patronage of Top Line's more easily accessible full-size vehicles, and the bridgehead was secured. Two more services, to provide evening journeys, started in June 1987 as this latest 'Battle of Hastings' was at its height and Southdown Bristol VRT double-deckers were added to the fray. Hastings & District ultimately paid the penalty as loser in this conflict.

Management Buy-Out

With the joint 'Top Line' operation safely established, a management-led team now prepared to make its bid for a privatised Southdown Motor Services Ltd. An off-the-shelf company, necessary for such a purpose, called Sharpton Ltd, was formed by Southdown's Philip Ayers, managing director; Roland Higgins, commercial director; Michael Gooch, engineering director; and David Charlton, finance director. Sharpton Ltd was successful and purchased Southdown from the National Bus Company on 2nd October 1987. Legal niceties aside, Southdown had become, for the first time in its history, a totally independent entity.

Sharpton Ltd paid the National Bus Company a net £7.0 million for Southdown in October 1987. It had faced four bidders at the final 'Sealed Bid' stage, and that bid was for a company whose Business Plan at the time forecast a loss. For comparison, the other 'half' of Southdown, Brighton and Hove, raised a net £1 million with a mere two

bidders in May of that year.

Predictably, the three Southdown 'divisions', already withering on the vine, now disappeared, redundant vehicles in large numbers were sold and a further round of belt-tightening began. Hailsham depot closed on 24th October 1987 and the Horsham travel office likewise in December. The year came to an end with Haywards Heath depot under threat.

With the Brighton & Hove Bus & Coach Company holding the centre ground, and Southdown's diminishing territory along the northern fringe of Sussex, the task of preserving the company as a homogeneous geographical unit grew more difficult by the month. Brighton & Hove now operated services at Haywards Heath, whilst Lewes Coaches, London Country (South West), Sussex Bus and Whitebush Travel were also represented in the town. It became clear that without further work, Haywards Heath depot did not have a future.

Following the privatisation of Southdown on 2nd October 1987, by means of a management-led buy-out, the concept of 'divisions' was dispensed with. Divisional logos quickly disappeared, and only the subtle differences of lower panel paintwork might give a clue as to previous allegiances. Another vehicle with a Devon accent, National 11351A/1R No. 55 (VOD 605S), is operating on the Old Steine-Henfield-Cowfold-Horsham Railway Station service on 6th August 1988.

The second of the pair of Bristol VRT double-deckers fitted by Southdown with trial electronic destination screens, on service in Bognor Regis High Street, bound for Chichester and Midhurst. Again, its previous identity is confirmed by the dark green skirt panels. The bus is No. 678 (EAP 978V).

A lifeline presented itself in early 1988. Kent County Council put five Sunday services in and around Tunbridge Wells out to tender and another between Forest Row and East Grinstead over which it had jurisdiction despite its being in Sussex – and Southdown won the contracts. Although traditionally Maidstone & District and London Country territory respectively, these locations were previously termini for Southdown services in the north-east of its operational area and so were not completely detached forays into foreign territory of the kind engaged in by others following de-regulation.

The vulnerable depot was chosen to provide staff and vehicles for this additional Sunday task, and two new services – from Haywards Heath to Tunbridge Wells and to Forest Row – were introduced, commencing on Sunday 6th March 1988, in order to place them in position for their weekly duties.

Sadly, however, and despite the dedicated efforts of its local employees, this comparatively modest expansion did not prove enough to save the Haywards Heath depot and Southdown closed it the following October.

'Hastings Top Line Buses Ltd'

In contrast, things were going well at Hastings and plans to regularise the Top Line operation were in hand. In the midst of rumours of a forthcoming merger with Southdown, Eastbourne buses were instead in discussion with the company on the fine detail of setting up Top Line as a separately accountable unit. Early in 1988, a shelf company called Wainland Ltd, with its registered office in Lewes, had been formed to carry this out. A board of directors comprised of officers from both Southdown and the Eastbourne municipality was set up and applications were invited for the post of manager of the new 'Top Line Buses Ltd'. Paul Southgate from Southdown's Portsmouth area was the successful candidate and took up office on the 1st May 1988. Drivers and local staff were now the direct employees of the new company, with Southdown primarily

responsible for engineering, financial planning and the administration of wages. An agreement for signature was drawn up in early August, but then both parties received a surprise note from Companies House. Someone who clearly did not intend using the title had already registered the name 'Top Line Buses Ltd'. A brief shake of the head later, the new company became instead 'Hastings Top Line Buses Ltd' with effect from 21st August 1988. Although administered locally from a Portakabin at St. Leonards, the registered office of HTLB was in Walwers Lane, Lewes.

From May 1988 vehicles for 'Top Line' were painted in yellow and black livery and the company house-style appeared in publicity and time-table leaflets, one of which carried warning enough to its rivals: 'We are looking for new areas in which to expand our Top Line service in 1989....' but they did not, and fare levels proved to be the decisive weapon.

'Pay-up Pompey'

Portsmouth was beset by considerable turmoil as a result of Deregulation. The full story belongs elsewhere, but briefly the relevant events at this stage were as follows: it had become clear by the end of 1987 that Portsmouth City Transport was sufficiently weakened by additional competition for it to be put up for sale. The competition had come from the minibuses of 'Red Admiral', owned by Pathfinder UK Ltd – a company formed for that purpose by Badgerline and Southampton City Transport. Portsmouth City Council issued a prospectus and invited bids by 10th February 1988. Southdown was to be involved in two

In 1988, Southdown and Eastbourne Buses bestowed separate company status upon their Top Line operation, under the care of directors drawn from both, and with its registered office at Lewes. Hastings Top Line Buses Ltd adopted an overall yellow and black livery and PCD 73R, a Leyland National 11351A/1R, originally Southdown No. 27, wears this in its original form at the Hollington Tesco terminus of the route from Ore on 25th March 1989.

Because of an unexpected hitch over the proposed registered name, it took Southdown and Eastbourne Buses from 1st May to 21st August 1988 to regularise the Hastings operation into Hastings Top Line Buses Ltd. The vehicles allotted to it from both operators were now repainted into its chosen separate livery. Southdown Leyland National No. 22 (BCD 822L) was transferred to the new company, whose registered office was at Southdown's Lewes headquarters, in 1989.

Most of the vehicles contributed to Hastings Top Line Buses Ltd by Eastbourne Buses were Leyland Atlantean AN68 double-deckers with East Lancs bodywork. Top Line No. 420 (GHC 523N) is a 75-seater painted in the original version of the yellow and black livery adopted in 1988. The vehicle is operating the Harrow Lane service from Malvern Way, Ore on 18th May 1989.

Leyland National BCD 823L (previously Southdown No. 23) is a 1151/IR/0102 model with 49 seats and room for 22 standing, which gives a fair picture of the carrying capacity ranged against the competing 26-seaters of Hastings & District Transport Ltd. The vehicle is at Priory Road, Ore on 19th May 1989, in the later, revised livery, without black skirt and with Top Line logo removed, Southdown-style, to the roof line.

Saloon buses also worked the 57 service from Malvern Way, Ore to Harrow Lane. Southdown No. 26 (PCD 126M) was one of 17 Leyland National saloons loaned to Hastings Top Line Bus Ltd in 1989, and is seen here at Ore on 23rd June, having attracted the first of its passengers for Ashdown House, Harrow Lane. Since these saloons, and a pair of Bristol VRT double-deckers also loaned by Southdown that year were not in Top Line livery, the slip boards saw further use.

ways. First, it was prepared to put up a third of the money necessary for an approach by PCT staff. This the council called anti-competitive and rejected. Secondly, Southdown made a bid in its own right, against rival offers from Badgerline, Provincial, Shamrock & Rambler, Southampton City Transport, Stagecoach Holdings, Trent and Southern Vectis.

The latter made the successful bid and prepared to set up what it would have called 'Solent Green Line' in the city. Then Southern Vectis decided that things were darker than they had been painted, attempted to revise conditions, but failed to reach agreement with the council. The latter tried to rekindle interest from the other bidders, only to find that they had joined Southdown as unwilling suitors. Only the depleted PCT staff, strongly backed by Southampton City Transport, were left in the field. So, 75 per cent of Portsmouth City Bus, as the new operator would be called,

After comparative trials with six vehicles in 1988, Southdown placed an order for its first new double-deckers since 1981. The selected combination was chassis by Volvo with bodywork by Northern Counties of Wigan. The latter, desparately short of orders, were so pleased to receive another order from Southdown after so long an absence that Alan Metcalf came down from Wigan to help Philip Ayers present ceremonial keys for the vehicles to the Lord Mayor of Portsmouth and the Mayors of Worthing and Eastbourne. Alan Metcalf (left) and Philip Ayers (right) are pictured at the Worthing ceremony.

came to be owned by municipally-controlled Southampton City Transport; a situation compounded when SCT bought a controlling interest (on 24th June 1988) in Red Admiral, the competing firm which caused such damage to PCT. Apart from successful trading, it was the political will of Southampton to maintain its own bus company which made possible such moves. It took a true-blue native of Portsmouth to realise what a bitter pill was this.

Southdown now had a 'Southampton look-alike' PCB to compete against in the Portsmouth area, save on service 53/54 where, despite the fact that both operators' publicity claimed it as their own, each accepted the other's return tickets – a positive gain for the poor passenger.

A Fighting Retreat

Meanwhile, in East Sussex, the retirement of Arthur Chapman, proprietor of the Lewes Coach Company, saw the purchase of his operations, premises and vehicles by Brighton Borough Transport Ltd on 1st May 1988. Thus Brighton Buses were to be found running way out into the countryside which was once Southdown's – a situation unthinkable in the days of the BATS agreement. But the competition was different rather than increased. A brighter note for Southdown was that Whitebush Travel of Redhill, which had set up at Horsted Keynes to run additional

Destined for use on the core routes from Brighton to Eastbourne and Brighton to Portsmouth, the twelve new vehicles were Volvo B10M Mark III models with 76 seats and room for 17 standees. They were fitted with factory installed electronic destination displays and the standard of finish was well up to the traditional mark, ensuring an immediately favourable response from the travelling public. Both on service 700 in the month of their arrival, August 1989, No. 304 (F304 MYJ) goes east, whilst No. 312 (F312 MYJ) seen below, travels west. It was to prove the last new vehicle delivered to Southdown in apple green and primrose livery.

Incorporating within its design the stylised independent Southdown 'S' this Bristol VRT carries an overall advertisement for Southdown 'Goldcards' a facility made available to the public in the Portsmouth area in 1989. Sold over the counter at local Post Offices, the card, which was transferable, offered 28 days of bus travel for £25. Travel to Hazelton Way on service 338, introduced in April 1988, would have been an acceptable use of the card. The vehicle is No. 685 (EAP 985V).

services from Haywards Heath, had overreached itself by June 1988, leaving Southdown to pick up some of the pieces thereafter. Whitebush Travel retreated to Surrey and ceased trading.

A firm pointer to the poor trading position of Southdown post de-regulation, however, was to be found in the 1988 summary of vehicle changes: no new vehicles taken into stock, and no second-hand ones either; whilst a total of 83 buses and coaches were sold. Many of these were Leyland Leopard coaches being withdrawn and not replaced as a result of the decision to close down Southdown's involvement with coaching, whilst the seven Leyland National saloons 'sold' to Hastings Top Line Buses Ltd could be counted as still 'in-house'; but the general pattern of contraction continued.

The Southdown management was by now well aware that its image was beginning to pale somewhat when comparisons were drawn with some of the vehicles now employed by rival operators. Brighton & Hove's contribution to the 700 (Brighton-Portsmouth) and 712 (Brighton-Eastbourne) for instance was likely to be a new Scania double-decker. The youngest reply Southdown could make was with seven-year-old Bristol VRTs. The company had fitted coach seats into some of them to upgrade the role of these double-deckers, but the fact was that in less competitive times they would instead have been downgraded to other, less strategic duties. In order to defend its competitive position on these and possibly other prime routes, Southdown decided to invest in some new double-deckers.

Comparative trials were carried out at various times in 1988 with six vehicles representing five chassis-builders (Dennis, Leyland, MCW, Scania and Volvo) and three coachbuilders (Alexander, MCW and Northern Counties). Philip Ayers and his team concluded that the Volvo B10M chassis with dual-purpose Northern Counties 76-seat coachwork offered the best value for what was intended to be a long-term purchasing policy and Northern Counties, struggling with their own considerable problems in the deregulated world, were clearly delighted to get another order from Southdown after such a long absence. At the time the selection was made, there was every intention to take delivery of considerably more than the twelve which actually entered the fleet.

The Volvos began to arrive in August 1989 and a pair of them were earmarked to participate in hand-over ceremonies at Portsmouth, Worthing and Eastbourne. They were to prove the last new vehicles to enter service in Southdown's traditional green and primrose livery. The ceremonies, which involved the Lord Mayor and Mayors respectively, included the presentation of the official key by either Alan Metcalf of Northern Counties or Philip Ayers. These were among the last public duties he would carry out as managing director of Southdown.

For some while it had been company policy to lend vehicles, and where possible drivers, to other operators in order to keep them actively employed. One such loan in the summer of 1989 – eight Leyland Leopard coaches to County Bus & Coach Ltd of Harlow, Essex – led to speculation that Southdown might be discussing rather more than the loan of coaches with that firm's parent group, Alan J. Stevenson's 'AJS Holdings'. Was Southdown's short existence as a totally independent operator about to come to an end? Yes it was but not as a subsidiary of AJS.

Apart from having been fellow bidders for Portsmouth City Transport the previous year, Southdown's first contact with Stagecoach Holdings PLC came just before the commencement of a Bus & Coach Council Conference at Eastbourne, where Philip Ayers met and subsequently talked at some length with Brian Souter, chairman and Chief Executive of the Group. As a result, Stagecoach made a formal approach to acquire both Southdown Motor Services Ltd and its property-owning associate Sharpton Ltd. Negotiations were conducted in various hotels in the south of England over a two-month period and the sale at considerably more than the original purchase price was completed on 16th August 1989 – although not announced until the 18th.

Philip Ayers took an early retirement from the industry: 'It was a hard decision to make. I enjoyed life, I enjoyed Southdown in particular – it was a wonderful company to work for. But it was the right decision for the company. We went at the right time. That manifested itself subsequently in preserving jobs for staff within the company. And Lewes, for all that people raised their eyebrows about the place to start with, has now become the hub of all Stagecoach operations in the South.'

Local honours have been bestowed for less.

Thought by many at the time of its introduction to the Southdown fleet (1982) to be the last word in saloon bus design, this Leyland National 2 survived in service throughout the days of independent Southdown to become Stagecoach property also. Seen at Chichester in full 'independent' livery and logos, this 11.6 metre 52-seater 405 DCD (No. 135) was originally RUF 435X. In common with most modern buses it warned its driver of problems with a repertoire of red and amber lights, buzzer and bell sounds – eat your heart out Alfred Mackenzie!

Chapter 10: Stagecoach's Southdown

Stagecoach Holdings PLC became one of the main operating beneficiaries of the government's decision to break up the nationalised bus industry and, where it could, municipal operations as well. Named 'Businesswoman of the Year' in 1990, managing director Ann Gloag had already established that Stagecoach sought 'a chequer board rather than a monopoly'. Only an embargo on the acquisition of contiguous bus company areas, loosely interpreted by the Department of Trade and Industry, seems likely to ensure that; yet, as its addicts declare, 'chess is war'. Stagecoach attracted equity funding in two stages. In 1989 several Scottish Institutions subscribed substantial cash to eliminate short term indebtedness. In 1993 the group was successfully floated on the London Stock Exchange to generate substantial investment funds.

Stagecoach: an Outline

A glance at the bus operators' map of Great Britain in the 'nineties and it looks as though some venerable giant has awaked in Scotland and left enormous footprints down the length of England. On reaching the south coast, he seems to have turned east and gone to Kent. The French, perhaps, viewed the large new hole under the Channel with alarm. But since it didn't happen in quite that order, an outline is appropriate.

Far from being elderly, or indeed to begin with a giant, Stagecoach proper was founded in 1980 by the offspring of Scottish bus driver Iain Souter. Ironically the initial capital was obtained from his severence pay when he was made redundant by Alexanders. The new company stemmed from an earlier business concerned with the hire of motor caravans and minibuses and whose first proper bus was bought second-hand for a proposed private hire trip to China which, in the event, did not proceed. Two further second-hand coaches were purchased when the provisions of the Transport Act, 1980 removed most of the restrictions on the operation of coach services. From 9th October 1980, these vehicles were employed on an over-night cut-price service between Dundee and London. Its success led to the purchase of brand new ones the following year.

David Souter, then marketing officer of the fledgling company, came up with the name 'The Stage Coach' at about the same time that far-away Southdown had selected the name for its core routes in the 700 series. Brian Souter was to become chairman and chief executive of what would develop into Stagecoach Holdings PLC – and the managing director Ann Gloag is their sister.

Stagecoach entered the stage carriage field in December 1980 when it took over A. & C. McLennan of Spitalfield, near Perth. Its resources were greatly strengthened by an upsurge of patronage during rail strikes in 1982 and, in 1983, it became involved in excursion work from Crieff, Dundee and Perth. This was also the year that the first acquisition of another operator took place (in Edinburgh).

Bus deregulation in 1986 saw the expansion of stage carriage work in Perth, and following the establishment of the subsidiary Magicbus (Scotland) Ltd, a range of services in Glasgow and district.

A shelf company necessary for the purchase of NBC subsidiaries on offer was formed in February 1987 and the remarkable expansion went into top gear; it was called Skipburn Ltd.

In April 1987, Skipburn acquired Hampshire Bus from NBC; Cumberland Motor Services followed in July and Stagecoach (Holdings) Ltd purchased United Counties in November. The corporate Stagecoach livery of white with tan, red and blue stripes was adopted for all such fleets the following year.

After gaining a foothold in Africa in 1989 (in the best BET tradition) Stagecoach bought Frontrunner Holdings assets, which included East Midland Motor Services, and then Ribble Motor Services in April 1989. Stephensons of Maryport and what remained of the Barrow-in-Furness municipal operation after previous activity by Ribble, followed. North of the border, Inverness Traction joined the group and was used to force Highland Omnibus to surrender its profitable heartland in that town. Existing operations in Perth and Dundee were strenthened. Then Brian Souter attended that Bus & Coach Council conference at Eastbourne and met Philip Ayers.

Brian Cox takes over

Upon purchase, Brian Souter became interim managing director of Southdown Motor Services Ltd. That role passed to Brian Cox on 1st October 1989. He was previously with Hampshire Bus for five years and had, of late, been dividing his time half-a-week in Scotland, where he lived, and half in Hampshire. He now moved house and

In September 1989 Cedar Travel of Worthing relinquished seven services, eight minibuses and the right to use the 'Cedarbus' trading name, which Stagecoach adopted briefly. Number 923 (E233 JRF), one of three Iveco 49-10 minibuses with Robin Hood bodywork involved, operated the Chichester 'Park and Ride' service.

Suitably modified with appropriate screen and door, another ex-Cedarbus vehicle, 904 (F564 HPP), was an MCW Metrorider integral 33-seat minibus. In an effort to pep up the competitive operation of the Wittering services from Chichester, those vehicles involved acquired a special 'Coastline' logo in addition to their Stagecoach-style 'Southdown' fleetnames. It was a title which would take on far greater significance in 1992. Together with its 8 permitted standees, a vehicle of this capacity would have been considered a full-sized single-decker, four decades previously.

The services to East and West Wittering were initially the sole users of the 'Coastline' fleetname. In 1990 Stagecoach's policy of transferring vehicles from its other subsidiaries enabled this Iveco Turbo Daily with 23-seat Robin Hood bodywork to be brought into the battle with Westring's Coaches of Wittering. It was previously with Magicbus (Scotland) Ltd and helped increase the service frequency from half to quarter hourly. The absence of 'Southdown' fleetname has more to do with the speed with which it was placed into service, rather than policy, at this stage.

Having purchased Portsmouth CityBus Ltd, Stagecoach engaged in a sizeable clear-out of older vehicles, notably ex-Portsmouth corporation Leyland Atlantean double-deckers. To fill the gaps left in the ranks of what, briefly, was 'Southdown Portsmouth', under the ex-PCB managing director Alan Barrett, Stagecoach drafted replacement vehicles into the city from other subsidiaries. Included was the hastily numbered 315 (KSA 180P) an Atlantean with Alexander bodywork, sent south from ex-East Midland subsidiary Frontrunner North West. It arrived in 1989 dressed in a not out-of-place green and cream livery and was destined to be used but briefly until sold the following year to Harry Blundred – who used it even more briefly.

Stagecoach's development policy for 'Southdown Portsmouth' was nipped in the bud by the Minister of State for Transport's warning that the purchase of Portsmouth CityBus might be referred to the Monopolies and Mergers Commission – as indeed it was, in February 1990. Ex-Ribble Leyland National UHG 757R demonstrates that things are on hold. Photographed outside Hilsea depot on 21st January 1990, the day that it closed, the vehicle has been repainted into Stagecoach colours, but is on service without identification logos. Number 757 had been a Philip Ayers purchase in 1986.

home to Sussex, making use of administrative facilities at the registered office in Lewes and at Chichester bus station. Roland Higgins and Michael (Mike) Gooch had remained with the company to aid the settling-in period, but departed soon after.

Stagecoach permitted no moss to gather in the Southdown area. The entire fleet, save a handful of historic vehicles retained for publicity purposes, was to be repainted in the Stagecoach house livery over an estimated three-year timescale, and even before Brian Cox was appointed, attention had been focussed successfully upon a previously unsatisfactory situation at Worthing where Cedarbus had been forced into a more competitive stance in the face of opposition by the previous Southdown management.

Probably because its priorities were at that stage elsewhere this latter day independent Southdown effort had not proven immediately successful. Late 'twenties style tactics like introductory fares, close rival headways and changed times of departure failed to woo sufficient custom away from Cedarbus. What the tactics had done, most likely, was to place the kind of pressure upon Chatfields's fleet which later caused severe maintenance problems; and the Traffic Commissioner to revoke his licence. Adverse local publicity, followed by a bout of staff resignations, had then compounded the problems.

Pending appeal against the Traffic Commisioner's decision, however, Chatfield decided to sell the Worthing routes (save the cross-town C1) to Southdown. On 24th September 1989, Stagecoach took over seven services, eight minibuses and the right to the 'Cedarbus' name for use in Worthing as a subsidiary of Southdown Motor Services Ltd. Chatfield retained the three remaining routes, but before the date of the appeal, surrendered his licence. Sussex Bus registered these routes on 27th October 1989, but it was to be Richard Wright, ex-traffic manager of Cedar Travel who would run them with a few ex-Cedar Travel vehicles latterly as Cedar Tavel 1990 – until January 1994, when Sussex Bus at last took them up.

Sharpton Ltd had been the vehicle by which the Cedar Bus purchase was carried out and it was soon to be put to similar use in both west and east of the traditional Southdown area.

'Pompey Pay-up'

Before the first month of his managing directorship was out, Brian Cox's domain had been increased by the Stagecoach purchase of Portsmouth Citybus Ltd. Rumours that the striped predator was about to descend upon the roost began in the local press in September. Southampton City Transport Co Ltd, unhappy about the returns from its jointly-owned Portsmouth subsidiary, was in discussion with Stagecoach; pressed by city officials, the wheels of the Office of Fair Trading clicked into gear and the Secretary of State for Trade and Industry was informed that a monopoly was about to be created in the city – which raised the eyebrows of the other uninvolved operators plying their services on Portsea Island.

Nevertheless, Southampton City Transport sold its 75 per cent stake in PCB to Stagecoach on 20th October 1989 and the PCB employee shareholders followed with their 25 per cent the following week. SCT withdrew to the other end of Southampton Water, taking several PCB vehicles with them as part of the price and claiming sole responsibility for service 727: Southampton, Portsmouth and Southsea. Michael Portillo, Minister of State for Transport, approved the sale, but warned that it might yet be referred to the Monopolies and Mergers Commission.

Above: Stagecoach's purchase of Portsmouth CityBus and the placement of its vehicles under Southdown control led to their appearing in hitherto unusual places in their red and cream livery. Ex-'London Buses' Leyland National 201 (THX 172S) pauses at Hampshire Bus' Winchester bus station, having been pressed into National Express service on route 075 to London.

Left: Leyland Atlantean/East Lancs double-deckers 'posted' to Havant bus station included 349 (CPO 349W), although its declared route to the Hard Interchange terminus in Portsmouth will take it back into home territory. 'Southdown-style' CityBus logos and livery remain, but the address block confirms that Southdown is its legal owner.

On duty at Leigh Park on 3rd March 1990, Atlantean/Alexander 343 (YBK 343W) was the first CPPTD bus to be repainted into Stagecoach livery. The first few were fitted with a rarely used number box. Initially such ex-CityBus vehicles traded simply as 'Portsmouth' – a Southdown subsidiary.

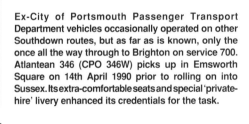

Ex-City of Portsmouth Passenger Transport Department vehicles occasionally operated on other Southdown routes, but as far as is known, only the once all the way through to Brighton on service 700. Atlantean 346 (CPO 346W) picks up in Emsworth Square on 14th April 1990 prior to rolling on into Sussex. Its extra-comfortable seats and special 'private-hire' livery enhanced its credentials for the task.

Leyland National 202 (THX 211S) also bears the succinct 'Portsmouth' logo, although it is one of those vehicles removed from the city to firmer ground following the enforced divestment of the Portsmouth operation. It has found employment on Southdown's Havant to Leigh Park Service.

From 1st January 1990 until divestment, the expanded and more descriptive 'Southdown Portsmouth' fleetname appeared on the ex-Portsmouth CityBus vehicles. Atlantean 354 (CPO 354W) is in Commercial Road, Portsmouth en route to South Parade Pier, Southsea on 1st September 1990.

Centre: For a while after Harry Blundred's Transit Holdings took over what was briefly Southdown's 'Portsmouth Division', the 'Portsmouth' part of the expanded fleetname on those vehicles remaining in the Southdown fleet was painted out, leaving a somewhat lop-sided logo. Leyland National 2, No. 124 (JNJ 194V) on Top Ten Bus facility service is an example.

Lower left: Also briefly under Southdown control, ex-Portsmouth CityBus, were some of the 'Red Admiral' minibuses, still in their appropriate livery, which had earlier done such damage to the prospects of CPPTD. Running a local service to Milton on 1st September 1990 is Iveco 49-10/Robin Hood 23-seater No. 960 (E960 LPX).

Thus Portsmouth Citybus became a subsidiary of Stagecoach rather than SCT and, after a brief two months trading simply as *Portsmouth* was, from 1st January 1990, to become *Southdown Portsmouth*, with ex-PCB managing director Alan Barrett in charge.

An immediate benefit for local passengers was that inter-availability of passes and tickets was restored after open competition, in stark contrast to the government's declared policy, had previously removed it.

The purchase brought Leigh Park depot into the Southdown fold. *Southdown Portsmouth*, however, based its Portsea Island operations upon the Eastney depot still owned by, and leased from, Portsmouth City Council. The days of Southdown's twin depots at Hilsea were thus numbered. A policy of peaceful co-existence was adopted toward Provincial and Basil Williams' Hants & Sussex, lately enjoying some useful service gains in the area.

The rationalisation which this arrangement permitted was now put in train with all speed. Services and timetables were streamlined, ticket machines standardised and previous duplication of effort removed. A sizable clear-out of travel-weary vehicles took place, particularly some of the older Leyland Atlanteans which had once been the pride of the Portsmouth Corporation fleet. In keeping with Stagecoach policy, more serviceable vehicles were transferred from other operators under its control for service in the city. This policy would lead to the increasing exodus of Southdown vehicles across the company area, in exchange for those of Stagecoach subsidiaries elsewhere, according to perceived needs.

The Portsmouth operation, however, was far from settled. Michael Portillo's warning became fact on 21st February 1990 when the Department of Trade and Industry did, indeed, refer the purchase of Portsmouth Citybus to the Monopolies and Mergers Commission. Its task was to establish whether 'a merger situation qualifying for investigation exists' in 'a substantial part of the United Kingdom'. That part was, for the purpose of the investigation, declared to be bounded by Southampton and Eastleigh (curious, because Stagecoach had vacated both locations in October 1987), Winchester, Havant and Chichester. Taking 25 per cent as its yardstick of accessibility, the commission found that Stagecoach subsidiaries (Hampshire Bus and Southdown) now provided 42 per cent of stage carriage services in that part.

The Commission's report, published in July 1990, concluded that the dominant position of Stagecoach in the area could deter competitors from entering the market. At the same time, it felt that the public interest had not been adversely affected. Rather than recommending that the purchase of Portsmouth Citybus should be undone, which would prove difficult in the light of the rationalisation process already carried out by Southdown, two basic safeguards were recommended in order to protect competitors from 'predatory retaliation'. They were: (1) if Stagecoach reduced its fares in competition with a competitor and that, as a result, that competitor should withdraw, then Stagecoach fares should remain at that level for a one year period thereafter, and (2) if Stagecoach increased its headways against a competitor and that competitor should withdraw, those headways should be maintained for one year. Stagecoach was also to publish information on its Portsmouth operations to demonstrate its accountability.

All acceptable to Stagecoach; but the Secretary of State for Trade and Industry, Nicholas Ridley, promptly stubbed-out the recommendations and directed that

As a result of its purchase of Southdown, Stagecoach of course inherited the company's share of Top Line, whose vehicles were running in its own distinctive yellow and black livery at Hastings. In September 1989, Stagecoach purchased the Eastbourne municipality's share also and in December acquired the competing Hastings & District Transport Ltd. Pending the merging of these two firms into a new 'Hastings Buses' operation, it continued the existing policy of loaning Southdown vehicles to Top Line. These joined No. 26 (PCD 126M) which had been on loan since January 1989 and was still in Southdown green and cream when photographed on 4th April 1990.

Below: In retaliation for the setting up by Southdown and Eastbourne Buses of the Top Line operation at Hastings, Hastings & District had devised its own 'Eastbourne & District' to compete in that municipality's own back yard. When Stagecoach acquired Hastings & District, it of course acquired also its subsidiary 'Eastbourne & District'. For a brief transition period and to ease local confusion, Stagecoach utilised that trading name on Southdown vehicles with its own livery modified on the lower panels to three blue bands. Southdown 252 (JWV 252W) demonstrates the variation on 20th August 1991.

Stagecoach should divest itself of its Portsmouth acquisitions.

Accepting the inevitable, Southdown spent the autumn reorganising *Southdown Portsmouth*. Leigh Park, not part of the Southdown empire until the purchase of Portsmouth Citybus, would be retained, together with Havant and Hayling depots, all of which would be administered from Chichester. Those operations now centred on Eastney, the ex-PCB depot with its lease running out, would be the ones which would be divested. At the same time, the better vehicles in the fleet were relocated elsewhere. This was not bloody-mindedness; Stagecoach already had a buyer in prospect by the end of the year and they knew what his vehicular policy would be.

The connection goes back to the summer of 1988 when that ex-Southdown officer, Harry Blundred of Devon General, decided to obtain an Operator's Licence to run a fleet of his preferred minibuses at Basingstoke. This was the territory of Stagecoach's 'Hampshire Bus' and the group had little hesitation in sending some vehicles down to Torbay to run a free service against Devon General. This effectively brought Harry Blundred, whom Brian Souter and Brian Cox had not previously met, to the table. 'Basingstoke Transit' was purchased by Stagecoach before it got going and, later in the year, Bristol VRT double-deckers, made redundant at Devon General by minibuses, joined the Stagecoach fleet. Both the chairman and Brian Cox went down to Exeter for the completion meeting and the latter recalls 'that we now knew Harry. Not long afterwards, he went to Docklands and we rented him a general manager, George Watson, for several months until the Stagecoach job for which he had been appointed was ready. Links were thus established and grew, so that when we realised that we had to find somebody to buy Portsmouth, we knew that Harry was acquisitive and would like to buy a bus company.'

Transit Holdings purchased what was now officially Southdown's 'Portsmouth Division' on 19th January 1991, brought in minibuses which were introduced as *Portsmouth Transit*; with *Blue Admiral* fleetnames for city services and *Red Admiral* for those going beyond the city boundaries, and garaged them at Hilsea West and Harts Farm, Havant respectively. Harry Blundred's team purchased some 100 vehicles from Southdown which they utilised until a four-phase introduction of the minibus fleet permitted their gradual withdrawal and disposal.

What had been sold was not Portsmouth Citybus; rather it was a large proportion of PCB plus a proportion of the old Southdown assets in the city. 'What we kept was the Havant operations of both Southdown and PCB. What we've got now in Portsmouth is an orphan-bastard of what PCB and Southdown once were; what Harry has got is a big brother orphan of the two!'

Hastings Buses

As if all this was not enough, there was turmoil also at the other end of the Southdown area – Eastbourne and at Hastings where Sharpton Ltd was again in acquisitive action. Hastings & District Transport Ltd, stung by the setting up of Top Line, had – in March 1989 – added to its earlier retaliation by introducing a frequent service of minibuses from the Langney area into Eastbourne, attacking the market of Eastbourne Buses in its own back yard. A second route followed in July, which confronted Southdown between Eastbourne and Polegate – the minibuses on both services carrying *Eastbourne & District* fleetname logos.

Eastbourne's municipally-owned company, put under some pressure by this move, had toyed with the idea of running its own minibuses, but regained an even keel by the sale of its 49 per cent share in Top Line to Stagecoach Holdings the following September. This made Top Line a wholly-owned subsidiary of Southdown.

There were now moves by Milton Keynes City Bus to regenerate an interest in the purchase of Hastings & District and co-ordinate this with the acquisition of Top Line from Stagecoach. Several preparatory arrangements were entered into but, in the event, the sale did not take place. Sharpton swooped for the fourth time in just three months and, on 8th December 1989, the Formia Group (the holding company for Hastings & District) was acquired by Stagecoach. Cinque Ports Travel Ltd, Eastbourne & District Transport Ltd, Hastings & District Transport Ltd and Hastings Coaches Ltd became subsidiaries of Southdown Motor Services Ltd and had their registered offices transferred to Lewes. A total of 104 public service vehicles was involved. The 16 coaches in the Hastings fleet were soon depleted, but joined by others from Portsmouth later as National Express work was reduced in 1990.

With ownership of both the previous contestants at Hastings now in its hands, Stagecoach set about merging the services

Stagecoach was now able to merge the services of Top Line and Hastings & District into one co-ordinated operation which was given the fleetname 'Hastings Buses'. Among the Southdown and Hampshire Bus Leyland Nationals sent to bolster the services in Hastings was Hampshire Bus 640 (LPR 940P). A 49-seat 11351/1R model, it had commenced service with Hants & Dorset Motor Services Ltd in 1976 as that company's 3652, and had passed to Hampshire bus in 1983 when NBC split up Hants & Dorset. Although sporting 'Hastings & District' logos it has wandered a little and turned up at Worthing on service 31 in May 1992.

A vehicle which looks like another ex-Hants & Dorset by virtue of its registration number – YLJ 332 – Leyland National series 2 NL116AL 11/1R, No. 132, which was new to Southdown in 1981 as RUF 432X. It carries an all-over advertisement for Sainsbury's of Rustington, near Littlehampton, primarily for use on a service to the store. At weekends, however, it was used on Worthing locals like this Lancing circular. Following the change of company name from Southdown Motor Services Ltd to Sussex Coastline Buses Ltd in April 1992, it was one of the first full-size vehicles to carry 'Coastline' logos.

Below centre: By no means all of the Volvo B10M double-deckers ordered by the independent Southdown company in 1989 were rushed into Stagecoach livery. But one of the first was 304 (F304 NYJ), specially painted in November 1990 for a fund-raising tour in aid of the BBC's 'Children in Need' appeal. The message is still in place on 6th July 1991 as the vehicle runs in from Havant on service 23 to South Parade Pier, Southsea, the traditional Southdown terminus in Portsmouth. It is followed by ex-Southdown BCD 824L, now of Provincial, re-established in Portsmouth after an absence of 52 years. Some of the Volvos were quickly dispersed elsewhere in the Stagecoach group, being moved to Fife Scottish.

Lower: Number 268 (JWV 268W), a dual-purpose seated Bristol VRT SL3/6LXB with ECW body, new to Southdown in 1981. The bus carries 'Top Ten Bus' labels – a marketing scheme designed originally for the competitive environment of Portsmouth. Following withdrawal from the city, all such vehicles were based at Havant, and the scheme was restricted to routes running into the city from there. 'Top Ten' provided the commuter with an opportunity to purchase a weekly ticket valid for ten journeys (five returns) for the price of nine. Route number 31 was introduced in January 1990.

of Top Line and Hastings & District into one operation under the fleetname *Hastings Buses*, rationalising sensibly in the way it had done at Portsmouth.

And, just as it had done in the case of Portsmouth, on 29th May 1990, the Department of Trade and Industry referred Stagecoach's acquisition of Formia Ltd to the Monopolies and Mergers Commission. On this occasion, Stagecoach was found to provide 36 per cent of the traffic in an area which included East Sussex, most of West Sussex, plus Ashford, Shepway and Tunbridge Wells in Kent. Again, the Commission's recommendation was not to divest, but to restrict Stagecoach's activities, particularly to reduce its 'scope for predatory retaliation against competitors'. Close liaison over proposed acquisitions and other matters was to be maintained with the Director General of Fair Trading.

As before, this was rejected by the Secretary of State for Trade and Industry, now Peter Lilley, who directed the Office of Fair Trading to discuss the sale of the Hastings operation with Stagecoach. The case was then put on hold because South Yorkshire Transport, which had received a similar directive, was going through a series of appeals, the outcome of which was likely to affect any directive on Hastings. SYT was also pursuing the basis of such references through the courts, ultimately to the House of Lords. The Secretary therefore elected to put the matter aside. In the event, the matter was finally settled in 1993 with Stagecoach, having given assurances on future procedures, being permitted to retain all its Hasting's operations.

New Divisions

Divested of its Portsmouth depot, Southdown was divided in January 1991 into two, rather than the originally planned three, new divisions. 'West Sussex' with Paul Southgate brought back from Hastings to take charge, comprised Bognor, Chichester, Havant, Hayling, Henfield, Leigh Park, Littlehampton, Storrington and Worthing whilst 'East Sussex' comprised Lewes, Eastbourne, Hastings, Rye,

Although registered in Brighton for Southdown, this Leyland Olympian is a now established Stagecoach standard vehicle. One of ten delivered in 1990, it is an ON2R56G13Z4 model with 85-seat Alexander bodywork and additional room for 12 standees. Number 706 (G706 TCD) is one of the eight from this batch which were allocated to Portsmouth initially for the planned 'Top Ten Bus' arrangement. All eight were 'rescued' from Portsmouth before divestment and relocated at Havant and elsewhere.

A pleasant surprise for traditionalists was the appearance in 1990 of Bristol VRT No. 276 (JWV 976W) repainted in full, lined-out, Southdown green and cream livery and old-style fleetname. Even the fleet number at the sides was in the right place. Based principally at Worthing, where it is seen operating the Lancing Circular service on 11th August 1990, the vehicle was celebrating the 75th anniversary of the founding of Southdown Motor Services. The message on the off-side panel also made it clear that Stagecoach intended being around for the next 75 years.

Bristol VRTSL3/6LXB No. 251 (JWV 251W), an ECW-bodied 75-seater new to Southdown in 1980, pictured at Waterlooville on 29th February 1992. Offering the 'Top Ten' ticket facility for regular passengers, it is en-route to Havant Bus Station. Service 39 was introduced on 20th January 1990 to run between Eastoke and Wecock Farm via Havant and Waterlooville, as part of the rationalisation of services in the area.

Leyland Olympian/Alexander No. 234 (G704 TCD), previously No. 704, photographed at Havant Bus Station on 11th January 1992. It awaits departure on route 21 The Hard/No. 22 to Havant, it became No. 21 in both directions under the control of Stagecoach and was retained for Southdown following divestment at Portsmouth in 1990.

Displaying the revised front with BET windscreens is Stagecoach standard Olympian No. 222 (J722 GAP), a dual-purpose 74-seater of 1991, operating the limited stop 'express' route between Portsmouth and Brighton. If the 'Southdown' fleetname on 234 had become noticeably small, here was notice that it was going to disappear altogether. Less than a month after the company name-change here was a full-size double-decker with 'Coastline' fleetname. The 'T' advertisement could almost refer to the new titles.

Lower: Rolling into Worthing from Portsmouth is Volvo double-decker No. 309 (F309 MYJ) similarly labelled, its electronic destination display winking in yellow and looking rather more fashionable than its younger companion as a result. Again, the combination of graphics lends the suggestion of double-entendre. 'Coastline Express' would seem to have a wider appeal than one might expect. Note the Southdown interpretation of Group livery.

Seaford and Uckfield, under Adam Yates, previously traffic manager with Hastings & District Transport Ltd. Paul Southgate had started his Southdown career as a conductor at Portsmouth. He was later to be appointed managing director of Stagecoach's subsidiary, Cumberland Motor Services.

These two divisional managers were directly answerable to Brian Cox as managing director of Southdown, there now being no appointment of traffic manager under the Stagecoach regime.

As formulated, the two units were largely co-terminous with the two name-sake county councils with their administrative centres at Chichester and Lewes, and which took very different stances towards public transport. 'It made sense to have one manager in West Sussex who understands how it works and another in East Sussex for the same reason, and there wasn't any connection between Eastbourne and Chichester, save history,

133

Now renamed and with its operations confined to the West Sussex and eastern Hampshire fringes of its company area, what had been Southdown Motor Services was left very much operating in the land of its early origins. Leyland National 17 (WYJ 171S), a 11351A/2R 44-seater of 1978, waits on the stand at Worthing on 16th May 1992, where its predecessors with the same fleetname had stood since 1915. That name was now fast disappearing from buses in regular service.

Both 683 and sister vehicle 684 (EAP 984V), a Bristol VRT SL3/6LXB with 74-seat ECW body, were painted in an overall advertisement livery for the *Evening Argus,* 'your own West Sussex daily newspaper' in 1992. Number 684 awaits departure from Midhurst on route 260 to Bognor Railway Station via Singleton, Lavant, Chichester and Pagham. The service traverses the wooded slopes of the Southdown Hills south of Cocking – in ancient times part of Hampshire.

Below: In complete contrast, No. 303 (F303 MYJ) leaves Western Road, Brighton for Eastbourne Pier on 23rd May 1992 in as-yet unchanged full livery of independent Southdown green and cream, fleet number and logo included, with only 'Hissing Sid', the stylised southdown 'S' missing from the days of its previous ownership. This time the advertisement concentrates one's eye upon a brand of cat food.

Right: In a rather pleasant gesture, Stagecoach preserved several speciments of Mackenzie's 'handwriting' on the front of vehicles still bearing the 'Southdown' logo, until the very last moment. Leyland National 113510A/1R of 1979 No. 105 (AYJ 104T) on a Worthing local service in May 1992 proudly displays a surviving traditional signature as it waits for a little boy and his grandfather to board.

Centre Right: After several years of competition, Stagecoach took over the vehicles and services of Easy Rider, the Bognor Regis-based operator. Just arrived and quietly ticking, after their last day of operation by Easy Rider – 16th May 1992 – three Freight Rover Sherpa 350 minibuses with Made-to-Measure 16-seat bodywork are at rest in Chichester garage. They are 968-9 (D318-9MNC) and 972 (E692 WNE); but saw only about a week's service with Sussex Coastline Buses before replacement.

Lower: Still carrying its original and portentous 'Coastline' logos, introduced in 1990 when minibuses were used on increased frequencies to the Witterings in competition with Westring's Coaches, No. 922 (G422 RYJ) is seen at Waterlooville in May 1992. An Iveco Turbo Daily 49-10 with 23-seat Phoenix bodywork dating from 1989, it is operating on Hampshire County Council contracted service 36, running south-east to Havant via Cowplain in the Forest of Bere.

but there was between Eastbourne and Hastings...it made geographical and political sense to move Eastbourne along to join it up with the Hastings operation. Obviously, we have the out-stations at Havant and Leigh Park which are in Hampshire, but all their vehicles are maintained in Chichester.'

Stagecoach asserts its Image

Instead of further Volvos, which proved to be the last new vehicles delivered in Southdown green and cream, Chichester was to receive some of the 1990 intake of new Leyland Olympians with Alexander double-decked bodywork, painted in full Stagecoach livery with *Southdown* fleetnames, as elsewhere in the group, in blue above the predominantly red *Stagecoach* logo.

In January 1992, neighbouring Hampshire Bus Ltd had its name changed to Stagecoach (South) Ltd with its registered office at Lewes Enterprise Centre, 112 Malling Street, Lewes. This became the holding company for all the Stagecoach subsidiaries in the south which now included 'Stagecoach: Hants & Surrey', the ex-Alder Valley South company. Brian Cox had responsibilty for them all,

as did Richard Alexander in the engineering sector.

With nomenclature now being altered freely to reflect what was actually happening upon the ground, Stagecoach now did what NBC had wanted Michael Sedgley to do in 1985. It turned the two Southdown divisions into separate companies.

Still hanging in there with 'Southdown' logos on 27th March 1993 is No. 301 (F301 MYJ) one of the Volvos purchased by independent Southdown in 1989. It was still performing the duty for which it was originally intended – the core route 712 between Brighton and Eastbourne. Despite the now-rare surviving fleetname, the vehicle was actually the property of South Coast Buses Ltd – a name very near that originally intended for Southdown way back in 1915.

Below centre: Stagecoach South was allotted a considerable number of new vehicles in 1992. Figuring large among them was an original Southdown allocation for forty Alexander Dash-bodied saloons on Dennis Dart chassis. On 25th October 1992 some of those already earmarked for 'Sussex Coastline' were instead transferred to the newly acquired 'Alder Valley South' operation. Six Darts await delivery to Aldershot and Hindhead, at Chichester Bus Station. Nearest the camera are K572-0-3 NHC respectively.

Below: Looking rather well in Stagecoach's modified livery at Chichester Bus station is T292 (FCD 292D) a Leyland Titan PD3/4 with Northern Counties bodywork, which was new to Southdown in 1966. Its longevity was not untypical of what proved to be a beautifully machined and highly successful combined effort by workforces in Leyland and Wigan. This example had been converted to a mobile office during the 1979 NBC-inspired MAP surveys, and when photographed in May 1992 was in use for driver instruction.

Old Names for New

And here nominal history began to repeat itself. The name 'Coastline' had been introduced by Brian Cox when it was felt necessary to buck up the Chichester operation, primarily as a competitive name on a small number of minibuses against the rival local firm, Westring's (it had previously been used – almost – by the 'Stagecoach Coastliner' from 1981 onwards). 'When we decided that it was time to make a change, we felt that Southdown's name had gone downhill very badly, particularly in Worthing and Chichester, because of bad performance.'

It was thought that the 'Coastline' name would be a good one for the whole West Sussex operation and the group set out to register the names 'Coastline Buses Ltd' and 'East Sussex Buses Ltd'. But, in yet another uncanny echo of the past, it was discovered that someone in Portsmouth had already registered, but again had no intention of using, both names beforehand.

Brian Cox was on business overseas at the time and his finance director and company secretary, having discovered that these names were therefore unacceptable at Companies House, were obliged (like their predecessors in 1915) to come up with two alternative names at short notice. West Sussex division would become 'Sussex Coastline Buses Ltd' they decided – and in the case of East Sussex 'as purely an off the top thing done in the flash of a moment', it was to be 'South Coast Buses Ltd' (and *South Coast* was precisely the name Mackenzie, Cannon and

Upper: Waiting at Brighton's Old Steine, terminus for local passenger transport since horse-bus days, is No. 578 (K578 NHC) one of the previous year's intake of Dennis Darts, en-route for Henfield, Cowfold, Lower Beeding and Horsham, on the long established route 107. Save for one vehicle – and that for one day only – all the Darts delivered for use by Sussex Coastline buses bore the 'Coastline' fleetname.

Lower: The long-legged capability of the Dennis Dart is epitomised here by the use of 579 (K579 NHC) on the 700 limited stop service. Stagecoach's livery sits happily upon the Alexander Dash bodywork, the upswept tricolour at the rear being complemented nicely by the vee-shaped effect of cab windows and windscreen – a 'happy accident' of design plus presentation.

A touch of Southdown green and cream is evident behind this August 1993 shot of No. 636 (XAP 636S) of 1978 at rest in Havant Bus Station. In contrast, 636 has already had its image moved even deeper into the Stagecoach fold. Whereas previously the standard Stagecoach fleetname logo had given emphasis to the subsidiary company's name with 'Stagecoach' beneath in small letters, from 1993 this arrangement was reversed. One had to look hard now to see that this was a Sussex Coastline vehicle.

With individual company identity similarly reduced to legal-ownership size, Dennis Dart 567 (K567 NHC) basks in the comparatively rare summer sunshine of August 1993. The jack-of-all-trades role allotted to the vehicle here – on a local service in Worthing – contrasts with the limited stop service duties allocated to the type from time to time.

A spell with Hampshire Bus as that firm's 384 explains why No. 604 (UWV 604S), now back in the 'Coastline' fold, carries both hand-drawn Hampshire Bus fleet number and black on white destination screen with names applied with a paint brush. In NBC days route 102 would have indicated a journey to the historic destination of Storrington – a Sussex Motor Road Car terminus in 1904 – but in the Stagecoach era, it represents a summer holiday service between Goring, Worthing and Shoreham.

Originally No. 92, 192 (AYJ 92T), a Leyland National 113510A/1R 52-seater saloon, new in 1979, provides heavy-weight relief on service 5 at Worthing. Normally the preserve in 1993 of MCW Metrorider integral 33-seaters, the headways of service 5 permitted 192 a rest in the midst of some brisk summer-time activity.

Not quite what it seems! Number 125, a Leyland National Series 2 NL116L11/1R 52-seat saloon dates from 1980, when it was taken into the Southdown fleet as JWV 125W. Between April 1989 and November 1990 it was re-registered LJY 145, and thereafter OUF 262W. The reason for this manoeuvre was to allow the vehicle to carry, as a holding exercise, a cherished registration number previously allocated to a coach which had been sold. This stemmed from independent Southdown's efforts to disguise the age of some vehicles, although Stagecoach itself also engaged in the transfer of 'cherished' registrations to its coaches.

Overall advertisement aside, this Leyland National Series 2 is simply identified as being owned by 'Stagecoach' with no further elaboration in the fleetname. Number 139 (FDV 829V), the same type as 125 (above) was new to Devon General in 1980, passed to Stagecoach's Hampshire Bus, before being transferred to Sussex Coastline Buses. It is en-route to Brighton on route 31 (the original number of the long-distance Portsmouth to Brighton service) revived by Stagecoach for the stopping version of service 700. It should not be confused with route 31, Havant to Hayling Island, which it certainly was by waiting passengers when both entered Havant Bus Station.

French had wanted for the company in the first place, instead of the-then berated *Southdown*).

Thus history was put straight, after a fashion, and on 2nd April 1992, Southdown Motor Services Ltd had its name formally changed to Sussex Coastline Buses Ltd; and a completely new company, South Coast Buses Ltd, formed from the Eastbourne and East Sussex operations of Southdown and of its subsidiary, Hastings & District Transport Ltd, *in toto*, took the name which had proven unacceptable in 1915. The only problem with these 'just like that' decisions is that it has left Stagecoach South with

two companies, each with the initials SCB, which was found to be somewhat confusing.

Southdown had been allocated 40 Alexander Dash-bodied Dennis Dart saloons in 1992 which, in the event, were delivered in *Coastline* and *Hastings Buses* logos save one, 501 (J501 JCD) which, for just one day carried *Southdown* fleetnames for a publicity photo-call outside Chichester bus station. It was the last new vehicle to carry the famous title.

Initially, South Coast Buses continued to trade as 'Southdown' and 'Hastings Buses' in the respective areas, but from the spring of 1993, these names were dropped and the *Stagecoach* name was brought into greater prominence on the vehicles. This was also the case with 'Coastline' and 'Hampshire Bus' (the eastern remains of Hants & Dorset Motor Services Ltd), to bring all Stagecoach South companies into line with 'Hants & Surrey', which had been similarly identified in relation to Stagecoach since the former's inception in 1992. Came 1994, and only three Bristol VRs remained in daily service in traditional livery, but Southdown bus stop signs lingered if one knew where to look. A reprise? Probably not, save for those special occasions like the traditional repaint for Bristol VRT No. 276 in 1990 which celebrated 75 years of Southdown service. Stagecoach is not without an intellectual sense of history, but its purpose is made clear on that same vehicle, which logo looked forward to 75 years of service from Stagecoach.

As intended by the management, the Leylands CD 7045, UF 4183, 409 DCD and 424 DCD remain with Stagecoach South in traditional Southdown apple green and primrose, primarily for publicity purposes. The two latter, PD3s, frequently turn up on service in times of need. Thus Stagecoach South acknowledges its debt to MacKenzie, Cannon and each and everyone who contributed to the achievements of the Southdown company.

New Directions

What then is the achievement of Stagecoach in relation to our subject? Brian Cox:

'We run Stagecoach South in a very decentralised, locally accountable manner. We take the view that the only way it will work is if the management and staff pull together; and the best way of achieving that is to make sure each local manager realises his depot's future depends upon its own performance. We are now fully upon local wage negotiations, for example; there is no commonality now. Every depot has separate wage negotiations and we have now got in Southdown (sic) very good relationships with the staff and I think we have turned the company around quite satisfactorily, both in terms of financial performance and in terms of its morale. We have had a phenomenal number of new buses this year which has done no end of good for that morale. So we try to work on a very low overhead. We run a very flat organisation, so that we know the people, we know what is going on; which backs up why we decentralised it rather than run it as a large amorphous unit. That's why we don't have a central traffic manager. Stagecoach South now extends from Andover in the west to Ramsgate in the east and it's a devil of a long way across between those places. We don't think that it would work with a centralised organisation, given the size and spread now of the Stagecoach South operation'.

Stagecoach aim at a 15 per cent pre-tax profit on turnover. Judging by the daily equity prices page in *The Times*, the group is well on course. Those who took up shares on floatation will have a sound investment.

Strictly speaking, if one wishes to pursue the history of Southdown beyond 1992, then it is solely 'Sussex Coastline' which should be concentrated upon. From both a nostalgic and a practical viewpoint, it is better to put a closure upon it from that date – and watch and record the fascinating onward march of Stagecoach South.

A humble and maturing Bristol VRT on service at Waterlooville is, sign of the times, tailed by Provincial saloon H523 CTR bound for South Parade Pier, Southsea, on a route once served by its electric tramways predecessor. Southdown had effectively 'seen off' that tramway in 1935, when it seemed highly unlikely that the emerald of Provincial would be on view there again. The 'T' advertisement on the VRT is designed to promote a detergent, some 58 years later. Perhaps its message could also be taken as appropriate to a similar 'cleansing' of Southdown.

Index